D0622449

The Creative Shrub Garden

The Creative Shrub Garden

Eye-catching combinations
for year-round interest

Andy McIndoe

Timber Press
Portland · London

ACKNOWLEDGEMENTS

I would like to thank everyone at Timber Press on both sides of the Atlantic for their help and encouragement, and for making this book possible. Special thanks to Sarah Rutledge Gorman for her meticulous work on the manuscript. I would also like to thank all of the garden owners and nurseries for allowing me to photograph their plants and for their help with pictures.

Copyright © 2014 by Andy McIndoe. All rights reserved.
Published in 2014 by Timber Press, Inc.

Photography credits appear on page 236.

The Haseltine Building
133 S.W. Second Avenue, Suite 450
Portland, Oregon 97204-3527
timberpress.com

6a Lonsdale Road
London NW6 6RD
timberpress.co.uk

Printed in China
Cover and text design by Patrick Barber
Layout and composition by Holly McGuire

Library of Congress Cataloging-in-Publication Data
McIndoe, Andrew, 1956–
    The creative shrub garden : eye-catching combinations for
year-round interest / Andy McIndoe. — 1st ed.
        p. cm.
    Includes bibliographical references and index.
    ISBN 978-1-60469-434-5
1. Ornamental shrubs. 2. Shrubs. I. Title.
    SB435.M144 2014
    635.9—dc23
                                    2013040985

A catalogue record for this book is also available
from the British Library.

Contents

Preface

I grew up in Warwickshire, in the heart of England, and started gardening as a child in the 1960s. We had a large garden that was typical of the time: half lawn, surrounded by flower beds; half for growing vegetables. I saw the vegetable area as a total waste of space, and I gradually encroached upon it with the various plant treasures I acquired in a variety of ways. The range of plants in gardens at that time was limited. Herbaceous perennials included Michaelmas daisies, goldenrod, Chinese lanterns, phlox, and peonies. Shrubs were relatively few. Most gardens, including ours, had forsythia, flowering currant, lilac, kerria, bridal wreath, broom, lavender, and perhaps mock orange. Foliage shrubs did not feature.

Cornus controversa 'Variegata' with *Sambucus nigra* f. *porphyrophylla* 'Eva' (front) and *Cotinus* 'Grace' (back) at RHS Rosemoor in Devon, England.

Through my time at university studying horticulture, and since then being in the garden industry, I have had the opportunity to work on and to visit many gardens of all sizes and styles. I have also started three of my own gardens from scratch. Like all gardeners, my tastes and favourite plants have changed over the years, but I have come to realize that the most important and rewarding are shrubs. No garden should be without these plants.

In this book I demonstrate how you can use shrubs in your garden, whatever its size, to create stunning planting combinations. I hope I will inspire you to grow them as the wonderful garden plants they are. I want you to enjoy their natural beauty, to choose the right ones for your situation, and to resist the urge to control them unnaturally.

Many gardeners think of shrubs as mere structure plants, the foundations on which to build planting schemes. But shrubs are far more than just the backbone of the garden. These are the most versatile and hard-working plants. You can rely on them year after year.

Gardeners grow shrubs for the beauty of their flowers, foliage, and fragrance, and for their winter stems, all of which enhance the garden by adding colour and interest at different times of the year. I am attracted to the beauty of flowers and captivated by their fragrance. In the winter garden, I never cease to be amazed by the brilliance of naked stems. However, for me foliage is the most important element. I believe the colour, texture, and shape of leaves lie at the heart of planting design.

I encourage you to examine your garden, or any garden you are cultivating, in a new light. Look at where the interest lies in all areas of the planting. Identify its shortcomings and think about possible changes and additions. I hope you will see what shrubs can bring to that picture.

This is a book for anyone who influences a garden, whether it is your own, a space you work on or maintain, or one for which you design in a professional capacity. This book will give you ideas and inspiration, simple planting schemes to follow, and plans you can adapt to your own requirements. The core of the book demonstrates how you can create a particular look or feel in your garden by choosing the right shrubs and putting them together creatively. You will also learn how to achieve a particular mood or style in any size garden. If you develop an initial selection of small shrubs and add medium-size and larger subjects, the planting schemes will work whether you have a courtyard, a balcony, or an extensive space.

I have written this book based on my experiences, and many of the examples and pictures are from my garden. Whether you use it as a reference book, dip in and out of it, or read it like a novel, I hope you enjoy it.

Happy gardening!

THE CASE FOR SHRUBS: AN INTRODUCTION

What do shrubs mean to you? Have you been bewitched by the sweet fragrance of an azalea on a warm spring day? Are you entranced by the delicacy and charm of the new leaves on a Japanese maple? Or perhaps you think of shrubs as big, boring beasts that take up too much room in your garden. Those bony characters you keep in shape with a stout pair of loppers and a pruning saw, more bare stems than leaves and flowers. Or perhaps they are neat bushes you trim into regular shapes with a pair of shears or a hedge cutter.

LEFT The deliciously fragrant deciduous azalea *Rhododendron* 'Irene Koster' has the added advantage of richly coloured fall foliage.

Acer palmatum 'Beni-maiko', one of the most delicately beautiful Japanese maples, displays soft red new foliage in spring.

Some gardeners think of shrubs as rhododendrons; a source of gorgeous colour for a few precious weeks, but perhaps rather green and boring during the rest of the year. Others call to mind hydrangeas, those vast, rounded mounds of flamboyant blooms that colour summer through to fall in shades of white, pink, and blue.

Some think of shrubs as gloomy evergreens that colonize dark, shady churchyards. Others picture annoying, litter-collecting thickets that get in the way of vehicles in supermarket parking lots. But those same shrubs, loved just a little, are precious, shining evergreens that thrive in shade and light up the dark corners of the garden. They are the same shrubs that illuminate the winter garden with their wand-like stems on a frosty winter morning.

Many gardeners consider shrubs to be reliable friends that fill the summer garden with flowers, fragrance, and foliage, and that colour the winter garden with bright

The deep scarlet stems of red barked dogwoods colour the garden picture on a freezing, foggy day.

stems and berries. As with many things in life, garden fashions change. Our affection for a particular group of plants fades, and we focus on another. Over the years shrubs may not always have been the flavour of the month, but they are the backbone of many gardens. But can shrubs be more than a foundation? Can they make up the whole planting scheme, or at least the majority of it, perhaps with a few embellishments in the form of perennials, bulbs, and seasonal bedding plants? Of course they can.

What qualities can shrubs offer that other plants cannot? They add permanence, structure, and presence throughout the four seasons, plus much more. This book shows you how shrubs can provide the inspiration and the palette of plants for exciting and colourful planting combinations that enhance the garden picture throughout the year.

You can improve shrubs by pruning to control their size and shape. However, once planted they stand firm; they do not need the regular lifting, dividing, and replanting that many perennials demand to maintain their performance and control their spread. For the most part, shrubs are low-maintenance subjects that will reward season after season. All they ask of the gardener is to

ABOVE Hydrangeas in rich shades of blue, mauve, and purple carpet the valley at Trebah Garden in Cornwall, England. The display lasts through summer and into fall.

RIGHT In this large garden, shrubs create a pleasing summer picture with flowers, form, and foliage.

choose well for the situation and to prune with a little thought and respect. Shrubs are undemanding garden plants that require only a modest initial financial investment, and they repay it many times over the years.

The evolution of shrubs

Shrubs are the foundation of successful planting in today's gardens. Smaller spaces and busy lifestyles mean that plants need to work hard to earn their keep. Most gardeners, from novices to old hands, welcome low-maintenance plantings. Shrubs offer so much with so little input. Other plants don't come close.

Shrubs in pots create a pleasing picture in a small space. They need little maintenance apart from regular watering, but they deliver great effect.

Nowadays a garden has particular significance as an extension of the home. Whether you live in your garden or look at it like a picture, its appearance is important. You want colour and interest throughout the year. A garden based on shrubs provides this very thing.

Gardeners have a wide choice of shrubs today. The variety of plants available has never been richer; the selection is vast compared to just a few years ago. The foundation of that palette is the work of the Victorians. Plant hunters, sponsored by nurserymen and wealthy collectors, unearthed an impressive number of plants, most of which remained in the gardens and estates of the wealthy. Gardening as we know it developed over the past fifty years. In Britain, in the first half of the last century gardening was focused around beans, potatoes, cabbages, a few cottage garden flowers, and the occasional shrub.

Most woody plants in gardens were roses, specifically hybrid teas and floribundas. These were the popular and fashionable plants of the day. Gardeners

The golden spring flowers of forsythia have been a staple in gardens since the beginning of the twentieth century.

Rosa Lady Emma Hamilton is a wonderful English rose of graceful habit with red-tinted, deep green foliage and globe-shaped, soft orange flowers.

always bought bare root, either from a shop or ordered via catalogue or at a flower show, and planted during late fall or winter. (Flower shows then were nothing like the Chelsea and Hampton Court of today; they were smaller, more regional affairs that focused on flowers and vegetables.)

New varieties of rose were in demand, and every year saw the introduction of fresh colour breaks and must-have varieties. The selling names of varieties became increasingly important, as they were what gardeners remembered and discussed. And there were negative aspects to this passion. The prevalence of roses in so many gardens led to the appearance and spread of diseases like black spot, rust, and mildew, which remain the banes of the rose grower's existence. This spread of disease was compounded by the demise of the coal fire for domestic heating. The sulphur in sooty air suppressed disease, while cleaner air gave it free rein. Another problem was the introduction of many weak and inferior varieties in order to meet the demand for something new.

Today's roses are different, and they are still some of our most popular shrubs—especially English roses, which combine the repeat-flowering qualities of hybrid tea and floribunda roses with the grace and charm of old shrub roses. Successful varieties have been bred for disease resistance, and their growth habit makes them perfect to combine with other shrubs in creative planting schemes.

Demand influences the palette of plants in our gardens. When a particular group of plants becomes fashionable, plant breeders and growers respond by producing new varieties. Herbaceous perennials and seasonal bedding plants are favourites in the United Kingdom, partly because of demand and popularity but also because of a relatively short lead time from initial hybridization to production of a commercial crop. Shrubs and trees are at a disadvantage when it comes to the introduction of new varieties, as they take much longer to grow.

Probably the biggest change in ornamental gardening over the past fifty years is how we buy our plants. I purchased my first shrub, *Magnolia ×soulangeana*, when I was nine or ten years old. I bought it from Woolworths, an early department store that sold everything from sweets to paint to bacon to flower bulbs. Most ordinary gardeners went to "Woolies" for everyday gardening bits and pieces that they did not get from a specialist seed shop. My magnolia was a typical Woolworths shrub: a stick with roots wrapped in peat and thin polythene, with a simple picture label promising eternal happiness and a lifetime of flowers. It needed a few years to grow and flower, but it eventually took over half the garden, leaving no room for those boring vegetables. Mission accomplished, if rather a long lead time!

Nurseries existed at the time, and those I knew of mainly grew summer bedding plants. Garden centres were just beginning, and I was taken on the occasional trip to visit our nearest one, which was probably twenty miles away. I remember buying *Hypericum calycinum*, which was my second or third shrub. I probably bought it because it was the only thing I could afford, rather than because I particularly liked it. This plant, hailed as good groundcover, was appearing everywhere. Sadly, it became another victim of over-exposure and monoculture. Its magnetism for rust has since rendered it worthless.

The difference between these two shrub purchases is that the hypericum was pot grown. The container-grown hardy plant had arrived, and it changed the way we garden. The range of shrubs expanded. No longer did the gardener have to choose from familiar favourites; an altogether richer palette became available, and with it a new adventure in gardening with shrubs.

The definition of a shrub

Just as botanists classify plants by family, genus, and species, gardeners classify plants as trees, shrubs, climbers, perennials, conifers, grasses, bedding plants, bulbs, and so on. Shrubs include any woody plant that does not die down to ground level in winter in temperate regions. A shrub also has more than one stem originating at or close to ground level. A tree is a woody plant with a single stem that then branches some way above ground level. However, it is not quite as clear-cut as that. There are

Magnolia ×soulangeana is sometimes regarded as a large shrub, often a tree. One thing is certain: it usually grows larger than the gardener imagines it will.

One of the most beautiful woody plants, *Cornus controversa* 'Variegata' is a shrub that becomes a tree.

ABOVE Phormiums are not truly shrubs, but are often used as such in planting schemes. They are valued for their bold foliage, architectural form, and exotic appearance.

LEFT *Juniperus ×pfitzeriana* 'Aurea' is just one of many conifers with an informal, interesting, shrubby habit and colourful foliage.

multi-stemmed trees, and some shrubs—such as bay, holly, rose, and euonymus—are often grown as standards. Gardeners tend to think of shrubs as smaller than trees, but that is not always the case. There are large shrubs and small trees.

Some conifers are clearly distinguished as trees. Pine, larch, cedar, and redwood all grow into statuesque specimens with soaring stems devoid of branches for many metres above ground level. Others make bushy, branched, rounded, or spreading individuals that are distinctly shrubby in character. For all intents and purposes they are shrubs, but for some reason many gardeners segregate them and classify them as conifers. This habit is probably reinforced by the fashionable gardener's unreasonable dislike of conifers in recent years.

When it comes to fashion, heathers often fall into the same category as conifers. However, they are more widely planted, as many gardeners realize their value as low-maintenance evergreen shrubs that can achieve excellent groundcover in a variety of situations that other plants find challenging, such as under trees and on poor soils.

Spiky architectural plants have enjoyed a high profile in recent years. Phormiums, yuccas, cordylines, and astelias offer contrasting form and texture to the rounded mounds of most shrubs and herbaceous perennials. Some argue that their sharp lines and photogenic qualities have earned them more attention than they deserve, but in some situations they are valuable plants. Botanically they are not shrubs, but practically they are used as such, especially in milder areas in temperate regions.

Roses, our much-loved and probably most popular garden plants, are the other main group of shrubby subjects that are classified separately. Bush roses are definitely shrubs, and many gardeners refer to some of the larger, bushier ones as "shrub roses." These are more likely to break out from dedicated rose beds and sit alongside shrubs and herbaceous perennials in the mixed border. Other types of roses could make this break if they tried a little harder—and if they had more encouragement from the gardener.

Some shrubs are limited in size, despite their woody stems. Most ericas and callunas, pachysandra, and vinca rarely grow above knee high. However, many shrubs have the ability to increase height and spread over a number of years. They often get bigger than expected. This may be their downfall, as they threaten the gardener's authority. As a precaution, introduce pruning at an early stage. This is a necessary task, even if it threatens the plant's performance and habit.

Lovely *Rosa* 'Ballerina' is one of the best shrubs. Its sprays of single flowers are wonderfully informal, so it mixes beautifully with other loose, arching shrubs, especially those with purple foliage.

LEFT Some perennials, such as striking *Euphorbia characias* 'Silver Swan', produce woody stems and are shrubby in character.

RIGHT Shrubs play a vital role in all layers of the planting picture, contributing structure, texture, and, most important, colour.

The fact that shrubs produce woody stems does not define them indisputably from other plants. Some shrubs usually grouped with herbaceous perennials, such as penstemons and euphorbias, produce woody stems that do not die down in winter in cool, temperate regions. A shrub may be evergreen or deciduous; it may be a broadleaf or a conifer; it may be grown for its flowers or just for its foliage or stems. It is always a perennial; in other words, it lives for a number of years, often many. A shrub is one of the vertebrae that make up the backbone of any garden, as it supports the planting and holds it all together.

The role of shrubs in the planting picture

Imagine a view of a garden as a picture. This is how you often see it from the window of a house, from the terrace, from a seat, or through a gateway. A pleasing picture has interest at all levels. In the layer of planting above eye level, trees play the major role; however, climbers and tall shrubs can also add interest. In the layer at eye level, shrubs play the leading role, while tall perennials and climbers lend support. Perennials, annuals, bulbs, and dwarf shrubs populate the layer below eye level. This is where the gardener focuses the most effort. It is a very accessible area, and it contains plants that often demand attention.

Shrubs can play an important part in all parts of the planting picture, but they dominate at eye level in the middle layer, the most visible and arguably the most important. Here well-chosen shrubs can add interest, colour, and variety throughout the year. Those with variegated and colourful foliage maintain the vitality of the garden in midsummer, when early flowering shrubs fade to green. Evergreens and shrubs grown for their winter stems keep the planting picture alive, while most deciduous shrubs retreat into dormancy during the coldest months of the year.

Shrubs are no less important in the upper and lower layers of the planting picture.

Tall shrubs can fill the role of trees and add the height that transforms a garden into a three-dimensional space. In small gardens, mahonia, photinia, and holly are good alternatives to small trees. In the lower layer, dwarf shrubs add structure and permanence among plantings of herbaceous perennials, grasses, annuals, and bulbs. Alternatively, you can use low-growing shrubs to create low-maintenance planting schemes that require little attention apart from occasional weeding, feeding, and maybe some pruning to keep their constituents in shape.

Making shrubs work in your garden

Many shrubs are malleable plants that you can easily shape to meet your requirements. You can employ them as hedges and screens, trim them into topiary shapes, and train them against walls and fences. These methods of using woody plants as a major part of the structure of a garden date back to the earliest years of garden design. Trimmed box and yew hedges planted and pruned to make patterns feature in gardens across Europe. The knot garden, parterre, and Dutch garden style have influenced gardens through the years and across the world.

Informal planting, often featuring a higher proportion of herbaceous perennials, was developed in the early twentieth century. "Informality contained within formality" is the style of planting often used to describe gardens such as Sissinghurst in Kent, England. Here neat box hedges, the influence of the ordered mind of Harold

ABOVE *Pittosporum tenuifolium* 'Tom Thumb', a dwarf evergreen shrub, makes a stunning planting partner for *Hakenochloa macra* 'Aurea'. When the latter turns parchment in winter, the combination is still pleasing.

TOP Box hedges and shaped yew create formal structure between the house and parkland landsape at Goodnestone Park, Kent, England.

Sissinghurst in Kent, England, is a garden designed with exuberant informal planting within the formal structure that shrubs provide.

ABOVE Shrubs deliver a complete planting picture throughout the four seasons of the year, with or without support from other plants.

RIGHT Contemporary planting with topiary box balls emphasizing a garden feature.

Nicholson, contain the exuberant planting of the expressive Vita Sackville-West. Perhaps it is this controlled use of shrubs as vegetable masonry that leads us to think of them as boring support plants that need to be kept in check.

Or perhaps we consider the shaping of plants as a fashionable art form. The ancient art of topiary is featured in gardens in times of affluence, and disappears in leaner periods. Topiary is time and labour intensive: either the money must be available to pay for regular trimming, or the gardener needs the time to do it. Topiary is used extensively in traditional and contemporary gardens, both formally and informally, in containers and in the open ground. Topiary is used as structure, ornamental enhancement, a focal point, green concrete, and even as a plant.

The time for shrubs has finally arrived. No longer are they just the backbone of the garden, playing a supporting role. They have come to the fore to take centre stage as stars of the garden show, stealing the limelight in terms of flowers, foliage, form, and fragrance. Designers and gardeners recognize their versatility, particularly as the palette of shrubs has become so diverse. It is time for us to open our eyes to shrubs' many attributes and to the rich planting choices they offer. It is time to get creative by designing your planting with shrubs.

CHOOSING THE RIGHT SHRUBS FOR YOUR GARDEN

With such a vast array of shrubs from which to choose, how do you go about selecting the best ones for your garden? This book offers lots of horticultural advice and plenty of limiting factors to think about, but ultimately a plant's basic appeal will always be the starting point. Whatever your taste or colour preference, and however analytical or creative your approach, something at the nursery or garden centre will grab your attention and beg to be planted. Remember that if your soil is unsuitable for the plant you want, you may be able to grow it in a pot in the right growing medium.

No matter how carefully designed or planned a garden is, most gardeners buy on impulse. We see a plant we like, and we buy it. We take it home, leave it in the pot for a few days (or weeks or months), find a space, and plant it—often with little regard for its ultimate size and spread or how it associates with its neighbours. If it thrives and looks good in a situation, we determine it was a solid choice and a good decision to plant it there. If it is a disaster, we claim that the label misled us or that we got poor advice, or simply put it down to the fact that the plant did not perform as it should have. If the plant is a short-term subject or an herbaceous perennial, you can easily rectify errors. But most shrubs are long-term garden plants that compose the fabric of your garden, so it is worth putting more thought into their selection and planting.

ABOVE Few of us can resist a butterfly lavender in bloom, regardless of whether we have the ideal growing conditions. This is a short-lived shrub; just buy it and enjoy it.

LEFT With so many shrubs available, it can be difficult to know which ones to choose.

The size of your garden

The size of your garden is an extremely important factor in your selection of shrubs. Before you go shopping, think about how much space you have to work with.

SMALLER GARDENS

If you have a small garden, you do not want plants that overpower; however, you do not necessarily have to choose dwarf compact shrubs. Look for light and airy plants, those with an open branch structure, or tall, slender specimens that use the vertical space. All of these fit in and make the garden look bigger. Lovely *Nandina domestica* is a good example. It has upright stems, fine branches in well-spaced layers, and small, delicate, evergreen leaves that often colour well in fall and winter. Ultimately it will grow to 1.5m (5 ft.) or more in height, but it provides light height, little weight, and year-round interest.

The more compact form, *Nandina domestica* 'Fire Power', is also suitable in a small garden, but has a totally different character. It is a more solid, rounded shrub that reaches only 60cm (2 ft.) in height but still has more than one season of interest.

Either will fit into a small garden, but the taller shrub will make the space look larger and will focus the eye on the middle layer of the planting picture. The smaller, more compact cultivar will draw the eye downward, filling the space and adding interest at ground level.

RIGHT In this large garden the birch, cercis, and physocarpus were planted first; the bed and additional planting came later.

BELOW *Viburnum opulus* is ideal in a country garden setting. It has white early summer flowers, plus wonderful fall foliage and glistening red fruits.

Nandina domestica is a tall, light, see-through shrub that provides height without weight.

Nandina domestica 'Fire Power' is a compact evergreen with wonderful fall and winter foliage colour.

LARGER GARDENS

In a larger garden you need a different approach. Small garden planting in a larger area looks diminutive and upsets the balance between space and planting, as space predominates and the planting disappears. You need a foundation of large, well-chosen structure shrubs to join the tree canopy with the lower layer of the planting picture. These shrubs need to be appropriate for the garden and provide colour and interest in that middle layer.

In country gardens, against a borrowed rural landscape, the choice has to be appropriate to the setting. Many shrubs that sit comfortably in an urban garden with fixed boundaries can look out of place in a country garden situation. Those with brightly coloured and variegated foliage, neat and manicured habit, or exotic form just do not fit in. Good transitional shrubs such as *Viburnum opulus*, *Sambucus nigra* f. *laciniata*, and *Cornus kousa* come into their own in this situation. These have a light, informal habit that would not look out of place in a country hedgerow.

I found it very challenging to move from a small cottage garden to a large plot of around two acres. I still came home with my little treasures and planted them in newly made beds that looked large at the time. I always positioned the beds safely near the boundaries. Nothing really made any impact until I broke away from the edges and introduced big, bold shrubs. I grouped them with trees and built the planted areas around them.

To reduce the amount of maintenance in a larger garden, plant a tree and two or three larger shrubs into circles cut in the grass. When they get going, remove the grass around them and create the planting area. This approach allows you to introduce an overall structure into the garden in the beginning and add the rest of the planting later, rather than doing everything at once. I have used this technique, and it certainly reduced the amount of beds to maintain in the early stages of garden development.

The size of the planting area

The size of the planting area is another major factor that influences our choice of shrubs. Beds and borders are often too small; you can improve most gardens by having fewer and bigger planting areas. Not many shrubs have an ultimate height and spread of less than 90cm (3 ft.). This is a sobering thought when you look at the narrow borders that frame the average garden.

Avoid planting the subjects in a border in a straight line unless you are making a formal border or a hedge. It is better to have a border that is considerably wider than 90cm (3 ft.) to enable the plantings to be grouped more naturally. A bed or border 1.8m (6 ft.) wide or more will greatly increase your planting possibilities; a border 3m (10 ft.) wide will present an even more exciting canvas on which to work. These wider

LEFT These narrow borders lead the eye into the surrounding landscape. The lavenders are trimmed after they flower. This practice keeps the planting in bounds.

BELOW *Euonymus fortunei* 'Emerald Gaiety' will fit into the narrowest planting area and make use of the vertical support. Here it is planted with variegated ivies.

planting areas allow you to get a variety of heights into a planting scheme and to give your shrubs the space to work together.

Borders that are less than 90cm (3 ft.) wide can successfully accommodate dwarf compact shrubs such as *Berberis thunbergii* 'Admiration', *Hebe* 'Caledonia', and *Convolvulus cneorum*. However, all the plantings will be at a low level. Or you could plant shrubs that will grow against walls or fences in very narrow borders or at the back of the planting, such as the ever-popular *Euonymus fortunei* 'Emerald Gaiety'.

Alternatively, you have to choose shrubs that respond well to regular trimming. This does not necessarily mean cutting into formal shapes, but just seasonal pruning to remove faded flowers, as you would do with lavenders and heathers.

In narrow borders, avoid shrubs that always need cutting back to contain them in the allotted space. This type of planting usually looks awful. It also detracts from the appearance of the individual plant and the garden as a whole, and is time consuming and inefficient in terms of garden management. Narrow borders can be effective if the planting is bold and the palette is limited. Repeating the same subjects along a narrow border unifies the planting and increases its impact.

The size of the shrub

The first question most gardeners ask about any shrub is, *How big does it grow?* However, it is very difficult to get concrete information on a shrub's ultimate size. Few shrubs reach certain dimensions and stop growing. They may slow down and spread, rather than getting taller, but they still continue to get larger. Ultimate size depends equally on growing conditions and variety. It is also very difficult for most gardeners to visualize overall size. A medium-size shrub, such as *Choisya ternata*, which can grow to 1.5m (5 ft.) in height with a similar spread, sounds enormous, particularly when you are examining a young plant in a pot at the garden centre. In most situations it will be around two-thirds that size because you will control it by pruning, and other shrubs and overhanging trees will compete to check its growth. However, in ideal growing conditions, left unchecked, it could easily reach 1.8m (6 ft.).

CHOOSING THE RIGHT SIZE

Considering the ultimate size of a shrub can be a challenge. Do you space your shrubs based on their ultimate size or their size in five years? If you want instant impact, you are more likely to plant close enough to fill the space in a year or two.

RIGHT An evergreen shrub such as *Choisya ternata* often grows considerably larger than the gardener initially imagines.

BELOW *Viburnum davidii* and sarcococcas in a narrow shady border alongside a path have sufficient weight and impact in this stone framework.

LEFT Pittosporums grow quickly to make an impact, particularly when used as part of an exciting foliage combination.

BELOW Shrubs that are trimmed purely to keep them from competing with one another do not create a pleasing planting scheme.

Most gardeners are impatient and want to see results quickly. This is particularly true of those who are new to gardening and not used to waiting for things to happen. A successful planting scheme will include some subjects that grow quickly and make an impact, and some that take longer to mature. Fast-growing shrubs that look impressive from an early stage include ceanothus, photinia, and pittosporum. These are good choices in new gardens where structure and perhaps screening is needed, or as an essential element in a planting combination. Other evergreens, such as holly and boxwood, are slow to reach a size and substance that makes an impact.

PRUNING TO CONTROL GROWTH

If a shrub gets too big for a situation, you can usually control its size by pruning. How much you rely on pruning depends on your style of planting and how much time and effort you are prepared to invest on a regular basis. If your scheme includes *Buxus sempervirens*, for example, you will need to trim annually to control size and shape. In most schemes where shrubs are allowed to grow naturally, you will need to prune only to prevent competition between shrubs and to improve their habit, or to remove old stems that have flowered to encourage new growth and flowering the following year. Gardeners never achieve pleasing planting schemes when they trim shrubs unnaturally from an early age to control their size and to avoid competition between individual plants. If you have to do this, you chose the wrong shrubs for the space or planted them too close to each other.

These pots of *Lavandula angustifolia* 'Hidcote' will be planted around 45cm (18 in.) apart so the mounds of foliage and flowers will join up when grown.

The lifespan of the shrub

Lavateras are short-lived shrubs. After three to five years they usually need to be replaced, but they have amazing flower power in the meantime.

Gardens do not stand still: they grow, develop, and change over the years. How quickly this happens depends on what you plant. There is little point in planting a choice, slow-growing shrub that will take several years to perform if you intend to live on the site for only a few years. It is preferable to grow it in a pot so you can take it with you, or to choose a faster-growing plant that will make a quick impact.

Many gardeners tend to think of shrubs as permanent garden plants. Buy a seasonal bedding plant and you know you will throw it away at the end of the season; buy a shrub and you expect it to live forever. It is always distressing when a large California lilac, which delivers a spectacular display of flowers every spring and is a major feature of your garden, suddenly deteriorates, sheds its leaves, and dies. Much soul-searching, investigation, and postmortem ensues, but the shrub has simply reached the end of its lifespan, which is usually about ten years. The same is true of many other shrubs from the Mediterranean region, such as cistus and lavender. These short-lived shrubs have an even shorter lifespan in cold, wet areas. Plant a lavender in damp, heavy clay and it may survive for only a couple of years; plant the same shrub on poor, well-drained soil in a dry region and it may still be going strong after ten years. Lavatera, abutilon, salvia, santolina, and some daphne all fall into this short-lived category. Even if these plants do not die after a few years, their appearance detracts from the planting. The remaining stems become woody with few leaves, flowering is poor, and the shrubs just look unhappy. The best solution is to remove and replace, rather than attempt rejuvenation.

The plan for the garden

When I plant a new bed from scratch, I start with long-term shrubs that will provide structure and interest in about five years. I plant these small and medium-size shrubs around 90cm (3 ft.) apart to allow them to reach their potential in that time frame. I have to control the spread of some of these shrubs with selective pruning—particularly the evergreens, where cutting some stems may be necessary to control size and shape. The size of the flowering shrubs is often controlled as part of the flowering cycle.

When I include dwarf shrubs such as heathers, or groundcover plants such as pachysandra or vinca, I plant them in groups of three or five, spacing the plants around 30cm (1 ft.) apart. I plant lavenders 45cm (18 in.) apart.

I fill the gaps in the planting with annuals that work in mixed plantings, such as *Nigella damascena* and *Salvia hormium*, non-invasive perennials like heuchera and *Salvia nemerosa*, or short-lived shrubs that can be removed at a later date, such as penstemon, lavender, and erysimum.

In public planting schemes, robust basic shrubs such as berberis, cornus, and deutzia are often planted in large groups at close spacing to achieve quick impact and low-maintenance groundcover. Do not be tempted to do this at home, as planting several shrubs of the same type close together in a garden situation rarely creates a pleasing effect. The individual shrubs soon compete with one another, and you will have to remove some to allow others the space to grow.

Climate, situation, and soil type

A few basic considerations will influence your shrub selection: climate, situation, and soil type.

ABOVE Deciduous shrubs like dogwoods are able to cope with the harsher climates of northern Central Europe and North America.

LEFT For *Daphne bholua* 'Jacqueline Postill', heavy snowfall is a relatively rare challenge in my garden in southern England.

CLIMATE

I garden in southern England, so I am fortunate to be working in a mild, temperate climate where I can grow a wide range of deciduous and evergreen shrubs. Winters are generally kind: temperatures regularly fall to −5°C (23°F) and occasionally to −10°C (14°F), and very occasionally the night temperature reaches −15°C (5°F). The climate is even milder nearer the coast, and in some coastal areas frosts are relatively rare.

Gardeners in northern Central Europe and North America have to deal with a much harsher climate. This limits their choice of broad-leaved evergreens and sun-loving Mediterranean shrubs, which are the foundation of the planting palette in dry areas of the southern United States and southern Europe.

The hardiness of plants is not an exact science, and rarely prevents the more experienced gardener from pushing the boundaries. Soil type, shelter, and altitude all influence hardiness. On heavy, wet soils, even a hardy subject recommended for a particular climatic zone may struggle to survive. The same is true on exposed sites, where wind chill pushes the temperature below that shown on the thermometer. The sequence of weather also has a profound effect. A long, mild fall with warm day temperatures and mild nights followed by a sudden freeze can unexpectedly damage plants that have not acclimatized, as well as those that have produced new growth at the wrong time of the year.

When you select shrubs, make sure the majority are suitable for your climatic zone and will comfortably survive. Choose sparingly those that are borderline hardy.

RIGHT A fleece jacket might have saved this cordyline from winter damage.

BELOW Frost can easily damage pieris if mild spring weather has stimulated the early production of tender new growth.

However, this does not mean you cannot experiment. Once you identify the favourable spots in your garden where shelter from walls, fences, buildings, or neighbouring plants will give additional protection, you can consider other shrubs that will find your zone more challenging. You can pamper some plants by giving them additional drainage at the time of planting—for example, coarse grit dug into heavy soils can work wonders. You can also plan to give added protection with horticultural fleece in severe weather, but you must put it in place *before* frost or snow occurs.

SITUATION

The amount of sun and shade in your site will definitely influence your choice of plants. Extremes of both are easier to choose for. Where a garden gets no direct sun at all, you need to choose shade-loving shrubs. A limited number of flowering shrubs will grow in these conditions, so foliage shrubs will provide most of the colour and interest. Where a garden is in an open, sunny situation without shade from buildings and trees, you need sun-loving shrubs, many of which flower. Gardeners in warmer, drier regions will be able to grow Mediterranean subjects and those with silver foliage. Those in cold regions will need to look to conifers and heathers to provide evergreen interest.

The in-between sites need a little more thought. Perhaps a neighbouring building casts a shadow for much of the day and most of the year, except in high summer. Deciduous trees have a profound effect, as a border may be quite sunny during the winter months but in dappled to heavy shade when a tree is in full leaf in summer. In younger gardens where new trees have been planted close to or within planted areas, the growing conditions in a bed or border are likely to change as the tree matures. You may have to adjust the underplanting as a situation becomes shadier.

Most flowering shrubs, including roses, need about four hours of direct sun during

In a shaded garden without direct sunlight, evergreen foliage shrubs can still create an interesting planting scheme with colour throughout the year.

ABOVE Most hydrangeas, such as *Hydrangea serrata* 'Bluebird', grow happily and bloom with some shade.

LEFT *Euonymus fortunei* varieties cope well with the shade and lack of water under trees.

the growing season to flower well. Without it, new wood will often fail to ripen sufficiently to produce flower buds for the following season. This is particularly true of spring and early summer–flowering shrubs like deutzia and philadelphus, which flower on wood produced the previous season. Often shrubs that flower on wood produced earlier the same season perform quite well in semi-shade, as they do not seem to have the same need for the sun to ripen the wood. Examples include many hydrangeas, ceratostigma, and potentilla.

There are many terms for describing the type of shade in a garden. *Partial shade* or *semi-shade* refers to a site that gets three hours or more of sun per day for most of the year. *Dappled shade* means the garden has some direct light, but the foliage of overhanging trees or large shrubs filters it. A structure that supports climbers, such as a pergola or a gazebo, could also provide dappled shade. *Deep shade* means the situation gets no direct sunlight and is in the permanent shadow of a wall, fence, or building, or perhaps the trunk of a mature tree.

Often the added challenge for plants in shade is lack of water because of the proximity of the structure or tree that is casting the shade. A building may create a rain shadow that prevents adequate rainfall from reaching the soil. A mature tree will draw water from the soil, competing with any shrubs or other plants in its vicinity.

SOIL TYPE

Gardeners worry a great deal about soil type. When asked about it, most report on how they feel about their soil rather than provide a real assessment of its pH and drainage qualities. Gardeners with heavy clay soils have a clear opinion of their soil because it presents a challenge when digging and usually remains wet and heavy long after other soils have dried out. Clay is usually seen as a limiting factor, but it is often the opposite. It is very good at holding water and nutrients and lending support to woody plants. It may be acid, neutral, or alkaline, and this information is often not included in its assessment. Gardening experts tend to make matters worse by suggesting soil analysis, which sounds horribly technical.

Remember that most plants grow on most soils. The exceptions are ericaceous and lime-hating plants, which need soils with a pH lower than neutral, or 7. These plants will not grow on more alkaline soils with a high pH, which prevent them from absorbing certain nutrients that are essential for growth. Other plants grow better on soils with a higher pH; these are known in the United Kingdom as "chalk-loving plants." They will often grow on acid soils too, but sometimes not as happily. You

Rhododendrons and other ericaceous plants need soil that is neutral to acid. If you garden on alkaline soil, you will have to grow them in pots.

Berberis thunbergii f. *atropurpurea* 'Rose Glow' is a good choice for heavy clay soils. In an open, sunny position it delivers the bonus of spectacular fall colour regardless of the pH of the soil.

can easily test soil pH by using a simple soil-testing kit or a pH meter. The latter is a better choice for those with large gardens because the pH may vary in different parts of the space.

The best initial guide for anyone planting a new garden is to take a look around the local area and see which shrubs predominate in other plots and in the native environment. This will give you an indication of which plants do well in your neighbourhood. I do not advise testing for the content of individual nutrients in the soil. It is much better to make them available by adding a good-quality, slow-release fertilizer at the time of planting and annually thereafter.

Challenging growing situations

Although most shrubs are tolerant, forgiving, and easy to grow, some situations present more of a challenge. For best results it is important to select subjects that will thrive rather than struggle in your conditions. Here are suggestions for shrubs to grow in frequently encountered soil conditions and extremes of exposure.

HEAVY CLAY SOILS

Heavy clay soils hang on to water, especially in winter. Clay soil is closely packed and has fine particles, so there are no air spaces, which makes digging difficult. However, clay soils are also fertile, and the right shrubs will grow well. If the soil is exceptionally wet in winter, plant higher than you would on normal, well-drained soil.

Abelia ×*grandiflora*
Aucuba japonica
Berberis thunbergii f. *atropurpurea* 'Rose Glow'
Choisya ternata
Cornus alba 'Sibirica Variegata'
Cotinus coggygria Golden Spirit
Deutzia ×*hybrida* 'Strawberry Fields'
Forsythia ×*spectabilis*
Hibiscus syriacus 'Hamabo'
Lonicera nitida 'Baggesen's Gold'

Magnolia ×*soulangeana*
Mahonia japonica
Osmanthus ×*burkwoodii*
Philadelphus 'Belle Etoile'
Potentilla fruticosa 'Primrose Beauty'
Ribes 'White Icicle'
Rosa Gertrude Jekyll
Spiraea 'Arguta'
Viburnum opulus 'Roseum'
Weigela 'Florida Variegata'

SHALLOW ALKALINE SOILS

Any ericaceous plants, such as rhododendrons and azaleas, are out of the question on shallow alkaline soils. But do not despair. There are plenty of shrubs from which to choose for this situation, including many of the most popular deciduous ones. On shallow soils, it is always beneficial to add compost and well-rotted manure, and to mulch to aid water retention.

The fine, flexible branches and light foliage of *Spiraea* 'Arguta', bridal wreath, cope well on exposed and windy sites.

Buddleja 'Lochinch'
Buxus sempervirens 'Elegantissima'
Cistus obtusifolius 'Thrive'
Cornus mas 'Variegata'
Cotoneaster franchetii
Elaeagnus 'Quicksilver'
Euonymus fortunei 'Emerald Gaiety'
Fuchsia 'Riccartonii'
Hebe 'Red Edge'
Hebe pinguifolia 'Sutherlandii'
Laurus nobilis
Philadelphus 'Virginal'
Potentilla fruticosa 'Abbotswood'
Rosmarinus officinalis
Sambucus nigra f. *porphyrophylla* 'Eva'
Sarcococca confusa
Spiraea japonica 'Little Princess'
Syringa 'Red Pixie'
Vinca minor 'La Grave'
Yucca flaccida 'Golden Sword'

EXPOSED, WINDY SITES

When planting on exposed, windy sites, avoid shrubs with large leaves and with fragile, brittle stems. Small, compact, wiry shrubs do well, as do those with small, tough, leathery leaves. The wind dries out the ground quickly in the absence of rainfall, so careful watering is essential to help plants to get established.

Berberis thunbergii 'Admiration'
Calluna vulgaris 'Robert Chapman'
Cornus alba 'Elegantissima'
Cornus sericea 'Hedgerows Gold'
Cotinus coggygria 'Royal Purple'
Cotoneaster atropurpureus 'Variegatus'
Erica carnea 'Myretoun Ruby'
Erica ×*darleyensis* 'Lena'
Euonymus fortunei 'Emerald 'n' Gold'
Hebe albicans
Hydrangea paniculata 'Kyushu'
Philadelphus 'Virginal'
Spiraea 'Arguta'
Spiraea japonica 'Anthony Waterer'
Viburnum opulus

COASTAL SITUATIONS

The warming effect of the sea is an advantage in the garden, and frosts and snow may be rare in coastal gardens in milder regions. However, some shrubs—particularly those with thin, delicate leaves—are sensitive to salt-laden wind. Shrubs with leaves protected by a woolly layer, like some silver-foliage plants, are a good choice, as are those with leathery or sticky, resinous foliage.

Brachyglottis (Dunedin Group)
   'Sunshine'
Choisya ×*dewitteana* 'White Dazzler'
Cordyline australis 'Torbay Dazzler'
Elaeagnus ×*ebbingei*
Escallonia 'Iveyi'
Euonymus japonicus 'Bravo'
Fuchsia 'Genii'
Griselinia littoralis 'Variegata'
Hebe 'Caledonia'
Hebe 'Midsummer Beauty'
Helianthemum 'Rhodanthe Carneum'
Hydrangea macrophylla 'Blue Wave'
Ilex aquifolium 'Argenteo Marginata'
Lavandula angustifolia 'Hidcote'
Phormium 'Yellow Wave'
Pittosporum tenuifolium 'Tom Thumb'
Pittosporum tobira
Rosa 'Fru Dagmar Hastrup'
Rosmarinus officinalis
Santolina chamaecyparissus

ABOVE *Brachyglottis* (Dunedin Group) 'Sunshine' thrives in coastal conditions and on dry soils. A felt coating protects its leaves well.

RIGHT Silver-foliage shrubs such as *Convolvulus cneorum* love hot, dry, sunny situations and cope with low winter temperatures if the drainage is good.

HEAVY SHADE

Perhaps the most challenging garden situation is low light, lack of water and nutrients, and competition from the hungry, thirsty roots of trees. Shrubs that can survive and compete will still need extra care when first planted. Avoid siting around the drip line of a tree, where the branches extend to, as this is where the tree roots are at their most active and there will be more competition for new planting.

Aucuba japonica 'Rozannie'
Buxus sempervirens
Camellia ×*williamsii* 'Jury's Yellow'
Cotoneaster dammeri
Euonymus fortunei 'Silver Queen'
×*Fatshedera lizei* 'Annemieke'
Ligustrum ovalifolium 'Aureum'
Lonicera nitida 'Maigrun'

Osmanthus heterophyllus 'Variegatus'
Pachysandra terminalis
Sarcococca confusa
Symphoricarpos ×*doorenbosii* 'Mother of Pearl'
Viburnum davidii
Vinca minor 'Ralph Shugert'

HOT, DRY, AND SUNNY SITES

Shrubs with aromatic leaves and silver foliage are nearly always a good choice on hot, dry sites in full sun, as are many plants from the Mediterranean region. Many of these shrubs are surprisingly hardy if the soil is well drained and dry in winter, and if you keep wet off the lower part of the plant by mulching the ground with a layer of grit or gravel. Even though these shrubs cope well with dry conditions, you still need to water them when you first plant.

Ballotta pseudodictamnus
Brachyglottis (Dunedin Group) 'Sunshine'
Buddleja Nanho Blue
Ceanothus 'Concha'
Ceanothus thyrsiflorus var. *repens*
Cistus ×*dansereuari* 'Decumbens'
Cistus ×*pulverulentus* 'Sunset'
Convolvulus cneorum
Cordyline 'Southern Splendour'
Cornonilla valentina subsp. *glauca* 'Citrinus'

Erysimum 'Bowles's Mauve'
Helianthemum 'Rhodanthe Carneum'
Helichrysum italicum 'Korma'
Lavandula pedunculata subsp. *pedunculata*
Phlomis italica
Potentilla fruticosa 'Abbotswood'
Rosmarinus officinalis
Salvia officinalis 'Purpurascens'
Santolina rosmarinifolia 'Primrose Gem'
Yucca flaccida 'Golden Sword'

ABOVE Always choose a shrub that is well branched and robust at the base.

LEFT Never buy a shrub just because it has a low price. It is worth purchasing a solid plant that has been well grown, looks healthy, and has a good root system and branch structure.

WET CONDITIONS

Most well-known garden shrubs resent waterlogged soil at any time of the year, but especially for long periods in winter. If these conditions prevail in your garden, your choice of woody plants is limited. If you use drifts of a particular plant to create a bold planting scheme, the effect can be stunning. It is essential to hard prune red-barked dogwoods and willows in late winter to maintain the effect.

Amelanchier canadensis
Calycanthus floridus
Clethra alnifolia
Cornus alba 'Aurea'
Cornus alba 'Gouchaultii'
Gaultheria shallon
Myrica gale
Physocarpus opulifolius 'Diablo'
Salix alba 'Britzensis'

Sambucus nigra f. *laciniata*
Sambucus racemosa 'Sutherland Gold'
Sorbaria tomentosa var. *angustifolia*
Spiraea ×*vanhouttei*
Symphoricarpos ×*doorenbosii*
   'Mother of Pearl'
Vaccinium corymbosum
Viburnum opulus

Healthy shrubs

Shrubs are an inexpensive commodity, especially when you consider the value they bring to a garden—usually through more than one season and over many years. It is worth a little additional investment to get the right plant. Despite the fact that they take months or years to produce, shrubs are living things that cannot be stored, and they need care to keep them alive. Avoid plants that have been hanging around the nursery or garden centre bed for a long time, shrubs that have been butchered by careless pruning, or specimens that generally look tired in pots infested with weeds and moss.

It is usually easy to spot plants that are from the current season's production. They have clean pots and unfaded labels. They do not appear to be too large for their containers, and their foliage and stems look clean and healthy. If you knock one out of the pot, the roots are white or cream and give reasonable coverage around the rootball,

ABOVE Sometimes a group of three smaller shrubs will do a better job than one large plant. These lavenders are a good example.

RIGHT It is worth investing in a larger key plant like *Choisya ×dewitteana* 'Aztec Pearl', which can gain you a year or more in maturity.

which should hang together without falling apart. (Note that there are exceptions to this rule, particularly with roses, which never make a good rootball. If you knock a rose out of its pot, the growing medium will fall away.)

If you are buying a shrub that will ultimately be a bushy plant with a number of branches rising from ground level, look for a well-branched individual. A philadelphus is a good example. If you buy one with one or two weak stems, plant it, and leave it to grow, it will continue to be a leggy, weak plant as it matures. You would need to prune it back hard after planting to encourage branching from the base if it is ever to make a decent specimen. You are better off buying a well-grown, well-branched plant in the first place.

Most garden centres offer different sizes of shrubs, from young ones in small pots that are little more than rooted cuttings to bigger specimens in much larger containers. The average plant in the United Kingdom is in a 2- to 3-litre (half-gallon) pot, and this size accounts for a large proportion of shrubs sold. However, there is an increasing demand for larger specimens in containers of 7 litres (1.5 gallons) or larger. These make a more instant impact in the garden and give more immediate maturity to a planting scheme. These cost more because they take longer to produce. You are, in fact, buying time.

Which is the best buy—the smaller, cheaper shrub that is often claimed to establish easily, or the larger specimen that costs more and may be more demanding in terms of watering and care once it is planted? It depends on your time frame. If you are not prepared to wait for a plant to grow, choose the larger specimen, unless it is a short-lived plant like lavender. As part a planting scheme, a group of three smaller lavenders may be a better choice to fill the space than one large specimen.

When I am planting a new bed from scratch or specifying plants for a scheme, I always choose a balance of larger specimens and standard-size shrubs. This gives the scheme variation in height, which conveys a sense of maturity to the planting at the outset. If you plant all specimen shrubs, there is no visual comparison in the planting scheme and the overall effect can be flat and immature. For the larger specimens, I choose long-term backbone structure shrubs that are worth a little extra investment, and those that can take longer to get established. *Choisya ×dewitteana* 'Aztec Pearl' is a good example. Although this is a reasonably fast-growing shrub, it can be slow for the first couple of seasons. It is likely to be an important element in the scheme by providing evergreen structure and foliage interest, so it is worth gaining a year or two by planting a larger specimen.

ABOVE The golden yellow flowers of evergreen *Sophora* 'Sun King' are a spring highlight and transform the shrub for several weeks.

LEFT *Sambucus nigra* f. *porphyrophylla* 'Eva' and *Brachyglottis* (Dunedin Group) 'Sunshine' make striking planting partners because they accentuate each other's attributes.

The bigger picture

When selecting for our gardens, we are ultimately attracted by individual shrubs that catch our eye. We often see plants as individuals and fail to consider what they contribute to the overall planting picture. Developing the ability to see how plants work together is the secret of creating successful and attractive planting schemes. The impact of two or three plants put together thoughtfully in a bed or border is usually far greater than the impact of the individual shrub. There are several factors to consider, including colour, flowering succession, fragrance, and shapes and textures.

COLOUR

Sambucus nigra f. *porphyrophylla* 'Eva' is a stunning deciduous shrub with dark purple-black feathery foliage and flattened heads of pinkish flowers. It is a striking plant in its own right, and it mixes well with many other shrubs and perennials. However, its foliage does not stand out against a dark evergreen and may disappear alongside other purple-leaved shrubs such as corylus and cotinus. However, planted in partnership with a silver-leaved shrub like *Elaeagnus* 'Quicksilver' or *Brachyglottis* (Dunedin Group) 'Sunshine', the sambucus foliage becomes all the more striking. Likewise, the rather utilitarian brachyglottis suddenly becomes all the more silver and velvety, transforming a basic shrub into a more sophisticated plant.

Most successful planting schemes have colour and interest over a long period, if not throughout the year. It is worth planning to include shrubs with different peak seasons of interest. This is where many planting schemes and gardens fail to deliver. Because some less-experienced gardeners are drawn to the garden only in spring, they are attracted to plants that perform at that time. The resulting gardens can run

TOP LEFT *Rosa ×alba* 'Alba Semiplena' is a deliciously fragrant summer-flowering rose of delicate beauty.

TOP RIGHT The dark black-purple leaves of *Physocarpus opulifolius* 'Diablo' are a striking contrast to white flowers and foliage.

BOTTOM LEFT *Syringa vulgaris* var. *alba* may not bloom for long, but it is lovely when it does.

BOTTOM RIGHT The lilac-like flower heads of *Hydrangea paniculata* are spectacular in late summer and fall.

out of steam as the season progresses. The biggest mistake you can make is to go to the garden centre and buy everything in one day. The plants that are stocked are likely to be those that look good at the time, so your choice may not include shrubs for other seasons.

FLOWERING SUCCESSION

Nearly all gardeners desire flowers. Even foliage fanatics are attracted by flowers' ephemeral pleasure, seasonal colour, and fragrance. The flowers of deciduous shrubs are part of the plant's seasonally changing picture, alongside the progression of foliage from new leaves in spring to fall colour and the skeleton of branches in winter. Flowers on evergreen shrubs are usually their seasonal highlight, adding a different colour to a constant picture of green or variegated leaves.

In temperate regions, with careful selection, it is possible to have a shrub in flower on every day of the year. But you also need to consider what each individual shrub is contributing when it is not in flower. Is the display of blooms worth waiting for? How long does it last? What does the shrub look like outside the flowering season? What can you plant alongside it to provide another display of flowers?

Consider a white lilac, like *Syringa vulgaris* var. *alba*. It produces large panicles of fragrant flowers in late spring on a large shrub with plain green foliage. For the rest of the summer and into fall it has plain medium green leaves and an unremarkable branch framework in winter. The flowering period is about three weeks. This is not a long-lasting display of flowers for the size of the shrub, and its contribution for the

ABOVE The light, bright, green-and-white foliage of *Cornus mas* 'Variegata' maintains the white element of this planting scheme from spring to fall.

LEFT *Osmanthus delavayi* is a smaller evergreen alternative to the white lilac in this planting scheme.

rest of the year is unremarkable. But if you love lilac and have the space, those fragrant flowers are worth waiting for, and their opulence and scent lift the spirits when seen against a blue spring sky.

One could argue that this is a good structure or background shrub for the back of a border, and it may fill the role of a tree in a planting scheme. It could be valuable in a large garden, but in a small one it probably does not work hard enough to earn its keep for the rest of the year. Where space permits, you could extend the season by planting it alongside a white shrub rose, such as *Rosa* ×*alba* 'Alba Semiplena', a tough and hardy rose with tall, arching stems carrying blue-grey leaves and large semi-double pure white blooms with golden stamens. The fragrance is delicious, and although the rose blooms only once, it does so for about four weeks.

Both the lilac and the rose would benefit from the company of a shrub with dark purple foliage, such as *Physocarpus opulifolius* 'Diablo', which has a robust, upright habit. It would also make a superb background for the white, lilac-like flower heads of *Hydrangea paniculata*. This plant lacks the fragrance of the other two, but it flowers from late summer well into fall, putting on a display for at least two months. In a dry fall and winter, the flowers fade to parchment and remain attractive throughout the winter months alongside the tan-coloured bare stems of the physocarpus.

Although none of these medium- to large-flowering shrubs has a particularly long flowering season, the group could produce nearly four months of flowers and a changing picture for nine months of the year. You will have to prune to maintain flower power, and this simple grouping will need space, at least 3m by 3m (10 ft. by 10 ft.).

You could also include an evergreen-flowering shrub in this grouping to prolong the season of interest. *Osmanthus* ×*delavayi* has arching stems and small dark green leaves, and in spring it has wonderfully fragrant tubular white flowers all along the branches. In the preceding combination it could take the place of the syringa in terms of flowering season, colour, and fragrance. However, its habit is different and its foliage colour is much darker, and it would disappear alongside the purple physocarpus. If you change the physocarpus for a light green-and-white variegated shrub, such as *Cornus mas* 'Variegata', the combination works.

Although *Philadelphus* 'Belle Etoile' flowers for only a few precious weeks, I anticipate its delicious fragrance throughout the year.

ABOVE *Myrtus communis* is a symbol of love and immortality.

TOP LEFT The aromatic foliage of *Laurus nobilis*.

TOP RIGHT The soft yellow, aromatic foliage of *Salvia officinalis* 'Icterina' highlights a birdbath feature in a paved area.

FRAGRANT FLOWERS

A garden should be a sensory experience, and fragrance is an essential element. I include philadelphus in as many planting schemes as possible. For the rest of the year the shrub may be rather green and ordinary, but for those three weeks when it is in bloom, the scent transforms the garden and I can forgive its shortcomings.

Shrubs to plant for fragrant flowers

WINTER
Daphne bholua 'Jacqueline Postill'
Daphne odora 'Rebecca'
Hamamelis ×intermedia 'Orange Peel'
Mahonia japonica
Sarcococca confusa

SPRING
Magnolia stellata
Osmanthus delavayi
Rhododendron luteum
Skimmia ×confusa 'Kew Green'
Syringa 'Red Pixie'
Viburnum carlesii 'Diana'

SUMMER
Buddleja 'Lochinch'
Elaeagnus 'Quicksilver'
Magnolia grandifora
Philadelphus maculatus 'Sweet Clare'
Pittosporum tobira
Rosa Gertrude Jekyll
Rosa 'Roseraie de l'Hay'

FALL
Abelia ×grandiflora
Choisya ternata
Clerodendrum bungei
Elaeagnus ×ebbingei

AROMATIC FOLIAGE

Fragrance comes not only from flowers, but also from aromatic foliage. Other than lavender, woody herbs are often forgotten as part of the shrub-planting palette. In garden centres and nurseries they are usually offered alongside other herbs for culinary and medicinal purposes, rather than grouped with shrubs grown for their ornamental value.

The various cultivars of *Rosmarinus officinalis*, *Thymus vulgaris*, *Thymus citriodorus*, and *Salvia officinalis* are wonderful shrubs for their foliage form and their aromatic qualities. When planted alongside paths and paved areas in full sun, they add to the sensory experience, as their aromatic foliage releases its fragrance when passers-by brush against or gently crush them. These are drought-resistant, sun-loving plants, perfect for poor soils where many others fail to establish.

Rosmarinus officinalis, both the species and cultivars such as *Rosmarinus officinalis* 'Miss Jessop's Upright', have the benefit of an early display of flowers. Although pink and white forms exist, the blue ones are the most valuable. They deliver a showy display of light to bright blue flowers amidst spiky silvery leaves. Few other blue-flowering shrubs put on such a delicate display, particularly early in the season.

Laurus nobilis, true laurel or common bay, is the best-known large evergreen shrub with aromatic foliage. This native of the Mediterranean is surprisingly hardy in cooler regions, but gardeners in harsher climates should avoid it. Many shrubs hailing from similar warm, dry areas have aromatic leaves; the oils that give them their fragrance also prevent desiccation.

Myrtus communis, myrtle, is one my favourite tender shrubs. I love its bright green, elegantly pointed leaves carried on fine stems, as well as its light green rounded buds in summer, which promise fragrant white flowers. The foliage is especially vibrant in summer, and I grow it in a pot on my patio so I can occasionally crush one of its pungently fragrant leaves. The smell transports me to the Greek island of Kos, to the Asklepion where Hippocrates taught medicine and I first came across this wonderful plant. It grows wild and its verdant leaves contrast with the hot, arid environment. Sprigs of myrtle are given to visitors as symbols of love and immortality.

My garden is really too cold for this shrub. I should choose a hardier subject, but its qualities overcome the power of reason. Emotion will always be the more powerful influence on our selection of plants.

ABOVE Any combination of shrubs looks livelier if it contains a variety of shapes and textures.

LEFT The silvery foliage and sparkling white flowers of *Hebe pinguifolia* 'Sutherlandii'.

Other shrubs to plant for aromatic foliage

Helichrysum italicum 'Korma'
Lavandula angustifolia 'Hidcote'
Lavandula pedunculata subsp. *pedunculata*
Perovskia 'Blue Spire'
Prostanthera cuneata
Salvia officinalis 'Icterina'
Santolina chamaecyparissus

ABOVE A neatly trimmed dwarf box hedge contains manicured mounds of lavender that soften and billow as they bloom.

RIGHT The golden cut foliage of *Rhus typhina* Tiger Eyes shines against the dark leaves of a purple hazel.

SHAPES AND TEXTURES

Successful plantings include various leaf shapes and different plant habits. Temperate gardens are generally full of round mounds, so anything with vertical lines is a contrast. This may be in the form of upright stems, or it could just be a shrub with narrow, spiky leaves.

Consider a planting of silver-foliage shrubs, most of which have a soft, silky appearance and gentle colouring. *Santolina chamaecyparissus* and *Convolvulus cneorum* both make low-mounded shrubs with silver foliage. However, their textures are totally different. The santolina has a woolly appearance and is quite soft and sticky to touch. The convolvulus is shiny and silky, and its narrow silver leaves reflect the light; it feels like satin when stroked.

On the other hand, *Helichrysum italicum* 'Korma', curry plant, has a more open, spiky appearance. Its narrow silver leaves are almost needle-like. Although the plant is a similar shape and stature to the other two, its texture is different again.

A grey-leaved hebe, such as *Hebe pinguifolia* 'Sutherlandii', would sit happily in the same planting scheme. The colour may be more green than grey, but it is closer to a silver-foliage shrub than a plain-leaved evergreen. The hebe has tiny, closely packed leaves that give it an altogether more solid appearance and a harder texture than the santolina, helichrysum, or convolvulus.

In a larger planting scheme containing several plants of the same subject, the shrub that predominates conveys its character to the overall scheme. So if santolina is repeated, the planting's overall texture will be soft and woolly, perhaps punctuated by shrubs of different textures.

This is one of the reasons why *Buxus sempervirens*, and the dwarf form *Buxus sempervirens* 'Suffruticosa', work so well when used to contain softer, more informal subjects in a parterre or knot garden. Box, with its twiggy, branched habit and tiny leaves, lends itself to clipping, and the medium to dark green leaves maintain a uniform colour when the shrub is clipped. But the clipped box also has a dense, solid texture that contrasts with the lighter, more open planting within.

Large, bold leaves in a planting scheme become stronger and more impressive when contrasted against a softer texture. Small-leaved groundcover shrubs such as *Lonicera nitida* 'Maigrun', *Vinca minor*, or *Pachysandra teminalis* are ideal subjects for underplanting bold evergreens such as *Fatsia japonica* and *Viburnum davidii*.

The textural contrast of hard and soft foliage in a planting is also accentuated by

including different-coloured foliage. A cut-leaved subject such as *Rhus typhina* Tiger Eyes becomes lighter and brighter when planted alongside the dark leaves of *Corylus maxima* 'Purpurea'.

Every shrub has a unique character, whether it is primarily grown for its flowers, foliage, or stems. Some shrubs have more ornamental attributes than others, but often it depends how they are used and which shrubs they are planted with. Foliage is the foundation of good planting. Look at the leaves of any shrub you are thinking of purchasing. Before you buy, consider what the foliage contributes and how it works with other shrubs around it. Be sure it is a good fit.

ABOVE A stunning, simple planting using *Sarcococca confusa* at RHS Wisley in Surrey, England.

LEFT A lively combination of *Photinia ×fraseri* 'Red Robin' and *Cornus alba* 'Elegantissima' is all the more colourful against a dark backdrop of *Prunus laurocerasus*, cherry laurel.

BASIC EVERGREENS

A plain evergreen shrub may not sound like the most appealing choice for your garden, especially if it does not produce flowers or berries. But these plants play a vital role in both formal gardens, where trimmed box and yew often feature, and informal situations.

Large plain evergreens, such as *Prunus lusitanica*, *Laurus nobilis*, and *Elaeagnus ×ebbingei*, are excellent screening and background shrubs. In a large garden they give the planting body and a foundation on which to build. When deciduous shrubs in the foreground lose their leaves, these basic evergreens maintain life in the planting and prevent it from becoming a mass of bony winter skeletons.

In a small garden, basic evergreen shrubs, such as *Sarcococca confusa* and *Viburnum davidii*, also play a structural role. These two plants also show the diversity of plain evergreens. The viburnum has dark green foliage that is strongly furrowed and ribbed. The sarcococca has small, shiny, deep green leaves on upright stems. They have very different textures and shapes, as well as distinct characteristics.

The versatility of *Sarcococca confusa* is shown in the mass planting created by Tom Stuart-Smith, Chelsea Flower Show award-winning garden designer at RHS Wisley in Surrey, England. Here waves of sarcococca contrast with feathery mounds of *Hakenochloa macra* and solid columns of plain green *Fagus sylvatica*. The picture changes in winter, when the foliage of hakenochloa and beech change to papery brown, while the sarcococca maintains its shining deep green foliage.

The flowers of sarcococca contribute winter fragrance, although their rather subtle floral display can go almost unnoticed. Some evergreens, such as camellias and rhododendrons, produce much showier flowers. An evergreen camellia could be considered a rather plain shrub for most of the year, but for one month the presence of gorgeous blooms transforms its appearance. This is why these shrubs are so popular: they play more than one role in a planting scheme.

Although variegated evergreens and deciduous shrubs with variegated and colourful foliage light up the planting, you can have too much of a good thing. Green comes in many shades. Combining bold and soft greens, and placing bright green leaves alongside deep green ones, will keep the planting lively when flowers are taking a break. Most planting schemes also need plain green foliage as a foil for showier subjects. Green foliage does not necessarily dilute the effect of other subjects; instead, it gives them space to shine. Rather like the green space created by a lawn in a garden, plain green leaves are there to set off the other colours of foliage, flowers, and stems.

Shrubs to plant for basic evergreen foliage

Aucuba japonica 'Rozannie'
Choisya ternata
Euonymus japonicus 'Green Rocket'
Griselinia littoralis
Lonicera nitida 'Maigrun'
Pittosporum tenuifolium
Pittosporum tenuifolium 'Golf Ball'
Prunus lusitanica 'Myrtifolia'

COLOURFUL FOLIAGE

While flowers are an ephemeral pleasure, foliage is more enduring. Foliage contributes colour and interest throughout the growing season—or, in the case of evergreen shrubs, throughout the year. Adding shrubs with gold, silver, purple, or variegated leaves means imbuing a planting scheme with enduring colour.

Evergreen shrubs, including conifers with coloured foliage, are particularly important in winter, when deciduous plants lose their leaves. Evergreen and deciduous shrubs also take on a leading role in midsummer, when the early summer–flowering

RIGHT The golden leaves of *Leycesteria formosa* Golden Lanterns will predominate in any planting scheme.

BELOW The colourful foliage of spiraea, salvia, and berberis maintains the colour in this planting scheme from spring to fall. The foxgloves are a seasonal highlight.

shrubs have passed, the roses are taking a break, and late summer–flowering shrubs have yet to perform. Variegated, gold-leaved, and purple-leaved shrubs can add considerable colour and variety in the middle layer of the planting picture at this stage in the season.

These plants are also invaluable when it comes to holding a colour theme together. If you plan a yellow scheme with flowers alone, the effect will be disappointing for much of the season. However, shrubs such as the golden-leaved *Leycesteria formosa* Golden Lanterns and the green-and-gold variegated *Cornus sericea* 'Hedgerows Gold' leave no doubt as to the predominant colour in a planting scheme from spring to fall. The green foliage of other shrubs and perennials provide a foil for the yellow.

A green-and-white scheme without green-and-white variegated foliage will be green for much of the year. If you add shrubs such as *Pittosporum tenuifolium* 'Irene Patterson' and *Euonymus fortunei* 'Emerald Gaiety', the picture will be green and white throughout the year. Again, plain evergreens such as *Choisya ternata* and *Osmanthus ×burkwoodii* make the white variegation seem stronger. The addition of a few white blooms—perhaps *Narcissus* 'Thalia' and *Pulmonaria* 'Sissinghust White' for spring and white *Cyclamen neapolitanum* for fall—add seasonal interest and increase the proportion of white in the planting.

ABOVE The bright green-and-white variegated evergreen foliage of *Pittosporum tenuifolium* 'Irene Patterson' will maintain the colour scheme throughout the year.

LEFT The bold gold-and-green variegation of *Cornus sericea* 'Hedgerows Gold' adds strong colour to the planting from spring to fall.

Variegated shrubs

Some gardeners claim to dislike variegated plants, which they consider unnatural, out of place, gaudy, artificial, and suburban. Variegated plants really only exist in gardens; they are rarely seen in the natural environment. They often originate as variegated shoots on plain green plants. The gardener then selects and propagates these oddities—partly for their novelty value but mostly for their ornamental qualities.

Many gardeners eschew variegated leaves because of an aversion to the bold gold-and-green variegations of some euonymus, elaeagnus, aucubas, and the like. Yellow is a loud colour in the garden. It shouts and attracts attention. When associated with dark green in the same leaf, the lively cocktail is just too much for the faint of heart.

The strong combination of hard yellow and green is difficult to combine with other colours, as it swamps our beloved pinks, blues, and other pastels and screams angrily with red. Yellow-and-green variegations partner happily only with their own individual hues: plain green leaves, pure golden foliage, and cream and pale yellow. They also contrast well with dark purple and wine foliage, but this combination is bold and strong, not soothing.

The soft combination of green and white is far more acceptable, even to plain-leaf purists. The strength of variegation has a major impact on how pleasing we find it.

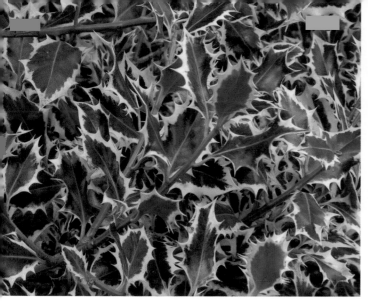

ABOVE The variegation in
the leaves of *Ilex aquifolium*
'Elegantissima' is clearly defined.

RIGHT The variegation of
Cornus alba 'Sibirica Variegata'
is soft, subtle, and gentle
against neighbouring plants.

Some variegation is clearly defined. Take *Ilex aquifolium* 'Elegantissima', for example, which is deep green with a clearly defined creamy white margin to each leaf. Although the variegation is defined, the colour combination is sophisticated.

In some cases the variegation is softer and more diffuse. *Cornus alba* 'Sibirica Variegata' has softer green-and-white variegated leaves with a hint of pink. The overall effect is more subtle, and the shrubs blends rather than contrasts with adjacent plantings.

Variegated pittosporums have small shining leaves that reflect the light. The overall effect of *Pittosporum tenuifolium* 'Variegatum' is light, soft, and sage green, and the variegation is visible only on close inspection. The same is true of variegated *Buxus sempervirens* 'Elegantissima'. Its tiny deep green leaves are boldly edged with cream, but the effect is soft and diffuse from a distance. This rich cream variegation is not enhanced alongside pure white variegations. It is at its best with deep green or more subtly coloured leaves, such as the soft yellow and copper foliage of *Osmanthus heterophyllus* 'Goshiki'.

Shrubs to plant for green-and-white variegated foliage

Cornus alba 'Elegantissima'
Cornus alternifolia 'Argentea'
Cornus controversa 'Variegata'
Cornus mas 'Variegata'
Euonymus fortunei 'Emerald Gaiety'
Euonymus japonicus 'Bravo'

Euonymus japonicus 'Microphyllus
  Variegatus'
Fatsia japonica 'Variegata'
Pittosporum tenuifolium 'Irene
  Patterson'
Vinca minor 'Ralph Shugert'

The warm copper and cream
variegations of *Osmanthus
heterophyllus* 'Goshiki'.

Shrubs to plant for yellow-and-green variegated foliage

Aucuba japonica 'Angelon'
Coprosma 'Lemon and Lime'
Cornus alba 'Gouchaultii'
Cornus sericea 'Hedgerows Gold'
Daphne odora 'Rebecca'

Elaeagnus ×*ebbingei* 'Viveleg'
Euonymus japonicus 'Chollipo'
Ligustrum ovalifolium 'Aureum'
Lonicera pileata 'Lemon 'Beauty'
Yucca flaccida 'Golden Sword'

Purple and bronze foliage

Purple, wine red, plum, and bronze foliage shrubs add depth and drama to a planting scheme. They are the foundation of any planting with hot colours, and the essential element in a red border. Alongside these hues other colours become louder and

stronger. Plant an orange hemerocallis alongside a deep purple cotinus and suddenly the daylily becomes even more powerful.

Purple-foliage shrubs are the ultimate mixers, as they can harmonize with just about any other colour. Their addition can be the salvation of a discordant planting scheme. A purple physocarpus or cotinus added as a backdrop to a planting scheme can amplify individual colours but have a calming effect on the combinations.

Although we usually use the term *purple*, shades vary from plum-black to wine red. Some, such as *Physocarpus opulifolius* 'Diable d'Or', have distinctly copper leaves. Purple-flowering shrubs are always at their best in open situations where they get several hours of direct sun each day. In shady situations they lose colour, often fading to brown or muddy green.

Only a few purple-leaved evergreen shrubs exist. Purple-black *Pittosporum tenuifolium* 'Tom Thumb' is particularly valuable, especially because its colour is most intense in midwinter.

Some designers are wary of dark purple–leaved shrubs and trees, and describe them as "black holes" in the planting picture. These specimens can appear heavy if poorly placed or planted in large, solid groups. Their presence is nearly always more successful when combined with other shrubs, perennials, or grasses in the foreground.

ABOVE *Physocarpus opulifolius* 'Diable d'Or' has glowing copper foliage, particularly at the tips of the shoots, in an open, sunny situation.

LEFT The deep blue *Clematis* ×*durandii* growing through a purple-leaved *Berberis thunbergii* f. *atropurpurea* 'Rose Glow' has a gem-like quality, even though it has few flowers.

Shrubs to plant for purple and wine red foliage

Acer palmatum 'Bloodgood'
Acer palmatum var. *dissectum*
   'Crimson Queen'
Berberis thunbergii f. *atropurpurea*
   'Admiration'
Cercis canadensis 'Forest Pansy'

Cotinus coggygria 'Royal Purple'
Hebe 'Caledonia'
Phormium Back in Black
Physocarpus opulifolius 'Diablo'
Sambucus nigra f. *porphyrophylla* 'Eva'
Weigela florida 'Foliis Purpureis'

Golden yellow foliage

Golden-foliage shrubs, or those with strong yellow variegations, are invaluable when you want to lead the eye to an entrance, a point in the distance, or a garden feature.

A gold-variegated evergreen, such as the widely planted *Euonymus fortunei* 'Emerald 'n' Gold', will light up a shady corner under a tree or at the foot of a wall. *Choisya ternata* 'Sundance' is one of the most widely planted golden-leaved evergreen shrubs. This eye-catching subject owes its success to its shining appeal as a young

ABOVE When the simple yellow-foliage *Lonicera nitida* 'Baggesen's Gold' is left to grow naturally, it creates a light, beckoning backdrop for a garden seat.

RIGHT *Choisya ternata* 'Sundance' loses its intensity in shade, becoming lime yellow and fresh green, but it remains a contrast to surrounding darker evergreens.

plant, as it simply stands out in any garden centre plant area or nursery bed. Sadly, it is often badly placed in gardens, left to sit in splendid isolation or as a large golden blob in the middle of a nondescript green border. But its colour ensures that it is always the focal point, regardless of whether it is well positioned. It can look stunning as part of a scheme containing yellow-flowering shrubs, bulbs, and perennials and other golden-foliage and yellow-variegated shrubs.

Like purple-foliage shrubs, most yellow-leaved shrubs lose colour in shade as green hues creep into their golden mantle. This may be an advantage in a planting scheme for semi-shade. The same dazzling yellow *Choisya ternata* 'Sundance' becomes softer and gentler in these conditions, and its foliage turns lime yellow.

Sun scorch can be a drawback of deciduous yellow-leaved shrubs when planted in full sun. They are usually fine when the new leaves unfurl in spring; however, the leaves often go brown at the tips, and in patches of the blades of the upper leaves, in strong, hot sunshine in summer. This is more of a problem on dry soil.

Shrubs to plant for golden yellow foliage

Choisya ×*dewitteana* 'Aztec Gold'
Cornus alba 'Aurea'
Cotinus coggygria Golden Spirit
Fuchsia 'Genii'
Leycesteria formosa Golden Lanterns

Philadelphus coronarius 'Aureus'
Pinus mugo 'Wintergold'
Rubus cockburnianus 'Golden Vale'
Sambucus racemosa 'Sutherland Gold'
Spiraea japonica 'Firelight'

COLOUR BALANCE

Colour balance is an essential element in any well-designed garden. This is particularly important in the foliage layers, which are the enduring aspect of the planting scheme. A common mistake is to make planting decisions while *in* the garden, rather than from the points where key plants can have the biggest visual impact. Sometimes the best way to assess the garden's colour balance is to take pictures from these significant viewing areas, such the living room window, the bedroom windows, the kitchen window, and the terrace.

It is particularly important to balance yellow, white-variegated, and purple foliage in the garden, as these are eye-catching elements amidst the green canopy. If you plant a yellow-leaved shrub on one side of the garden, for example, you also need yellow on the other side. It does not necessarily have to be at the same level, but the two sides need to balance. A purple-leaved tree, such as *Prunus cerasifera* 'Nigra', on one side

ABOVE In this garden the addition of a purple-leaved shrub in the foreground would balance the red-leaved maple. It would also accentuate the perspective by drawing the eye through the vista.

ABOVE LEFT The foliage colour, especially from dark purple–leaved shrubs and trees, is well balanced through this planting picture.

LEFT The solid form of clipped box balls contrasts with the open structure of *Cornus sanguinea* 'Midwinter Fire' in winter.

ABOVE The light, airy stems of *Perovskia* 'Blue Spire' add an ethereal quality in this narrow, sunny border.

ABOVE RIGHT A mass planting of deciduous azaleas create a riot of colour beneath pine trees at The Sir Harold Hillier Gardens in Hampshire, England.

of a garden could be balanced with a purple-foliage shrub like *Berberis thunbergii* f. *atropurpurea* 'Rose Glow' on the other. The berberis is low growing, so it will balance the tree more successfully if planted toward the foreground.

The same is true for white-variegated foliage if it plays a dominant role. This does not mean you need to use more specimens of the same shrub elsewhere in the garden; you can simply plant shrubs or trees that will convey the same foliage qualities. You can also use this distribution of colour to accentuate the perspective, perhaps by siting more muted tones or shorter subjects in the distance.

REPETITION AND MASS PLANTING

You can repeat particular shrubs or groups of shrubs to draw the eye through the planting picture of a garden or through a particular vista. Repetition emphasizes a theme in the design, and it can create a powerful rhythm along a pathway or route. Shrubs with a bold form, such as clipped box balls, are often used to provide a degree of formality that contrasts with the informal shapes of other shrubs. A group of formal shapes clustered around a feature provides contrast to the rest of the planting and increases the impact of the seat, sculpture, birdbath, or statue. You can use naturally compact shrubs, such as *Hebe* 'Red Edge' or *Cistus obtusifolius* 'Thrive', in a similar way.

Repeating a low shrub, such as lavender or groups of lavenders, along the front of a border ties the theme together by carrying the same soft colour and texture through the scheme. The blue of the flowers and the soft silver foliage can work alongside everything else in the planting. Sometimes a row of the same shrub in a narrow border can be more effective than a mixed planting of several different varieties. This can be a light airy subject, such as *Perovskia* 'Blue Spire' for a sunny border, or a more spreading, climbing shrub, like *Euonymus fortunei* 'Emerald Gaiety', in shade.

In private gardens we are often averse to planting a particular shrub if it is already growing elsewhere. However, if you like a shrub that does well in your garden and contributes in more than one season, consider planting more of the same. If you are looking for a plant for a particular situation, do not dismiss the possibility of repetition in favour of another shrub that will be less successful. Remember that repetition often unifies the planting and helps you avoid fragmented planting schemes.

Mass plantings of shrubs can make the most dramatic features in large gardens, whether they are groups of the same subject or shrubs that flower at the same time. Rhododendron gardens are a good example, as the whole planting erupts in a spring festival of colour before it fades into mounds of green for the rest of the season. Hydrangeas can achieve a similar effect in late summer and fall, but their season is longer.

Layers of the planting picture

We tend to think of shrubs as subjects mainly for the middle and lower layers of the planting picture. But some of these versatile plants can fill the role of trees, while others will hug the ground.

SHRUBS TO USE AS TREES

Tall, upright shrubs, or those with a canopy on one or more stems, easily fill the role of trees in planting schemes. You can also train some shrubs as standards, where the lower branches are removed to leave a clear stem with a crown of branches and foliage. These shrubs are ideal in small gardens and close to buildings, where a standard tree may be problematic because of its spread or the extent of its root system.

The most popular shrubs that work as trees are varieties of *Acer palmatum*, Japanese maples. Their stature and vigour vary. Some achieve small tree proportions relatively quickly, while other types stay within the middle and lower layers of the planting picture. Regardless of their size, these shrubs have character and exquisite foliage that changes with the seasons. There are many varieties from which to choose, although a reliable favourite is *Acer palmatum* 'Bloodgood', a vigorous variety of upright growth with spreading branches and wine red foliage.

Photinia ×fraseri 'Red Robin' is one of the most popular of the shrubs that lend themselves to being trained standards. Its evergreen foliage and bright red new growth make it a popular choice to grow in pots and to add height to a small garden. The foliage is dense if you prune the shrub regularly, so it can be a useful screen if grown as a large standard. When pruned less severely it often produces large clusters of pink-white flowers in spring, which are attractive to bees and pollinating insects.

Other evergreen shrubs that lend themselves to training as standards include *Pittosporum tenuifolium*, *Prunus lusitanica*, *Ilex aquifolium* varieties, and, on a smaller scale, *Euonymus fortunei* varieties.

Sambucus nigra f. *porphyrophylla* 'Eva' is sometimes grown on a single stem. In a planting scheme its dark, divided foliage is dramatic when carried above the underplanting, and it casts little shade. The lovely white spring-flowering shrub *Exochorda macrantha* 'The Bride' makes a wonderful standard, with soft green foliage gently

ABOVE *Acer palmatum* 'Bloodgood' and *Photinia ×fraseri* 'Red Robin' fill the roles of small trees in pots on this terrace.

LEFT Removing the lower branches from this *Pittosporum tenuifolium* transforms a solid evergreen shrub into a small, compact-headed tree.

BELOW Lovely *Prunus incisa* 'Kojo-no-mai' is a hard-working shrub for all seasons and ideal for the smallest garden. In a pot it has the presence of a tiny tree.

LEFT *Eucryphia ×nymansensis* 'Nymansay' can make a tall, narrow tree in a sheltered woodland garden. The late-summer flowers are spectacular.

MIDDLE In milder areas the variegated *Cordyline australis* 'Torbay Dazzler' can make a stunning small, exotic tree.

RIGHT The sensational fall foliage colour of *Cornus florida* f. *rubra*.

cascading on arching branches. It is spectacular when covered with ice white blossoms in late spring.

Flowering dogwoods are some of the most magnificent shrubs to grow as trees, and some can reach large proportions. *Cornus* 'Porlock' grows quickly as a young plant and flowers from an early age. Most cultivars of *Cornus florida* have a slender conical habit and a distinct pagoda shape. Their early summer flowers are spectacular, as are the fiery colours of their foliage in fall. The curly twigs of *Cornus florida* f. *rubra* carry deep pink waved bracts in early summer, and the curled foliage turns to shades of orange and red in fall.

Those gardening on acid soils could consider *Camellia japonica* as an evergreen alternative to a tree. It is particularly successful in shade, and you can train it as a standard. Alternatively, eucryphias are an inspired choice, particularly because they flower later in summer when few shrubs are performing. These upright evergreens can reach large proportions in ideal growing conditions. *Eucryphia ×nymansensis* 'Nymansay' has deep green foliage and large single white flowers with red-brown stamens in late summer. Its form is strong and columnar when young and becomes broader with maturity. A shrub in full flower is a magnificent sight.

In milder regions gardeners often grow *Cordyline australis*, cabbage palm, as an exotic subject on a single or multiple stems. Its sword-shaped green leaves make an architectural crown. In a large garden, this plant can be very striking when viewed from a distance; in a small space it can grow larger than originally imagined. The coloured foliage forms, such as *Cordyline* 'Red Star' and *Cordyline australis* 'Torbay Dazzler', are occasionally seen as large, mature specimens.

The upright habit of mahonias makes them suitable alternatives to trees in small spaces. They have the advantage of evergreen foliage and yellow, often fragrant flowers in the winter months. The more upright varieties tend to flower in early winter, and they have whorls of leathery, prickly evergreen leaves on upright stems. *Mahonia ×media* 'Winter Sun' is a good example.

For those with tiny gardens, certain shrubs impersonate trees on a very modest scale, particularly when grown in pots. In a well-chosen container, the lovely dwarf cherry *Prunus incisa* 'Kojo-no-mai' is almost a hardy bonsai. This wonderful shrub has zigzag twigs and a cloud of delicate white blossoms with a hint of pink in early spring. The small serrated leaves are dark green through summer, turning orange in fall.

ABOVE Many shrubs make very effective groundcover by reducing the need for cultivation and suppressing weed growth.

TOP LEFT *Pachysandra terminalis* is a very useful glossy evergreen groundcover shrub with suckering stems that produce closely packed upright stems with whorls of shining foliage. Plant under the shade of variegated shrubs to create a green carpet.

LEFT *Pachysandra terminalis* 'Variegata' is a variegated form with effective creamy white–edged dark green leaves. It is excellent for groundcover in any green-and-white scheme, and a good choice with *Cotoneaster atropurpureus* 'Variegatus'.

Shrubs to use as trees

Acer palmatum 'Sango-kaku'
Berberis thunbergii 'Helmond Pillar'
Cercis canadensis 'Forest Pansy'
Cornus alternifolia 'Argentea'
Cornus controversa 'Variegata'

Euonymus europaeus 'Red Cascade'
Fatsia japonica
Prunus lusitanica
Rhus typhina Tiger Eyes
Syringa vulgaris

SHRUBS TO USE FOR GROUNDCOVER

We tend to think that groundcover plants have to hug the ground, but it is worth remembering that any shrub is creating effective groundcover if it covers the bare ground, prevents the emergence of weeds, protects against soil erosion, and makes cultivation unnecessary.

Low and spreading shrubs, such as *Vinca minor*, *Cotoneaster dammeri*, and *Hedera helix*, hug the ground surface. This type of groundcover shrub often takes time to establish. In the early stages, weed seedlings and undesirables may colonize the spaces between the creeping stems. You will have to manage this situation. Many gardeners use membranes on the soil surface as a preventive measure, but this method also prevents the shrub stems from rooting into the ground, and the groundcover effect can be equally ineffective.

The natural groundcover of calluna, daboecia, and ulex on cliff tops in Cornwall in southwest England.

Pachysandra are very dwarf evergreen groundcover shrubs that enjoy shady situations on reasonably moist soils. They are not good on chalk. Plant in groups of three or more plants 60cm (2 ft.) apart. No pruning is required. The suckering groundcover shrub *Pachysandra terminalis* is useless if planted using a membrane. This shrub needs an open soil surface to allow the underground stems to throw up shoots that gradually create an effective groundcover mat of evergreen foliage.

Alternatively, there are mounded and smothering shrubs that are low and broad with a dense branch framework. Heathers are a good example. This type of groundcover occurs in the natural environment, like the vegetation of Cornish cliff tops, where erica, calluna, daboecia, ulex, and other low, tough woody subjects create an undulating carpet by holding on to the thin soil and preventing weaker annual seedlings and grasses from emerging.

You can use heathers—botanically callunas and ericas—in a similar way in gardens. They tolerate exposed sites and some shade, and once established they cope with poor soil and dry conditions. The varieties of summer-flowering heathers, *Calluna vulgaris*, need neutral to acid soil. Gardeners with alkaline soils will be more successful with *Erica carnea* and *Erica ×darleyensis* varieties. These winter-flowering heathers are often the best on all soil types to achieve good groundcover.

Other low-mounded shrubs achieve effective groundcover in sun or shade. Under the canopy of trees, the bold mounds of *Viburnum davidii* with *Euonymus fortunei* 'Emerald Gaiety', perhaps combined with *Hedera helix* 'Green Ripple', would soon cover the soil surface in evergreen foliage. In sun, the mound-forming *Hebe* 'Red Edge' planted with *Salvia officinalis* 'Purpurascens' and *Helianthemum* 'Rhodanthe Carneum' would be equally effective.

Some shrubs have horizontal, spreading branches and dense leaf cover. These are also good groundcover plants, and particularly useful as the lower layer under larger shrubs. *Lonicera nitida* 'Maigrun' is often used in this way. Its herringbone branches carry small evergreen leaves, and it quickly gives effective cover on the poorest of soils. You could use *Leucothoe* Lovita in a similar way in semi-shade on acid soils.

Some groundcover shrubs are just too vigorous and successful for most gardens. Both *Vinca major* and *Rubus tricolor* have a bad reputation for getting out of hand too

quickly. On rough ground and steep banks, where other shrubs struggle to survive, *Rubus tricolor* will cover anything with its vigorous horizontal stems and dark green leaves. *Vinca major* becomes rather straggly and unruly, and is a better choice for a neglected corner of the churchyard.

Vincas, or periwinkles, are tough, easy to grow, trailing evergreen shrubs. They have a reputation for being rampant and invasive. This is true of *Vinca major*, so the varieties of *Vinca minor*, the small-leaved, lesser periwinkle, are the ones to grow. This is an excellent groundcover plant with long, trailing stems that root into the ground as they go. It thrives on most soils and is excellent in shade. Trim back as necessary in spring or fall.

ABOVE Dark green leaves edged with white and deep sky blue flowers make *Vinca minor* 'Ralph Shugert' one of the most attractive vincas.

LEFT *Lonicera nitida* 'Maigrun' and *Euonymus fortunei* 'Emerald 'n' Gold' work together to create effective and colourful groundcover.

Shrubs to plant for groundcover

Cotoneaster atropurpureus 'Variegatus'	*Hebe pinguifolia* 'Sutherlandii'
Cotoneaster dammeri	*Pachysandra terminalis*
Cotoneaster horizontalis	*Pachysandra terminalis* 'Variegata'
Erica carnea	*Rubus cockburnianus* 'Golden Vale'
Erica ×*darleyensis*	*Vinca minor* 'Illumination'
Euonymus fortunei 'Emerald Gaiety'	*Vinca minor* 'La Grave'
Euonymus fortunei 'Emerald 'n' Gold'	*Vinca minor* 'Ralph Shugert'

OTHER PLANTS

In most planting schemes, gardeners will include other plants alongside the shrubs, like perennials, bulbs, and seasonal bedding subjects. These supporting acts fill the gaps in the planting, particularly in the early years when the shrubs are reaching maturity. Hardy annuals that can be sown directly into their planting positions are useful here, as are short-lived perennials with a light and airy habit that sit happily in mixed plantings. These include popular subjects such as *Verbena bonariensis*, *Digitalis lutea*, and *Knautia macedonica*. On most soils these plants seed freely, and once established in a scheme they seed and conveniently relocate to fill any available space.

Other subjects also add colour and seasonal interest to the scheme. Spring- and summer-flowering flower bulbs are particularly useful for this purpose. They fit in anywhere, they are easily planted, and their performance is reliable. You need to

ABOVE *Allium cristophii* adds a different flower form and sparkling lilac early summer colour to a planting of low shrubs.

RIGHT The bursting lipstick buds of *Magnolia* 'Susan' against the early wine-coloured leaves of *Berberis thunbergii* f. *atropurpurea* 'Rose Glow'.

consider the drawback of fading foliage, but well-positioned tulips, alliums, and narcissi can lift a planting scheme and can create some of the most stunning planting combinations in any garden.

Many perennials also fit in and provide seasonal interest alongside the shrubs, while others fill the gaps beneath them or add interest early in the season before deciduous subjects gain their foliage. Heucheras, pulmonarias, brunneras, and primulas all provide excellent foliage and flower interest under the semi-shade of mature shrubs, and they can add to the impact of the leading subjects.

But our first considerations are the main subjects in the planting scheme: the shrubs. These other additions are purely enhancements, and they will come later. You may well be thinking about including them, but they will not hold together a year-round, long-term planting scheme.

Putting shrubs together

Numerous factors influence our choice of individual shrubs, but it is most important to choose those that work together to make an impact, whether subtle or powerful. We want shrubs that sit well together and bring out the best in their neighbours. We want shrubs that contrast and complement, with different leaf forms, textures, flower colours, and seasons of interest. We want combinations that excite, calm, please, and stimulate the senses. For me there is no greater pleasure than bursting buds that promise further delights as the season unfolds. This is where the creative part of gardening with shrubs really begins.

Digitalis lutea, Salvia nemerosa, and the annual *Nigella damascena* are good subjects to drift among shrubs and fill gaps in the planting.

CREATING STUNNING PLANTING EFFECTS USING SHRUBS

This chapter explains how to combine shrubs to reflect a mood or style that suits you and your garden. You will discover that by choosing a specific cocktail of plants you can conjure a little magic in your planting design, whatever size your garden.

ABOVE *Cornus controversa* 'Variegata' and *Viburnum opulus* 'Roseum' come together to create a wonderfully frothy but calming green-and-white combination.

LEFT I would never have thought to plant *Allium cristophii* to grow through a golden-leaved spiraea, but the effect is soft and pleasing.

Over many years of creating gardens at flower shows, I have learned how shrubs can tell a story. A plant's shape, foliage, texture, and habit often evoke a specific garden style. This may be because of the plant's frequent use in a certain type of planting, or simply its appearance. I often use these qualities to create planting effects. If you put together plants with similar qualities, you can achieve a specific style of planting that can lead the imagination to where you want to take it.

We are all inspired by things we see, touch, smell, taste, and experience. Whenever I visit a garden, a particular combination of colours or textures imprints itself on my memory. When I travel I see things that inspire me; memories I want to preserve and use beyond a hasty shot with the camera. Sometimes I see a plant that really surprises me out of context, which changes my perception of how it can be used.

I have been rather sceptical about the value of mood boards—collections of pictures, colours, and ideas that reflect the look you are trying to create. I have always done this in my mind—or have I? Perhaps my version of a mood board is collecting plants in pots outside the back door. The plants wait patiently for a slot to become available. By the time one opens up, I have forgotten what I was trying to create and I have lost the inspirational picture, whether a colour, a mood, a place. At the heart of the idea is a simple, hard-working planting combination that captures the essence of the inspiration. This is something to build on, to add more shrubs that fit the scheme to occupy more space in a larger garden, to add enhancements in the form of perennials and bulbs for seasonal colour.

This section features a selection of simple groupings of reliable shrubs. These planting combinations can create different moods and project different planting styles. They all work in a variety of situations, but it is important to choose an appropriate style that works with your house and sits well alongside the rest of the garden. In larger gardens it may be possible to isolate different styles of planting in separate areas of the overall garden vista. Visitors can then discover distinct plantings while journeying through the garden. Many well-known great gardens use this principle to showcase a white garden, an Italian garden, a Japanese garden, and others within an overall classic traditional style.

Soft pinks and lilacs are always easy to live with. *Phlomis italica* and roses create a warm summer-afternoon mood in this planting.

Most of us with smaller gardens choose one theme for a bed, a border, or the whole garden. It should be a theme or style that pleases you and that you will be happy to live with for a long time. Imagine you are choosing an important picture, rather than just painting the walls of a room. The endurance and longevity of shrubs will enable you to create a planting picture that will last and give you pleasure through the seasons and the years.

The shrub selections

Each selection of shrubs starts with three small to medium-size shrubs that work together as a planting combination. I then suggest three additional, usually medium-size, shrubs that would combine well with the basic combination to create a larger planting. For those with larger gardens and big planting areas to fill, I suggest larger shrubs that work as a backdrop to the previous selections. All these shrub selections will work as the entire planting scheme, but if you want to add other plants to enhance the scheme, I also suggest one or two perennials, bulbs, or climbers. These add variety and emphasize colour during part of the season.

You may need to modify schemes according to your climate, your situation, and your palette of available plants. Alongside each selection I list other shrubs that you might want to consider. I have modified these selections for the urban garden styles to allow for restricted space. All these subjects may be grown in pots.

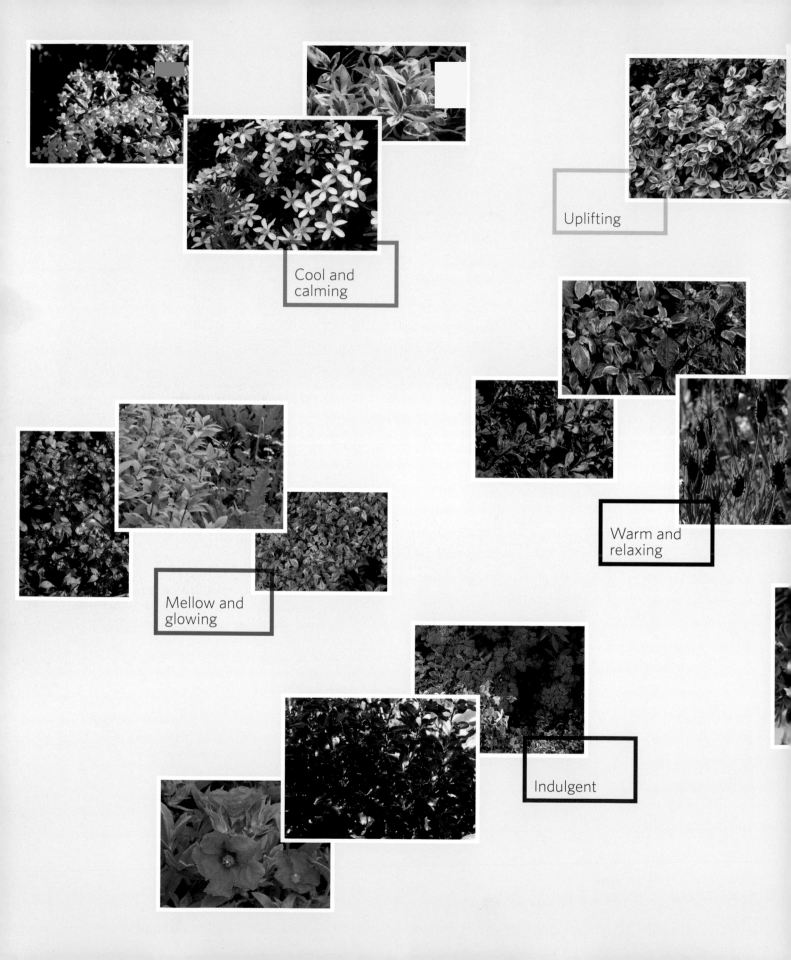

Uplifting

Cool and calming

Warm and relaxing

Mellow and glowing

Indulgent

Moods

These planting schemes are designed to reflect certain moods, and they are based on the influence of colour. We all favour certain hues, and our preferences can change along with the time of day and how we feel. Colour can be calming, uplifting, exciting, and relaxing, and in a garden we are receptive to its influence. You will likely enjoy your planting scheme for many years, so it is important to choose one you want to live with for some time.

Colour changes with the time of day. Some schemes work best in low light, others in bright sunshine. If you mainly enjoy the garden in early morning and evening, choose colours that work with the light at those hours.

Your garden is very personal. It is an extension of your personality. You should not see it as a fashion statement, or feel the need to be on trend. These planting schemes are designed to illustrate how just a few plants can work together to achieve an effect; they are by no means exclusive of other subjects. All gardeners should have their guilty pleasures. You can still have seasonal injections of other hues, even if you restrict your planting to a limited colour palette. We all like to live a little dangerously when the mood strikes us.

Reflective

Cool and calming

Green and white variegations with evergreens and pure white blooms

A green-and-white scheme is gentle on the eye, simple and sophisticated, and easy to live with. We all crave colour in our lives, and bright flowers and foliage can be very attractive. Most of us find green-and-white to be pleasing and calming, and a relief from the pace and stress of everyday life.

For me, a green-and-white theme has a cooling effect on the warmest days, but it is at its best in early morning and evening, as white can become glaring in full sun. At the start of the day green-and-white is uplifting and refreshing, like a cool shower or a freshly pressed white cotton shirt. After a day at work it is a reviving gin and tonic or a cold glass of white wine in the garden in the soft light of evening. These colours capture the cool smell of mint and the condensation on a glass of ice water. White flowers, like white lilies and white water lilies, have purity and definition against green foliage.

Lush green waterside plantings around the sparkling white splash of a cooling fountain creates a cool and calming green-and-white cocktail.

Where would this scheme work?

This scheme would suit both traditional and contemporary settings. It is ideal in a small garden or courtyard, as the simplicity and lightness help to create an illusion of space. It is also ideal in semi-shade. All these shrubs will grow happily with some shade, although the deciduous flowering shrubs need some direct sun to flower successfully. In shadier situations I would choose more of the foliage options.

Euonymus fortunei 'Silver Queen'

Osmanthus delavayi

Choisya ×dewitteana 'White Dazzler'

The basic combination

These shrubs will succeed in large, deep pots, 40cm (15 in.) in diameter or larger, and they would be ideal in a courtyard or on a terrace in semi-shade. In the open ground I would plant them at least 75cm (30 in.) apart.

My starting point is compact evergreen *Choisya ×dewitteana* 'White Dazzler', which I choose for its narrow dark green leaflets and clusters of sparkling white flowers in spring and fall. It flowers best with some direct sunlight. For shadier situations I would choose *Choisya ternata*, which grows larger but can be controlled with careful pruning.

Although *Osmanthus delavayi* is another plain evergreen, it has small, very dark green leaves on arching stems—a very different habit and colour from the choisya. In spring, small white tubular flowers sparkle on its branches and fill the garden with their sweet perfume.

Euonymus fortunei 'Silver Queen' is one of the finest small variegated evergreens, with warm green-and-white leaves on spreading stems. It maintains the green-and-white scheme when the choisya is not in flower. You could position it against a wall or fence where it will climb and form an eye-catching backdrop to the dark green foliage of its planting partners.

Pittosporum tenuifolium 'Irene Patterson'

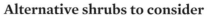

Alternative shrubs to consider

Cornus alba 'Elegantissima'
Cornus controversa 'Variegata'
Deutzia pulchra
Escallonia 'Iveyi'
Euonymus fortunei 'Emerald Gaiety'
Hebe albicans
Hydrangea paniculata 'Limelight'
Philadelphus 'Virginal'

Deutzia pulchra
Perfect sprays of
exquisite white flowers
in summer against
dark green leaves.
It is a larger shrub
for larger gardens.

**Cornus controversa
'Variegata'**
An altogether larger
version of *Cornus
alternifolia* 'Argentea'.
It is stunning in a larger
space as its layered
branches develop.

Hydrangea arborescens 'Annabelle'

Viburnum plicatum 'Summer Snowflake'

Expanding the scheme

These additions are interchangeable with those for a large garden. If you are selecting additional plants for large pots, the pittosporum, cornus, and magnolia are the best choices.

Viburnum plicatum f. *tomentosum* 'Summer Snowflake' is a more compact and upright form of this lovely shrub, with lace-cap flower heads poised along the branches from early summer into fall. It would work well planted behind either the choisya or the euonymus.

I would choose ice-cool green-and-white

Pittosporum tenuifolium 'Irene Patterson' to plant alongside the deep green osmanthus. This pittosporum is one of the brightest and whitest shrubs.

Delightful *Hydrangea arborescens* 'Annabelle' is particularly good in shade and is lovely from the moment the lime green flowers appear right through their transformation to cream, then white, then green again. Because of its relaxed nature it is perhaps best to plant it behind the euonymus, which will lend some support.

The basic combination

In a large garden

My additions for a larger garden are modest in size, and you can also use them in a smaller space. One of my favourite shrubs is frothy *Cornus alternifolia* 'Argentea', with its fine layered branches and delicate green-and-white leaves. It is light and lovely enough to fit into any garden, but would be essential in a more extensive green-and-white scheme.

I would also try and find room for the delightful *Magnolia stellata* 'Water Lily' for its blooms of great purity, which open from silky winter buds. The summer foliage may be rather ordinary, but you can transform it with the addition of a white large-flowered clematis, such as gorgeous *Clematis florida* var. *normalis* 'Pistachio'.

Clematis florida var. *normalis* 'Pistachio'

Magnolia stellata 'Water Lily'

Cornus alternifolia 'Argentea'

Pachysandra terminalis

Galanthus nivalis

Narcissus 'Thalia'

Bulbs & perennials

A good green groundcover plant helps to keep the scheme fresh and verdant by obscuring brown soil. Evergreen ground-cover *Pachysandra terminalis* would be an excellent choice for underplanting the deciduous shrubs.

For spring-interest single snowdrops, *Galanthus nivalis* are essential in any green-and-white scheme. They also provide that spring fillip we all need at the end of winter.

Narcissus 'Thalia' is my favourite narcissus. I love its delicately poised pure white blooms, and I would add clumps of it to contribute pure white in spring to follow the snowdrops.

Indulgent

A rich scheme of purple foliage, cerise and red flowers, and heady fragrance

Luscious tulips in red, purple, and pink, plus black violas, add rich and indulgent colour between a pink cordyline, red-leaved berberis, and wine red maple.

Rich purple foliage, cerise and red flowers, and heavy, delicious fragrance come together to create an indulgent planting scheme that exudes an atmosphere of warmth and well-being, the feeling I get from a good glass of red wine or piece of a delicious dark chocolate. These colours are deeper and more intense than those of a warm summer afternoon. The shades are velvety and silky, opulent and extravagant.

I associate these colours with the jewel hues of rhododendrons, and certainly the ericaceous world contains a wide palette of shrubs that deliver rich hues. However, I want a scheme that will work on any soil and will maintain its mood throughout the seasons, so foliage has to be the foundation.

This indulgent scheme is easy to love. It is daringly strong but balanced, with soft, subtle, quieter notes. I like to think of it as a glass of fine port with strength at first encounter and a warm glow to follow. Or maybe a delicious blackcurrant fool drizzled with rich fruit syrup; a little sharp on the tongue, but then sweet and satisfying. This is a mood to evoke any of your guilty pleasures.

Where would this scheme work?
This scheme would work in an open, sunny situation on any well-drained, reasonably fertile soil. All the shrubs in this selection grow well on alkaline soils. This versatile scheme suits gardens of any size and character. The shrub selection and the mood of the planting blend in easily with softer pastel shades, so the scheme does not need to sit in isolation to achieve the desired effect.

Spiraea japonica 'Anthony Waterer'

Cistus pulverulentus 'Sunset'

Pittosporum tenuifolium 'Tom Thumb'

The basic combination

These shrubs should be planted at least 75cm (30 in.) apart in the open ground. All are suitable to grow in containers; choose pots at least 35cm (14 in.) in diameter and of similar depth.

Pittosporum tenuifolium 'Tom Thumb' is my first choice for this scheme. It is dense and compact, and it provides structure as well as deep colour and texture. The rich dark purple shining leaves will warm the winter garden. Through the rest of the year they are a moody foil for the brighter colours of the shrub's planting partners.

In contrast, *Cistus* ×*pulverulentus* 'Sunset' has soft green foliage that is velvety and gentle against the metallic sheen of the pittosporum. The silky cerise, golden-eyed blooms shine like gems against the foliage throughout the summer months. The sunnier and warmer the situation, the better.

Spiraea japonica 'Anthony Waterer' may be familiar, but few shrubs produce such a long-lasting and richly coloured display of flowers. The abundant crowded heads of red flowers have a rich opulence and a velvety texture that are attractive to bees and butterflies as well as the gardener.

Philadelphus 'Belle Etoile'

Sambucus nigra f. *porphyrophylla* 'Eva'

Rosa 'Roseraie de l'Hay'

Alternative shrubs to consider

Acer palmatum 'Bloodgood'
Berberis thunbergii f. *atropurpurea* 'Rose Glow'
Cercis canadensis 'Forest Pansy'
Hibiscus syriacus 'Hamabo'
Physocarpus opulifolius 'Diablo'
Rosa Gertrude Jekyll
Weigela florida 'Foliis Purpureis'

Weigela florida 'Foliis Purpureis': Subtle green-purple leaves and mauve-pink trumpet flowers make this shrub a softer addition; its small stature would work well in the basic combination.

Hibiscus syriacus 'Hamabo': Hollyhock-like flowers of soft shell pink with a deep red eye could provide the fall encore in this scheme. This shrub is late into leaf, so I do not recommend it for small gardens.

The basic combination

Expanding the scheme

Plant these additions at least 90cm (3 ft.) apart. The sambucus provides light height, and you can easily contain it by pruning. You could also use it in the basic combination, but I do not recommend it for pots for more than a couple of seasons.

Lovely *Sambucus nigra* f. *porphyrophylla* 'Eva' is one of the first shrubs I choose for many planting schemes. The finely cut purple-black foliage reminds me of the feathers of an exotic bird. The flat pink flower heads have a soft, lacy texture that provides a pretty contrast to the shining leaves.

Every indulgent planting scheme needs a rose with fragrance and soft velvety petals. I have chosen *Rosa* 'Roseraie de l'Hay' for its opulent cerise-purple blooms with soft petals that reveal rich cream stamens at the heart of each flower. The fragrance is powerful and delicious. The pleated, bright green, healthy foliage provides the perfect setting for the blooms throughout summer.

Philadelphus 'Belle Etoile' captures the essence of the summer garden, as its creamy white single flowers fill the air with the powerful fragrance of orange blossom. Each bloom is blotched with maroon-red at the base of the petals, which picks up the colours of the rose and spiraea. The philadelphus has only the one season of interest, but you can extend it by planting a small-flowered clematis to grow through its branches. If you prefer an evergreen shrub, substitute *Abelia* 'Edward Goucher' for the philadelphus.

Cotinus coggygria 'Royal Purple'

Abelia 'Edward Goucher'

In a large garden

These two large shrubs are ideal to plant as a backdrop to the basic combinations. They both have the potential to grow large, so ideally plant at least 1.8m (6 ft.) apart.

Although *Abelia* 'Edward Goucher' is a smaller abelia, it needs a little room to spread and its evergreen leaves on arching stems are a valuable addition. The pink flowers in fall extend the season, especially as the pretty deep pink calyces remain on the branches well after the flowers have fallen.

Few shrubs have the rich, velvety appearance of *Cotinus coggygria* 'Royal Purple'. This smoke bush produces deep red-purple smoky flower heads, but the rounded wine-purple leaves, whorled around the branches, are the main feature.

Bulbs & perennials

Papaver somniferum 'Black Paeony'

To start the season, rich purple tulips are the ultimate indulgence. *Tulipa* 'Passionale' is a short, single, long-lasting variety with elegant purple blooms emerging from a wrapping of waxy green leaves. It is stunning against the foliage of the pittosporum.

Red-black *Dianthus barbatus* (Nigrescens Group), sweet william, is biennial but still a rich addition to the basic combination. The dark flowers and leaves are particularly gorgeous with the spiraea.

Papaver somniferum 'Black Paeony' is also easily raised from seed, and the crumpled

silk blooms are a stunning addition in early summer. The blue-green seed heads remain attractive for many weeks after the flowers have faded.

For the ultimate summer fragrance, choose *Lilium regale*, the best garden lily for permanent planting. The waxy white, purple-backed trumpets add an extravagant seasonal highlight, and the scent is bewitchingly wonderful.

Tulipa 'Passionale'

Lilium regale

Dianthus barbatus (Nigrescens Group)

Mellow and glowing

Sunset shades of rich gold, orange, copper, and deep blue with a hint of purple

The rich tones of this scheme create a mellow feeling of warmth and satisfaction. In low light they have the sweetness of toffee and the glow of brandy; in bright sunshine, the vibrancy of cayenne. These shades make shades of orange appealing to gardeners who would never choose this colour.

These are my favourite hues, and perhaps the reason I love fall so much. When those warm tints creep through the fall foliage of deciduous trees and shrubs, they light up the landscape. They glow in soft light, and are surprisingly luminous on dull days and at twilight.

I am always drawn to the mellow warmth of terra-cotta pots, and I love the way they work with any colour of flower or foliage. Blue has similar properties, but it is particularly effective with orange and gold. It reflects low rays of light and becomes more dramatic early and late in the day.

These colours capture the magic of a sunset over the sea. They change as the sun sinks, becoming richer but softer. For me they evoke that mellow feeling at the end of a day in the sun. They make me feel good, and they lift my spirits in any weather.

A glowing sunset over the sea is heart-warmingly mellow and reassuringly familiar, but with notes of deep mystery.

Where would this scheme work?
This scheme is designed for an open, sunny position and could suit any style of garden. However, it is ideal for a traditional rather than a contemporary property, perhaps with terra-cotta tiles or brick in the hard landscaping. All shrubs are tolerant and easy to grow on any well-drained soil, but are best in the open ground rather than in pots and containers.

Spiraea japonica 'Firelight'

Abelia ×grandiflora 'Kaleidoscope'

Ceratostigma willmottianum

The basic combination

When planted together, the three shrubs in the basic combination offer interest in all seasons. In the open ground I would plant to 75–90cm (30 in.–3 ft.) apart. Bear in mind that the abelia is evergreen, so it is probably best in a central position.

Spiraea japonica 'Firelight' presents a changing picture from the moment the first glowing orange young leaves emerge in early spring. The sunset shades remain at the tips of the shoots throughout the growing season against the warm gold of the mature leaves. The flower clusters are deep pink, perhaps a little surprising, but they work in the scheme, particularly in the presence of blue.

The evergreen *Abelia ×grandiflora* 'Kaleidoscope' continues the colour through winter. Its foliage is a lively cocktail of rich gold and green with red-orange in the mature leaves and at the tips of the shoots. The pink flowers blend seamlessly into the sunset picture.

Ceratostigma willmottianum, hardy plumbago, adds deep blue blooms late in summer and fall, which is perfect against the flame shades that colour some of the dark green leaves. In colder areas this will die back in winter, but leave stems and seed heads in place and enjoy them over winter.

If you want the colour of winter stems, substitute *Cornus sanguinea* 'Midwinter Fire' from the following additions for the ceratostigma, but add the geranium and muscari from the enhancements.

Berberis ×stenophylla 'Etna'

Cornus sanguinea 'Midwinter Fire'

Rosa Lady Emma Hamilton

Alternative shrubs to consider

Cotinus 'Grace'
Hamamelis ×*intermedia* 'Robert'
Lavandula angustifolia 'Hidcote'
Nandina domestica 'Fire Power'
Phormium 'Evening Glow'
Potentilla fruticosa 'Tangerine'
Rhododendron 'Nancy Evans'

Hamamelis ×*intermedia* **'Robert':** On neutral to acid soil in a larger garden I would definitely consider a copper-coloured witch hazel like this, both for its glowing winter flowers and its rich gold or red-orange fall colour.

***Nandina domestica* 'Fire Power':** In a small space, this evergreen would be a good addition for its olive green summer foliage and rich red-orange winter colour.

Expanding the scheme

The basic combination

These are all medium-size shrubs that are best planted around 90cm (3 ft.) apart. If you add only one, choose the cornus for the length of its season of interest.

Cornus sanguinea 'Midwinter Fire' is one of the most satisfying garden shrubs. Although the flowers are virtually unnoticeable and the summer foliage is plain pale green, few plants add so much colour in fall and winter. The fall foliage is warm and glowing, and the winter stems set the winter garden aflame.

Berberis ×*stenophylla* 'Etna' is a small-growing form of this well-known berberis, with arching stems and dark green leaves that contrast well with the lighter foliage. These dark lines in the sunset picture intensify the flame shades. In spring the arching stems of the berberis light up with tiny blood-orange flowers.

The scent alone of a rose will lift your mood, and *Rosa* Lady Emma Hamilton is warm and fruity, which is appropriate for its soft orange glowing blooms. Its red-flushed dark foliage makes it particularly appropriate in this mellow scheme.

Physocarpus opulifolius 'Diable d'Or'

In a large garden

Ceanothus 'Concha'

Wherever possible I include *Physocarpus opulifolius* 'Diable d'Or' in a mellow planting scheme, especially alongside *Rosa* Lady Emma Hamilton. This shrub needs a little space to allow its branches to arch naturally, displaying the deep copper foliage and ruby fruit clusters to advantage. The glowing tips of the shoots are particularly vibrant in early summer.

This would make it the perfect planting partner for dramatic *Ceanothus* 'Concha', which will be a smoking mass of deep blue in late spring and early summer. The dark evergreen leaves of the ceanothus make an excellent backdrop to the rest of the planting throughout the year.

These two shrubs need to be planted 1.5m (5 ft.) apart and a similar distance from the other grouping. The ceanothus is not a good choice for cold sites or heavy, wet soil.

Bulbs & perennials

Geranium 'Rozanne'

Deep purple *Allium atropurpureum* would add depth to the pink flowers of the spiraea in early summer, with tall stems carrying those rich wine flowers above the lower shrubs.

Blue is such a wonderful mixer and a mellow contrast to the warm red-orange tones of the planting, bringing them to life and increasing their intensity. Geraniums are an obvious addition. *Geranium* 'Rozanne' forms a sprawling mound studded with saucer-shaped blue flowers, and unlike other geraniums it blooms from early summer right through fall. Plant it alongside the smaller shrubs, or beneath the larger ones, but give it space to spread.

Muscari armeniacum, grape hyacinth, produces its rich blue flowers at just the right moment to create a striking partnership with the new leaves of the spiraea and the orange flowers of the berberis. If you want to contain it, cut off the seed heads when the flowers fade.

Allium atropurpureum

Muscari armeniacum

Reflective

Shimmering white and soft blue, with highlights of silver foliage

Soft blue and silver shades induce a feeling of relaxation. Along with calming white, these are the colours for meditation and contemplation. They are beautiful in the early morning and soft light of evening. These are colours to sit and enjoy, to immerse yourself in to get your life in perspective, or perhaps to get you in the mood for gentle reviving exercise in the open air.

These are the colours of still, reflective waters and expressive skies; early morning sun shimmering on a gently rippling sea; grey clouds parting to reveal a silver lining, promising fair weather to come. Leaves and petals reflect the light, while tiny flowers echo raindrops falling on a sheet of still water.

Fragrance enhances the planting by adding the power of aromatherapy to the scheme. These flowers smell like summer, and they are at their best in the early morning and evening, when their fresher, sweeter notes are more apparent.

This scheme may be cool, but it has a very different quality from the green-and-white combination. You will never tire of this scheme. It is easy to blend it into neighbouring plantings, including pinks, mauves, and darker blues and purples.

The surface of still water reflects the contrast of the large leaves of gunnera beneath the silver stems and delicate branch tracery of birches beneath a watery sky.

The basic combination

The shrubs in the basic combination should be planted at least 75cm (30 in.) apart in the open ground. They could also be grown in pots in loam-based compost. Choose containers that are at least 35cm (14 in.) in diameter. Light blue-grey glazed pots would enhance the scheme and maintain the colour throughout the year.

Soft silver-green foliage and shining white single flowers make *Potentilla fruticosa* 'Abbotswood' the perfect plant to lead this scheme from early summer through to fall. Although it may have little to offer in winter, it makes up for it during the summer months.

The evergreen *Hebe albicans* makes the perfect planting partner for the potentilla, with its fresh green foliage and sparkling white flower spikes. This shrub brings year-round vitality to the scheme and adds the benefit of summer flowers.

Perovskia 'Blue Spire', Russian sage, adds magical blue and silver to the scheme. Slender stems carry the bright blue late-summer flowers; they remain into winter as sparkling silver wands. The whole plant is delightfully aromatic and adds a light, ethereal quality alongside its more compact planting partners.

Hebe albicans

Perovskia 'Blue Spire'

Potentilla fruticosa 'Abbotswood'

Where would this scheme work?

This scheme would suit an open, sunny position, but all subjects will tolerate some shade. All will grow on any well-drained, reasonably fertile soil. The pale colours make the scheme suitable for a small garden, where they will impart an illusion of space. This scheme would also work well in coastal gardens away from direct salt spray.

Hydrangea macrophylla 'Ayesha'

Philadelphus maculatus 'Sweet Clare'

Choisya ×*dewitteana* 'Aztec Pearl'

Expanding the scheme

These additions need to be planted at least 90cm (3 ft.) apart. Both the philadelphus and the hydrangea have the potential to grow larger in the long term in ideal growing conditions.

The fragrance of *Philadelphus maculatus* 'Sweet Clare' is heavy, sweet, and spicy, reminiscent of orange blossom. The shrub's fine arching stems and tiny leaves have a silver-green sheen that is delightful with the white summer blooms that cling to the underside of the stems. 'Sweet Clare' has lightness, movement, grace, fragrance, and subtlety—all perfect qualities for this scheme.

Hydrangea macrophylla 'Ayesha' is quite unlike any other lacecap or mophead hydrangea, as it has flower heads of small, incurved florets. The delicate and beautiful individual florets reflect the light and cast shadows upon one another, changing with the direction of the sun. 'Ayesha' needs neutral to acid soil to display its pale blue flower colour; on alkaline soils the flowers will be mauve-pink. To maintain the blue element in this scheme, substitute *Ceanothus* ×*delileanus* 'Gloire de Versailles' for the hydrangea.

With its aromatic evergreen foliage and scented flowers, *Choisya* ×*dewitteana* 'Aztec Pearl' adds to the scheme throughout the year. It has a lightness and beauty lacking in many more solid evergreen shrubs, with the benefit of exquisite white flowers twice a year.

Alternative shrubs to consider

Choisya ×*dewitteana* 'White Dazzler'
Exochorda macrantha 'The Bride'
Hydrangea paniculata 'Floribunda'
Hydrangea paniculata 'Kyushu'
Pittosporum tenuifolium 'Irene Patterson'
Rosa glauca Pourr
Viburnum plicatum f. *tomentosum* 'Summer Snowflake'

Rosa glauca Pourr: The steely blue-grey foliage of this rose is a welcome addition to this scheme. The shrub has a slender, upright habit, so it will fit in with any of the above combinations.

Hydrangea paniculata 'Floribunda': Lacy lilac-like heads of white flowers in late summer on upright stems maintain the effect through fall.

Buddleja 'Lochinch'

Elaeagnus 'Quicksilver'

In a large garden

These shrubs for a larger garden need some space. Ideally you should plant at least 1.5m (5 ft.) apart. If allowed to grow unchecked, in time the elaeagnus might grow to 4m (13 ft.) tall and could take the place of a small tree.

Elaeagnus 'Quicksilver' is the perfect background for this scheme. From late spring it is a cascade of slender silver leaves that shimmer in the sunlight. In early summer it fills the garden with heavy fragrance from its tiny but potent flowers.

The shining silver foliage of the elaeagnus is lovely alongside the silver-green foliage and lilac-blue flowers of *Buddleja* 'Lochinch'. Its scented spikes appear in late summer and attract butterflies and bees to the planting picture.

The basic combination

Bulbs & perennials

Narcissus 'Thalia'

Agapanthus Headbourne Hybrids

This scheme is at its best through summer. To extend the season, you could add blue-and-white spring-flowering bulbs like the delicate white *Narcissus* 'Thalia' and blue-and-white muscari in pots or under the stems of deciduous shrubs.

Few summer-flowering perennials possess the intense blue colour of *Agapanthus* Headbourne Hybrids. This is one of the hardiest strains, and it flowers freely in cooler regions. If given the sunniest position in the scheme, it will delight with its bright blue sparkling flower heads and striking seed heads that follow.

Nigella damascena 'Miss Jekyll', love-in-a-mist, is a lovely annual with soft blue flowers carried in a haze of fine foliage. You can sow it directly into the flowering positions and allow it to seed itself in subsequent seasons. Nigella is also an excellent choice for filling the gaps between newly planted shrubs.

Nigella damascena 'Miss Jekyll'

A seat by the lake or a rowboat: either could be the perfect place to relax and enjoy the garden on a warm afternoon.

Warm and relaxing

Warm summer shades: pink, mauve, blue, and soft white

The colours in this scheme recall a warm summer's afternoon in the garden. They are easy-to-live-with shades that create a relaxed and dreamy mood in the planting. These are the subtle hues that many of us are drawn to in fashion and in our homes. They convey an aura of comfort and security. They are slightly sleepy and never stimulating and exciting, but also never boring.

The sweet and familiar character of these colours is echoed in the foliage and the fragrance of the flowers. Some depth of colour, in the form of wine purple foliage and flowers, accentuates the lightness of other subjects in the scheme. Flower heads composed of tiny individual blooms add a lacy effect to the planting.

This scheme means sunshine, china cups and saucers, strawberries and cupcakes. It means time spent enjoying the garden, the sound of insects gathering nectar, the scents of summer. It is an unhurried Sunday afternoon, a time to recharge the batteries; although simple and familiar, it conveys a rare quality of life in today's busy world.

Cornus alba 'Sibirica Variegata'

Berberis thunbergii f. *atropurpurea* 'Rose Glow'

Lavandula pedunculata subsp. *pedunculata*

The basic combination

Of the three shrubs in the basic combination, only the lavender retains foliage in winter, but the cornus has dark red stems for winter colour and the berberis has a very long season of interest. For more evergreen content, you could add *Hebe* 'Red Edge' to the planting.

Although you could grow some of these subjects in pots, this planting is designed for the open ground. All the plants will succeed on any reasonably fertile, well-drained soil. I would plant them at least 75cm (30 in.) apart. For greater impact, you could plant the lavender as a group of three plants 30cm (1 ft.) apart.

My starting point is *Lavandula pedunculata* subsp. *pedunculata*, butterfly lavender. This plant captures the essence of the mood with its menthol-and-lavender-scented foliage with a hint of warm eucalyptus. The lilac-blue flowers with delicate wings are the spirit of a warm summer's day. The shrub starts to flower in early summer and has a long season.

Berberis thunbergii f. *atropurpurea* 'Rose Glow' has wonderful warmth with wine purple leaves and pink suffused tips to the shoots. When partnered with pink flowers, these blend seamlessly with other subjects in the planting. This rich foliage colour accentuates the paler shades of the planting partners.

Cornus alba 'Sibirica Variegata' is compact and hard working, but also light, delicate, and a changing part of the picture through the year. It has red stems in winter and delicate green-and-white variegated leaves in spring, it becomes tinged with pink in summer, and in fall it turns pink-purple studded with white berries.

The three subjects work together to create a pleasing and varied picture throughout the year.

Where would this scheme work?

These colours suit an open, sunny position. Although they are still softly pleasing in the low light of morning and evening, they are at their best bathed in sunlight. They work well in a large or a small space, and they blend easily with the surroundings when used in country gardens. These shades have an air of casual informality and suit naturalistic gardens. They work well alongside a fresh green lawn and have a softening effect alongside paving and in gravel.

Pittosporum tenuifolium 'Elizabeth'

Ceanothus ×delileanus 'Gloire de Versailles'

Hydrangea arborescens Invincibell Spirit

Expanding the scheme

If you prefer a flowering subject, you could substitute the hydrangea in these additions for the cornus in the basic combination. It will work beautifully alongside the berberis, but will lack the winter interest.

Hydrangea arborescens Invincibell Spirit blooms throughout summer, with lacy flower heads the colour of crushed strawberries against soft green leaves. Unlike some *Hydrangea arborescens* varieties, this one is more upright and will not flop over its neighbours.

Ceanothus ×delileanus 'Gloire de Versailles' has a charming, light, gently arching habit, with lovely open flower heads of soft sky blue. It flowers in summer and again in fall, adding the magic of summer skies to the scheme for long periods.

Pittosporum tenuifolium 'Elizabeth' has a softer, lighter character than many evergreens, with its shining gently waved, green-and-white variegated leaves that blush pink toward the margins. In summer it picks up the colour of the cornus and maintains it during winter.

Alternative shrubs to consider
Deutzia ×*hybrida* 'Strawberry Fields'
Perovskia 'Blue Spire'
Rosa Gertrude Jekyll
Sambucus porphrophylla 'Eva'
Spiraea japonica 'Anthony Waterer'
Syringa 'Red Pixie'
Weigela florida 'Foliis Purpureis'

Deutzia ×hybrida 'Strawberry Fields': Elegant arching stems of soft green leaves surprise with sprays of dainty pink flowers in early summer.

Rosa Gertrude Jekyll: The most fragrant of the English roses, with glowing pink double blooms produced throughout summer on a large shrub. You can grow it as a climber, perhaps as a backdrop behind a smaller planting.

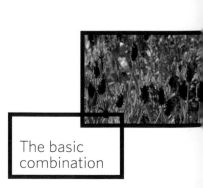

The basic combination

In a large garden

My choices for a larger garden are medium in stature. You can substitute them for any of the additions in the previous selection.

Philadelphus 'Belle Etoile' may flower only once, but when it does the sweet orange fragrance of its single flowers will fill the garden. No scent captures the relaxed warmth of the summer garden like this one. The deep maroon blotches at the base of the warm white petals pick up the purple foliage of the berberis.

No summer garden is complete without the beauty and scent of a rose. *Rosa* 'Cornelia' is a lovely hybrid musk rose with sprays of strawberry pink flowers flushed gold in the heart of each bloom. The fragrance is hauntingly beautiful throughout the day, and this variety repeats, so you can enjoy it through summer and fall.

Rosa 'Cornelia'

Allium cristophii

Philadelphus 'Belle Etoile'

Sedum 'Herbstfreude'

Tulipa 'Queen of Night'

Bulbs & perennials

In spring the silky purple-black blooms of *Tulipa* 'Queen of Night' are a soothing feature in any garden filled with vibrant spring colour. They add depth to the planting and are stunning against the pretty variegated foliage of the pittosporum.

Different flower forms add another dimension to any planting scheme. The lovely *Allium cristophii,* with its sparkling silver-lilac flower heads, never fails to please. The seedheads remain beautiful through fall.

Sedum 'Herbstfreude' has ice green leaves and flattened heads of pink flowers that turn red-brown and then mahogany. At their peak the blooms are a magnet for bees and butterflies and blend beautifully with the late flowers of the rose and hydrangea.

Uplifting

A lively, refreshing cocktail of yellow and green

Sunrise across the countryside in Hampshire, England. The pale golden morning light illuminates early mist over trees and fields—a wonderful start to any day.

Yellow is an exciting colour. It raises the metabolic rate and lifts the spirits. It is the hue of spring and of daffodils, forsythia, and celandines that reflect the welcome bright sunshine. Yellow has the power to lighten shade and bring a little precious sunshine into a dark corner of the garden. In this scheme it is uplifting, cheerful, and a welcome sight.

Sometimes yellow can be a little too bold, especially in its strongest and harshest form. A single yellow shrub in a border of green foliage screams for attention and cannot associate happily with its neighbours. But away from too much direct sunlight golden yellow foliage assumes a lime green hue, while green-and-yellow variegated leaves become softer and more subtle. This is how I like to see yellow shades in the garden. They feel fresher, and more like a spring morning than the hard sun in the middle of a summer day. I find them pleasantly exciting, rather than frantic attention grabbers.

I enjoy this uplifting scheme at any time of year, but I find it particularly pleasing in the dull, grey days of winter, so I want shrubs that provide plenty of evergreen interest. Often their colour is stronger in winter, especially under deciduous trees where they are treated to more light without the overhead canopy of foliage to obscure the sun.

Euonymus fortunei 'Emerald 'n' Gold'

Lonicera nitida 'Baggesen's Gold'

Choisya ×dewitteana 'Aztec Gold'

The basic combination

The choisya and lonicera in the basic combination have the potential to grow into medium-size shrubs, although you can restrict both by careful pruning. In the open ground you should plant them at least 90cm (3 ft.) apart. The euonymus is lower growing and spreading, so you can plant it closer. You can grow all of them in large pots in a courtyard or on a balcony. Choose containers at least 40cm (15 in.) in diameter.

Choisya ×dewitteana 'Aztec Gold' is a sparkling shrub with waxy, aromatic leaflets that give the plant a light and textural appearance. Even with a fair amount of sunshine it retains plenty of green colouring in the lower leaves, making it a good planting partner for green-and-gold variegations.

Euonymus fortunei 'Emerald 'n' Gold' is an ideal planting partner. It has a low, sprawling habit and will cover the ground beneath the feet of either of the other two shrubs, or will cling to a wall or fence behind them. Its cheerful, small, gold-and-green appearance enhances the plain golden foliage of the other two shrubs.

Some shrubs have great versatility, and *Lonicera nitida* 'Baggesen's Gold' is one of them. When allowed to grow freely it makes a large, loose shrub with straight twigs and tiny golden yellow evergreen leaves. You can trim and shape it, and use it as a young plant for colourful foliage in pots and containers. Here it adds another leaf form and a lighter habit that is such a pleasing contrast in the combination.

Where would this scheme work?
This scheme would work in semi-shade in any size garden. You could plant under the light shade of overhanging trees or in the semi-shade of surrounding buildings. In heavier shade without any direct sunlight the yellow foliage will become greener. It will still be a contrast to dark green foliage, but without the same lightening quality. This scheme is ideal in an urban garden and would create an illusion of light and space in a small or narrow area. All shrubs will grow on any well-drained, reasonably fertile soil.

Hydrangea paniculata 'Limelight'

Euonymus japonicus 'Chollipo'

Cotinus coggygria Golden Spirit

Expanding the scheme

These three medium-size shrubs should be planted at least 90cm (3 ft.) apart in the open ground, but in ideal growing conditions you can give them a little more room. You can fill the space between them with more plants of the euonymus from the basic combination.

Euonymus japonicus 'Chollipo' has similar gold-and-green variegation to that of *Euonymus fortunei* 'Emerald 'n' Gold', but with larger, shining leaves and an upright habit. It is bold and beautiful, one of the finest evergreen shrubs with this colouring, and it will maintain a powerful presence throughout the year.

In semi-shade the lovely *Hydrangea paniculata* 'Limelight' adds a lighter, frothier quality to the planting in late summer and fall, when its upright flower panicles explode in a cloud of soft green florets. It needs some direct sunlight to flower well, so it is not a good choice for deep shade, but it is surprisingly tolerant.

Cotinus coggygria Golden Spirit is a refreshing change from the popular purple-leaved varieties of smoke bush. If you give it a fair amount of sun it will produce smoky flower heads in summer, but these are of little importance compared to the vibrant rounded leaves, which are bright lime yellow in spring and become yellow-green in summer. This is one of the most exciting yellow foliage shrubs, and it creates a strong focal point in any planting scheme.

Alternative shrubs to consider
Elaeagnus ×*ebbingei* 'Viveleg'
Euonymus japonicus 'Microphyllus Pulchellus'
Ligustrum ovalifolium 'Aureum'
Lonicera pileata 'Lemon Beauty'
Rhus typhina Tiger Eyes
Skimmia ×*confusa* 'Kew Green'

***Ligustrum ovalifolium* 'Aureum':** The golden privet adds a smaller leaf and another lighter, more open growth habit to the planting scheme.

***Elaeagnus* ×*ebbingei* 'Viveleg':** Bright green evergreen foliage, each leaf edged with gold; this is a good alternative if planting in a sunnier or drier situation.

In a large garden

The cornus will grow bigger than you imagine, and the cotinus smaller. Plant these two at least 1.5m (5 ft.) apart and be prepared to prune the cornus.

With dark red stems, showy green-and-gold variegated foliage, and rich fall tints, *Cornus sericea* 'Hedgerows Gold' is a shrub for all seasons. It is a vigorous specimen with upright stems displaying large, bold leaves. It makes a bright background and will lighten the darkest corner.

Many of the red barked dogwoods work well in combinations, and *Cornus alba* 'Aurea' is no exception. It adds dark red stems in winter and soft gold foliage in summer, and it assumes a quieter lime yellow hue in shade. It has a pleasing effect when partnered with 'Hedgerows Gold'.

Cornus sericea 'Hedgerows Gold'

Cornus alba 'Aurea'

The basic combination

Alchemilla mollis

Narcissus 'Jack Snipe'

Digitalis lutea

Bulbs & perennials

Good groundcover enhances this scheme. Any of the dark green–leaved varieties of *Vinca minor* is a good choice; their blue, white, or purple flowers are a bonus in spring and summer.

I love anything with a lime green colouring, and no plant does that better than *Alchemilla mollis*, lady's mantle. It has soft green leaves that carry water droplets like beads of mercury, and the laciest flowers of lime green from early summer. Although herbaceous, it makes excellent groundcover under the larger shrubs.

Digitalis lutea is another perennial that drifts gracefully between the shrubs and adds spikes of vertical interest, and is perhaps the most subtle and beautiful foxglove. Gently arched spikes carry slender lime green bells that soften the stronger presence of the shrubs.

Despite their bold contribution to the winter garden, the gold and green evergreens become lighter and brighter in the presence of the cheery spring flowers of *Narcissus* 'Jack Snipe'. Brightly poised blooms on strong stems herald the longer days with creamy white petals and primrose trumpets.

Coastal

Mediterranean

Japanese

Exotic

Urban
contemporary

Cottage
garden

Tropical

Country garden

Styles

The style of planting in any garden should be appropriate to the property and the location, but that does not mean you have to stick to a formula. If you select the right shrubs and put them together with a little thought, you can create a style of planting that will achieve the garden you desire.

Certain plants suggest particular climates or regions of the world, even if they are a long way from home. Anything with silver leaves or aromatic foliage evokes sunshine for me. Shrubs with big leaves have a tropical feel. Manicured shrubs with colourful leaves communicate a cultivated, suburban garden. Berries and hedgerow flowers convey countryside. Use these qualities to create a style, but always choose subjects that will thrive in your situation.

I hope these style schemes will inspire you. They are by no means exclusive of other subjects, but they show how to achieve a style with shrubs. Planting style is all about the plants, and shrubs provide a way to achieve it. This is what real garden design is all about. Often gardeners place too much emphasis on creating a stage set to reflect a particular style, or invest too much in the hard landscaping element and neglect the planting.

Urban traditional

Coastal

Sea cliffs carpeted with a colourful tapestry bask in the summer sunshine. These low shrubs, with their tiny leaves and wiry stems, are well equipped to cope with exposure to the elements.

Silver leaves, compact evergreens, and summer flowers blow a sea breeze into any sunny garden

Exposed but favoured—perhaps that describes a coastal garden? No shade from trees, just open skies and abundant light. No still, damp air, but a light breeze on even the calmest days. The warming effect of the ocean is a blessing, but the scorching effect of salt can be a curse. Plants are often short and compact, hugging the ground for shelter. Or they may be grey or silver to reflect the light and avoid desiccation.

I imagine a coastal planting scheme set against pebbles or salt-washed boards. The shrubs and their planting companions are silver, sea lavender, and shell pink, almost an extension of the stones and shingles. Shrubs are never lush and luxuriant, but always modest and whispering on the breeze. Some move gently; others are wiry and resistant to the lively movement of air.

Some shrubs seem to have salt in their sap. Escallonia recalls the sticky-leaved hedges of the seaside. Lavatera is reminiscent of the hollyhocks that stand to attention against the whitewashed walls of seaside cottages. The aromatic foliage of lavender, rosemary, and thyme fill the air with their vaporized oils on warm summer days.

Where would this scheme work?

This scheme is ideal for a small seaside garden sheltered from the ravages of the salt wind by a wall or hedge of escallonia, elaeagnus, or olearia. Alternatively, it would suit any small sunny garden away from the coast where you want a light, simple planting effect. It is designed for an open, sunny position and well-drained stony or sandy soil. You can surround the shrubs with gravel or pebbles to keep the winter wet off the foliage, reduce maintenance, and enhance their appearance.

Convolvulus cneorum

Coronilla valentina subsp. *glauca* 'Citrinus'

Hebe 'Frozen Flame'

The basic combination

These shrubs will grow on any well-drained soil and are very tolerant of poor soil. If you plant in the open ground, space them at least 60–75cm (2 ft.–30 in.) apart. You can grow them in pots at least 30cm (1 ft.) in diameter, which makes them ideal for a patio, a small, sunny courtyard, or a balcony.

Lovely *Convolvulus cneorum* has silky silver leaves, a soft, loose habit, and shining white flowers with yellow throats and deep pink undersides. The reflective quality of this superb little shrub mirrors the ripples on the sea and promises fair weather to come.

The primrose yellow, pea-like flowers of *Coronilla valentina* subsp. *glauca* 'Citrinus' are reminiscent of the vetches found nestling in the short, tough grass of clifftops. With its long flowering period, curling stems, and small grey-green leaves, it is perfect to grow against a low wall.

Hebes are a familiar sight near the coast, but *Hebe* 'Frozen Flame' is a good choice even for colder situations. It may be hardy, but the purple-pink winter colour of its foliage is warming alongside its cool planting partners. Blue flowers attract summer bees and insects.

Escallonia 'Apple Blossom'

Alternative shrubs to consider

Ballotta pseudodictamnus
Cistus ×purpureus
Euonymus fortunei 'Emerald Gaiety'
Hebe pinguifolia 'Sutherlandii'
Helichrysum italicum 'Korma'
Hydrangea macrophylla
Phlomis italica
Rosmarinus officinalis
Santolina chamaecyparissus

Phlomis italica: Suckering upright stems with thick, felted, creamy grey leaves and mauve-pink flowers give this shrub with a soft, warm, and welcoming appearance.

Helichrysum italicum 'Korma': You can substitute this sparkling, silvery form of the aromatic curry plant for the convolvulus in the basic combination, or add it to any of these schemes.

Lavatera ×clementii 'Mary Hope'

Hebe 'Midsummer Beauty'

Expanding the scheme

Plant these medium-size shrubs at least 90cm (3 ft.) apart. The lavatera is a short-lived shrub; if you want a longer-lasting alternative, substitute *Phlomis italica*.

Lavatera ×clementii 'Mary Hope' is a compact form of the popular woody mallow. Strong, upright stems carry open shell pink blooms with darker eyes, reminiscent of hollyhocks. This shrub gives the scheme those vertical lines and fluttering summer flowers I associate with seaside gardens.

The dark green, leathery leaves and pretty summer flowers of escallonia are a familiar sight near the coast. *Escallonia* 'Apple Blossom' is smaller than other varieties and has masses of apple-blossom pink flowers in summer. It is a good planting companion for roses, and works well with the rose included in the larger scheme.

Hebe 'Midsummer Beauty' is quite different from the dwarf compact hebe included in the basic combination. This is a much larger shrub with willowy leaves and long, lilac-pink bottlebrush flowers that bees and butterflies adore.

The basic combination

In a large garden

The griselinia is an excellent evergreen background shrub. You can prune it to control size or clip it into shape as a hedge. It is a good shrub to plant for shelter in a coastal or exposed situation.

Griselinia littoralis 'Variegata' always reminds me of the sea because of its seaweed green stems and rounded, shining leaves that appear so different from other broad-leaved evergreens. The creamy variegation in the foliage softens, lightens, and contrasts with the plain green foliage of the hebe and escallonia.

Roses grow well by the sea. The air keeps them free of disease, they enjoy the light, and the flowers are unblemished by still, damp air. *Rosa* Rosy Cushion suits this coastal scheme with its simple single flowers in pretty shades of pink. It is never without flowers through the summer months. You can substitute it for any of the shrubs in the selections for expanding the scheme.

Griselinia littoralis 'Variegata'

Rosa Rosy Cushion

Eryngium ×*zabelii* 'Jos Eijking'

Thymus serphyllum

Bulbs & perennials

All the following plants will grow well in gravel, and the erigeron is particularly good in pots.

Charming little daisy *Erigeron karvinskianus* will grow just about anywhere and will wander among the shrubs. It seeds and spreads prolifically, and cheers every situation with its golden-eyed delicate flowers.

Thymus serphyllum, creeping thyme, forms ground-hugging mats of tiny, deep green, aromatic leaves. In summer, brightly coloured flowers attract the bees. This plant is a must for any gravel garden or gaps in paving.

No coastal style scheme would be complete without sea holly. *Eryngium* ×*zabelii* 'Jos Eijking' has intricate steely blue flower heads carried on stiff stems. Surprisingly, eryngiums grow best with adequate moisture in the soil, so add some organic matter when planting.

Erigeron karvinskianus

Cottage garden

Familiar flowers for a sunny, homey garden: roses, wallflowers, and lilacs

A cottage garden makes me think of roses around the door, honeysuckle, narrow beds filled with simple summer flowers along a straight pathway, lupins and hollyhocks, an apple tree, and a wigwam of runner beans or sweet peas. There might be a holly tree to keep evil spirits away, as well as a gooseberry bush and rhubarb. In late spring, big red poppies billow and flop over their neighbours in the border, followed by a prized red double peony that the neighbours envy. In winter, maybe a Christmas rose blooms in a sheltered corner near the front door before spring wallflowers and primroses light up a sunny border.

Although not always included in the cottage garden palette, a number of shrubs have the right personality to portray this style. Simple single flowers should abound, mostly in soft colours. A cottage garden is associated with the countryside, and thus will be a haven for wildlife, so shrubs that attract bees and butterflies are an obvious choice. Cottage garden borders are often populated with migrants from the surrounding countryside, so shrubs that sit happily in a rural environment predominate.

Cottage garden style is homey, easy to live with, familiar, and comforting. This is no place for sharp lines, architectural leaves, and exotics. The winter is a sleepy season, awaiting the energy of spring and the warm contentment of summer.

A traditional cottage garden provides a cozy corner to sit and enjoy the sunshine, the scent of summer flowers, and the sound of birdsong and buzzing bees.

Spiraea japonica 'Little Princess'

Where would this scheme work?

This style suits a small garden or a designated bed or border in a larger space away from the shade of trees and buildings. All the shrubs are flowering, so they need sunshine. All are easy to grow and thrive on any well-drained, reasonably fertile soil, but most tolerate poor soil. Cottage garden style sits easily in a country garden setting, but it also will work in an urban setting to bring a little of the countryside into the town. It suits traditional and older properties, and it works well with cottage perennials and wildflowers.

Erysimum 'Bowles's Mauve'

Potentilla fruticosa 'Primrose Beauty'

The basic combination

In the open ground, plant these shrubs at least 75cm (30 in.) apart. Although you can grow any of the selections in the basic and expanded schemes successfully in pots, they do not provide winter interest. If translating this scheme to containers, include some evergreen subjects, such as *Euonymus fortunei* or *Buxus sempervirens* varieties, to provide interest throughout the year.

I start with shrubby wallflower *Erysimum* 'Bowles's Mauve', even though it does not live long and usually needs to be replaced after a couple of years. This plant is the essence of the cottage garden and has one of the longest flowering seasons of any shrub I know; expect to find it in bloom from early spring to early winter. The poorer and drier your soil, the better the wallflower will like it.

Spiraea japonica 'Little Princess', with its mauve-pink pincushion flowers, would make a lovely planting partner for 'Bowles's Mauve'. It too revels in poor soil and flowers through summer, attracting bees and butterflies along the way.

I always associate the simple buttercup with the countryside, so *Potentilla fruticosa* 'Primrose Beauty' is perfect for the cottage garden. In winter it may be unprepossessing, but from early summer through to late fall, pale primrose single blooms stud this bee-friendly shrub.

Rosa 'Ballerina'

Syringa 'Red Pixie'

Hydrangea serrata 'Bluebird'

Expanding the scheme

These additions are relatively modest in size, and you can mix them with any of the basic combination. However, allow a little more space for the rose because of its spreading habit.

Rosa 'Ballerina' has the light, pretty, simple character I want for my cottage garden style. Although it is only lightly fragrant, it blooms through summer and produces graceful sprays of small, single, pink, white-eyed flowers.

The rose will make a wonderful planting partner for *Hydrangea serrata* 'Bluebird', no matter what kind of soil you have. The flowers will be truly blue only on acid soil; they are mauve-pink on alkaline soil, but just as pretty. The pointed leaves are flushed burgundy, and the flowers last from early summer through fall. It is an altogether dainty but hard-working shrub.

The lilac tree is a familiar sight in cottage gardens, but it takes up a lot of space and has only a short season. *Syringa* 'Red Pixie' is a small lilac with dainty little leaves and profuse delicate pink, early summer flowers. It also adds the magic ingredient of scent.

Alternative shrubs to consider
Abelia parvifolia 'Bumblebee'
Buddleja Nanho Blue
Ceratostigma willmottianum
Ilex aquifolium 'Elegantissima'
Kolkwitzia amabilis
Rosa Rosy Cushion
Sambucus nigra f. *porphyrophylla* 'Eva'
Spiraea 'Arguta'

Kolkwitzia amabilis: Beauty bush has soft leaves and masses of soft pink and gold flowers in early summer.

Ilex aquifolium 'Elegant-issima': A lovely holly with cream-edged deep green leaves. It has no berries but is a good addition to the scheme throughout the year. Keeps witches away too!

The basic combination

In a large garden

Abelia ×grandiflora

Many evergreen shrubs look out of place in cottage garden style, but *Abelia ×grandiflora* is an exception. It can grow to form a very large shrub if left unattended, but it adds year-round interest with its arching stems and small, shining, dark green leaves. The pink flowers light up late summer and fall, and the deep pink starry calyces remain for much longer.

The flowering currant is one of the most traditional flowering shrubs, and it deserves its place in this style. *Ribes* 'Koja' delights with its hanging clusters of ruby red flowers produced as the aromatic leaves unfurl. The soft green foliage makes a good backdrop for the rest of the scheme through summer, and even the tan stems look good in winter.

Ribes 'Koja'

Primula vulgaris

Bulbs & perennials

Primula vulgaris, the humble primrose, would be excellent to naturalize under any of the deciduous shrubs. The leaves are evergreen and the lovely soft yellow flowers start to appear in late winter. Other colours may turn up if it has hybridized with polyanthus and hybrid primrose plants.

Although red poppies are stunning, I choose lovely *Papaver* 'Patty's Plum' for this scheme. The soft mauve-grey blooms will work with any shrubs in this selection, and the poppy plants die down quickly after flowering and take up little space.

The hybrid hellebores work well among the shade of deciduous shrubs. They bloom for months from winter through spring and add attractive semi-evergreen foliage, which is particularly valuable in early winter.

Papaver 'Patty's Plum'

Helleborus ×hybridus

A country garden blends seamlessly with trees and shrubs in the natural landscape. There are no neatly trimmed shapes here; plants grow freely and naturally.

Country garden

Shrubs to attract bees, butterflies and wild birds to a sunny garden in a rural setting

Many popular garden shrubs look out of place in a rural setting, whereas others make a seamless transition with those in the field and hedgerow. Shrubs with strongly variegated and highly coloured foliage can be jarring, whereas those with small flowers in clusters, plain green or grey leaves, and a loose natural habit blend beautifully. This is no place for the manicured, trimmed, or trained.

Country style is about shrubs that are popular with wildlife, including bees, butterflies, and birds. Single flowers, rich in pollen and nectar, are popular with insects, while wild birds will appreciate shrubs that produce edible fruits and berries.

Country gardens are often larger than those in towns. Therefore, larger-growing shrubs, requiring little in the way of pruning and aftercare, naturally convey the country garden message. Some of these will be cultivars of widespread native species. Most of all you want a style of planting that sits happily with long grass and needs no neatly edged beds.

The country garden is at its peak in high summer, when meadows and hedgerows are filled with flowers. Spring interest comes from perennials and bulbs that grow, bloom, and flower under the branches of deciduous shrubs and trees. However, the overall picture has another peak in fall, when the foliage of deciduous trees and shrubs colour richly and shining berries and fruits ripen on the branches.

Where would this scheme work?
This style of planting naturally suits a rural setting and is the perfect transition from garden to natural landscape. Gardens adjoining open countryside or using the borrowed rural setting are perfect. The scheme suits a sunny position, but most subjects will tolerate some shade from neighbouring trees. All shrubs will grow happily on any well-drained, reasonably fertile soil. This scheme is designed for the open ground and is not suited to growing in containers.

Rubus spectabilis 'Olympic Double'

Rosa 'Fru Dagmar Hastrup'

Cotoneaster franchetii

Fruits of *Rosa* 'Fru Dagmar Hastrup'

The basic combination

The shrubs in the basic combination grow larger than many other subjects in the initial selections in this section. They should be planted more than 90cm (3 ft.) apart, ideally with even more space for the cotoneaster.

I associate the countryside with *Rosa canina*, dog rosa, with its delicate, single, pale pink fragrant blooms. Therefore my starting point is *Rosa* 'Fru Dagmar Hastrup', rugosa rose. When the single shell pink blooms open, they have golden yellow stamens that are lovely against apple green foliage. This rose grows on the most hostile site, and deer and rabbits usually leave it alone. Tomato-like shining red fruits replace the blooms in late summer and last into winter.

Rubus spectabilis 'Olympic Double' is a perfect partner for the rose. It produces its showy cerise rosette blooms before the rose buds open. The first buds of the rubus usually open in spring, before the bright green leaves unfurl on tan-coloured stems, and they continue until early summer. This is another tough country character, and its suckering habit shows off its free spirit.

The semi-evergreen *Cotoneaster franchetii* provides winter foliage, single white flowers in spring, and red-orange berries in fall. Unlike most evergreen shrubs, it is airy and arching, with small leaves that are silver on the underside and give a light effect. Together with its planting partners it makes a pleasing picture throughout the year.

Viburnum opulus 'Roseum'

Buddleja 'Miss Ruby'

Expanding the scheme

These additions are medium-size to large shrubs that have the potential to reach more than 1.8m (6 ft.) in height with similar spread, so you will have to provide the space to allow this. Only the buddleja needs regular, hard pruning in late winter for best results.

The lovely *Viburnum opulus* 'Roseum', a selection of the British native guelder rose, is a pure delight in spring, when green flower clusters appear on the branches. Each one is like a green man or a spirit of the country-side. These green globes soon expand into

cream and then white pendant snowballs. The whole flower cycle captures the advent of spring and its ascent into summer.

The buddlejas may be imposters in the country garden, and certainly seedlings are often uninvited visitors. However, their summer flowers are welcome for their colour and fragrance, and butterflies appreciate their rich nectar source. *Buddleja* 'Miss Ruby' is a stunning hue of red-cerise, lovely with the rose and continuing the colour of the earlier rubus.

Alternative shrubs to consider
Cornus alba 'Sibirica'
Cornus sanguinea 'Midwinter Fire'
Euonymus alatus
Euonymus europaeus 'Red Cascade'
Ilex aquifolium 'Pyramidalis'
Rosa ×alba 'Alba Semiplena'
Symphoricarpos ×doorenbosii 'Mother of Pearl'
Syringa vulgaris var. *alba*
Viburnum opulus

Cornus alba 'Sibirica': A wonderful shrub for its red stems in winter and rich fall colour. Plain green leaves in summer make this a useful backdrop to herbaceous perennials.

Ilex aquifolium 'Pyramidalis': Common holly is one of the few bold evergreens that looks like it belongs in an informal country scheme. This selection produces plenty of berries that birds appreciate in winter.

The basic combination

Physocarpus opulifolius 'Diablo'

In a large garden

Both the sambucus and the physocarpus can grow to more than 1.8m (6 ft.) high with a similar spread. They are interchangeable with either of the shrubs in the expanded selection. The sambucus benefits from hard pruning in late winter in the first couple of years to promote strong growth.

Sambucus nigra f. *laciniata* captures the atmosphere of a country lane lined with cow parsley in early summer. The finely cut leaves and huge lacy flower heads are frothy and exuberant, perfect against a blue summer sky. Drooping clusters of red fruits follow as summer turns to fall.

Although most coloured foliage looks out of place in this scheme, deep purple mixes here as well as it does in the urban garden. *Physocarpus opulifolius* 'Diablo' adds dramatic depth to the background; it maintains a country look with its hawthorn-like flowers and dark red fruit clusters.

Sambucus nigra f. *laciniata*

Bulbs & perennials

Most of the shrubs are deciduous, and you can underplant them with shade-loving bulbs and perennials that flower before the leafy canopy of the shrubs fully develops. Any of the pulmonarias or lungworts are a good choice. *Pulmonaria* 'Roy Davidson' is a lovely variety with sky blue flowers and attractively spotted foliage that makes good ground cover in the shade of the shrubs.

Digitalis purpurea, common foxglove, has ascending spires of pendant flowers that hail the onset of high summer in the countryside. On poorer soils it will seed freely and drift through the planting to add another dimension.

Hyacinthoides non-scripta, English bluebell, has exquisite blue flowers carried in gently arched garlands in late spring. If you allow it to seed and keep cultivation to a minimum, it will naturalize and colonize the ground between larger shrubs.

Pulmonaria 'Roy Davidson'

Hyacinthoides non-scripta

Digitalis purpurea

Exotic

Blooms in wild silk colours against a backdrop of luxuriant leaves

The blooms of rhododendrons have an air of eastern promise, especially the blossoms with contrasting flares of hue that inspire rich and vibrant colour associations. In this scheme I see wild silk colours torn from a tea picker's sari. I imagine rich velvet textures and precise but intricate patterns. I want the planting to capture the atmosphere of cool, shaded courtyards and hot sunshine. Deep green and purple foliage enhance exotic flower forms in brave, bold colours. Rhododendrons, azaleas, magnolias, and tulips—treasures of the flower world evoke a sense of mystery.

The principal colours of purple and orange clash softly, but with louder notes of excitement. Clusters of small blooms jingle around the sweeping melody of opulent flowers. Although evergreen foliage holds the rhythm throughout the year, the flowers call the tune in loud bursts of seasonal sound.

The picture is one of colourful faraway places—nowhere in particular, but with echoes of India, Morocco, and Persia. It captures the atmosphere of 1001 nights in a temperate garden every time those rhododendrons bloom in spring and the hydrangea expands its lacy heads in fall.

A stone goddess stands serene amidst a flowering forest of silky precious blooms and delicate leaves.

Where would this scheme work?

This scheme is best suited to a medium-size to larger garden on neutral to acid soil. The first selection would suit a much smaller garden, and these subjects are suitable for growing in pots. Although the colour is adventurous, it would work in a traditional or contemporary setting and is ideal under the light, dappled shade of trees.

Rhododendron 'Blue Danube'

Leucothoe keiskei 'Royal Ruby'

Nandina domestica

The basic combination

For containers, use a lime-free, loam-based compost for the evergreen azalea and leucothoe. All subjects are best with some shade, and all dislike hot, dry conditions.

Evergreen azaleas are wonderful in pots and small gardens. When in flower, the blooms are like shimmering silk. *Rhododendron* 'Blue Danube' has large open blooms of rich purple that are glorious against its bright green leaves and the red and orange tones of its planting partners.

Arching stems and regularly arranged and defined leaves make *Leucothoe keiskei* 'Royal Ruby' an outstanding small evergreen shrub. The leaves turn rich red in winter, and the colour remains through spring alongside the azalea's violet blooms.

Nandina domestica, sacred bamboo, adds light height and a delicate tracery of leaves reminiscent of an ornate fretwork screen. The leaves colour in fall and winter, compensating for the lack of blooms on the flowering shrubs. In sunlight the frond-like leaves cast intricate shadows on the plants beneath.

Hydrangea aspera Kawakamii Group

Rhododendron 'Mrs. T. H. Lowinsky'

Berberis darwinii

Alternative shrubs to consider

Acer palmatum 'Shaina'
Cercis canadensis 'Forest Pansy'
Cotinus coggygria 'Royal Purple'
Enkianthus campanulatus
Leptospermum scoparium 'Red Damask'
Magnolia 'Susan'
Rhododendron 'Arabesk'
Sophora 'Sun King'

The layered branches and magnificent red-purple leaves of **Cercis canadensis 'Forest Pansy'** would make the perfect backdrop for all shrubs in this planting scheme. Do not disregard it even if space is limited; you can prune it in winter to restrict its size.

Most magnolias have a rather exotic air, and the slender, cerise-purple tulip flowers of **Magnolia 'Susan'** are definitely from another land. These are full of eastern promise and will delight in spring when they appear before the leaves are fully unfurled.

Expanding the scheme

The basic combination

These additions are medium-size shrubs that could reach 1.5m (5 ft.) or more with a similar spread. None are particularly fast growing, and you can control the size of the berberis by pruning after flowering. You can grow the rhododendron in a large container with lime-free compost. It would make a splendid specimen on its own or with the other additions and the basic combination.

Rhododendron 'Mrs. T. H. Lowinsky' is a delicately exotic rhododendron. The copper-ochre flare at the back of the bloom makes it the perfect partner for coppery leaves. The delicate mauve-pink petals also work beautifully with purple foliage. The shining deep green leaves are a textural contrast to the dark holly foliage of the berberis and the soft velvet leaves of the hydrangea.

Hydrangea aspera Kawakamii Group adds an unexpected floral element to the scheme in late fall. Delicate lacy heads of purple-pink are spangled with pink-white florets that float above luxuriant velvet leaves. This is one of the most beautiful late-flowering shrubs.

The dark leaves and sparkling orange flowers of *Berberis darwinii* remind me of the beads and sequins of a ceremonial costume. The blossom's brilliance is a stark contrast to the soft shades of the rhododendron, yet it amplifies the orange in the flare in the rhododendron flower.

Where space allows I would add *Rhododendron* 'Firelight' to the scheme. The warm pale orange blooms speckled with deep pink are unusual in their hose-in-hose formation. They have a bell-like quality, and their rich, fruity colour softens the orange notes in the scheme toward the mauves and purples of other plants. You could also substitute this delicious subject for the rhododendron in the additions.

The heart-shaped leaves of *Cercis chinensis* 'Avondale' are bright green and then golden before they fall, and they are defined and beautiful like the pattern on a fabric. Before the leaves appear, the bare stems are clothed in purple pea flowers as the berberis erupts in a shower of orange, creating a picture that is clashing, eye-catching, and full of spring promise.

In a large garden

Cercis chinensis 'Avondale'

Rhododendron 'Firelight'

Lilium henryi

Tulipa 'Ballerina'

Bulbs & perennials

This scheme is about creating shocks of colour, and adding flower bulbs is the best way to achieve it. No other group of plants fits in as easily or offers such a range of colours and flower forms.

Tulips always conjure images of Persia, their native land. The elegantly beautiful *Tulipa* 'Ballerina' is the perfect choice for its warm orange blooms with pointed petals. Even gardeners who claim to dislike orange will enjoy this tulip. It survives in the ground from year to year if the soil is well drained.

Later in the year I would like to see *Lilium henryi* with its orange flowers on long,

delicate stamens spaced on tall stems that rise high above the planting like towering minarets. Just two groups of three bulbs will add a spectacular dimension to the combination in late summer.

Few plants have such colourful foliage as heucheras. For this scheme I would choose lovely *Heuchera* 'Creme Brulee' with its soft caramel-coloured, gently waved leaves. A group of three plants alongside the rhododendron would pick up the copper flare in the flower. If you are growing in containers, this is an excellent choice with the plants in the basic combination.

Heuchera 'Creme Brulee'

Olives, woody herbs, and the parchment remains of spring flowers cling to a rocky, sun-drenched Cretan hillside.

Mediterranean

Drought-tolerant shrubs in an easy-to-care-for scheme for a sunny spot

Picture the warm tones of the Mediterranean landscape: red-brown soil and sand-coloured rock blend with low-mounded shrubs adapted to withstand the summer sun, heat, and exposure. To resist desiccation in times of drought, some have small, tough leaves while others sport silver foliage. Colourful flowers appear in spring and early summer, before water is in short supply and shrubs assume a more parched appearance. Some of these blooms appear on the shrubs, while others emerge from bulbs growing between the shrubs. They all add a light, vertical dimension to the planting.

In the glaring Mediterranean midday sun, the landscape becomes less defined as a haze of grey, green, and sand blankets everything. In early morning the mounds of woody stems and foliage become more defined, each one taking on its own unique soft colouring.

The landscape is full of aromatic woody herbs, and their pungent fragrance drifts on the warm air. Scent is as an important quality of this style of planting.

You can adapt the Mediterranean style to the climate of temperate regions. In many cases, heavier summer rainfall means you can incorporate small-leaved hebes that would not succeed in a true Mediterranean environment but are reminiscent of the region's plant form and character.

Where would this scheme work?

The Mediterranean style suits an open, sunny position and poor soil. It is ideal alongside paving and decking and in gravel areas, and it sits well in contemporary and coastal designs. This is low-maintenance shrub planting, simple and minimalist. You can also use it for a container-planting scheme for paved areas, balconies, and courtyards. Light-coloured terra-cotta pots and pale sandstone paving would reflect the character of the rocks and soil of the Mediterranean landscape.

Salvia officinalis 'Purpurascens'

Santolina rosmarinifolia 'Primrose Gem'

Lavandula angustifolia 'Hidcote'

The basic combination

These low shrubs are normally planted as small pot-grown plants, but they have a deceptively broad spread and grow quickly. Space them at least 60cm (2 ft.) apart in the open ground. If you are growing in containers, use terra-cotta pots at least 30cm (1 ft.) in diameter and plant in loam-based compost with added grit for good drainage.

Santolina rosmarinifolia 'Primrose Gem', with its mounds of soft grey foliage and pale parchment yellow flowers, is a gentle, sociable shrub that sits well with any other sun lovers. The flowers of most cotton lavenders are loud and inappropriate, whereas these blossoms are a charming feature in summer.

The santolina is the ideal partner for wonderful *Salvia officinalis* 'Purpurascens', common purple sage, which has grey-mauve foliage that is darker at the tips of the shoots. This shrub is the perfect mixer and softener, and one of the most valuable plants in a sunny, dry position alongside paving or decking or in gravel. The spikes of bright blue flowers in early summer are a magnet for bees.

To add colour and more fragrant foliage, I have chosen my favourite English lavender, *Lavandula angustifolia* 'Hidcote'. This compact, long-lasting shrub will retain a mound of silver foliage in winter.

Expanding the scheme

These small additions are only a little larger than, or similar in stature to, those in the basic combination, and they are interchangeable if you want a wider choice of options.

Hebe 'Red Edge' is truly a plant for all seasons, with its tough grey-green leaves that flush deep red-purple at the tips of the shoots in winter. It is a strong, textural mound in the planting and will cope with cooler, moister conditions than most of the shrubs in this scheme.

Cistus obtusifolius 'Thrive' may not be the largest-flowered sun rose, but it makes up for it with quantity by blooming from early summer through to fall. The flowers are at their best in the morning, and they scatter the surrounding ground with confetti of white petals by evening. Small green leaves contrast with the soft silver and mauve-grey foliage of other subjects.

Ballotta pseudodictamnus is a shrub from the Mediterranean landscape, and its soft green upright stems, which carry the felted flower heads, burn to golden parchment by late summer. It has a more open habit and softer texture than its planting partners, and it loves dry, warm weather.

Ballotta pseudodictamnus

Hebe 'Red Edge'

Cistus obtusifolius 'Thrive'

Alternative shrubs to consider

Brachyglottis (Dunedin Group) 'Sunshine'
Cistus ×*dansereuari* 'Decumbens'
Cistus ×*pulverulentus* 'Sunset'
Hebe pinguifolia 'Sutherlandii'
Helichrysum italicum 'Korma'
Rosmarinus officinalis
Santolina chamaecyparissus

Cistus ×*dansereuari* 'Decumbens': A stunning cistus that spreads its deep green foliage beneath the large shimmering white flowers and has blotched red-purple at the base of the petals.

Rosmarinus officinalis: Common rosemary is the perfect addition to add height and vertical lines to the planting. Its wonderfully aromatic foliage and blue spring flowers are welcome in any garden.

In a large garden

These two larger shrubs are still relatively modest in size and would be ideal in pots on a sunny balcony or terrace, with any of the smaller plants grouped around them.

Pittosporum tobira 'Variegatum' looks like it belongs on the terrace of a villa. It captures the atmosphere of warm sunshine, especially when the fragrant cream flowers open at the ends of the shoots in summer. These blooms have the heavy, sweet scent of jasmine we associate with the Mediterranean night.

Myrtus communis, common myrtle, adds that surprising bright green that occurs in the Mediterranean alongside the softer shades of parchment, gold, and olive. Its aromatic foliage is a delightful partner for the creamy white late-summer flowers.

Myrtus communis

Pittosporum tobira 'Variegatum'

The basic combination

Allium cristophii seed head

Bulbs & perennials

Allium cernuum

Alliums work perfectly with this style of planting, not only for their stunning flowers but also their seed heads, which are reminiscent of the parched umbellifers that often appear in the Mediterranean landscape. *Allium cristophii* is one of the finest, with its sparkling lilac flower heads and enduring seed heads that last until fall. Planted among the shrubs, the withering foliage of the alliums will not detract from the overall effect.

Allium cernuum extends the season by producing its firework-like flowers in summer. Delicate blooms on fine stems surprise with their cerise-purple colouring. They are particularly striking emerging through a haze of *Stipa tenuissima*, one of the loveliest grasses for a hot, dry situation. On well-drained poor soil, the grass and alliums will seed and drift among the shrubs, softening and adding movement throughout.

Japanese

Elegant, precise, and understated, an illusion of space in the smallest of gardens

Stepping stones wind their way between moss, rocks, and low green shrubs beneath the ancient trees in this peaceful and serene Japanese garden landscape.

Delicate blossoms carried on bare stems and the fine tracery of maple leaves are the essence of Japanese garden style. The colours and shapes of flowers and the landscape feature in fabrics, paintings, ceramics, and many other aspects of Japanese life. Anyone who has walked through old Tokyo or a busy Japanese town has experienced a fusion of colours and designs. These designs are often bold and simple, and flowers and leaves that recall the brushstrokes of a painting, the line of a roof tile, or the pattern of a rice bowl convey Japanese style.

Japanese gardens are usually considered minimalist, as every plant is carefully positioned and controlled to maintain its presence. Shrubs rarely feature; the soft landscape is created from small trees, carefully chosen perennials, and moss. However, many shrubs can be used to create the same atmosphere, and the planting can be more naturalistic, as it is in the Japanese landscape.

I have been fortunate to visit Japan on a few occasions—never in the cherry blossom season, but this is still my starting point in creating this style. Japanese maples are essential, and they are used extensively in gardens and also appear in the natural landscape. I associate azaleas, hydrangeas, and enkianthus with this style too, as they feature in the areas I have visited. Some are included in the list of additions.

Prunus incisa 'Kojo-no-mai'

Acer palmatum 'Beni-maiko'

The basic combination

In the open ground, plant these shrubs 60–90cm (2–3 ft.) apart. If you are growing in pots, choose containers at least 35cm (14 in.) in diameter and 30cm (1 ft.) deep.

My starting point is delicate little cherry *Prunus incisa* 'Kojo-no-mai' for its fragile white blossoms in spring and rich fall colour. I have grown this prunus very successfully in a pot for a number of years; I love its zigzag branches and bonsai effect. It conveys the presence of a tree in a small space.

I have partnered the prunus with lovely small-growing Japanese maple *Acer palmatum* 'Beni-maiko'. It has coloured tissue-paper leaves that are cerise pink in spring, becoming soft green flushed with strawberry, and then colouring richly in fall. The branches are fine and arching; even as a young plant it has great charm.

If gardening on acid soil, or growing in a container filled with lime-free compost, the third plant I would choose is evergreen *Leucothoe* Lovita. This is a low, compact shrub with arching stems and precisely pointed deep green leaves that turn rich red in winter, adding colour when the other two shrubs have lost their foliage. The leaves in winter remind me of brushstrokes of red lacquer paint.

As an alternative to the leucothoe, for sunnier positions and alkaline soil, you could use *Chamaecyparis obtusa* 'Nana Gracilis'.

Leucothoe Lovita

Where would this scheme work?

This scheme would be perfect in a small garden or courtyard that enjoys some shade, and all shrubs would be successful in containers. If you plant in the open ground, well-chosen gravel or pebbles around the plants, perhaps with a few larger stones, would accentuate the Japanese effect. Using just a few well-chosen shrubs with different forms and seasons of interest, and giving each plant its individual space, can make a small space appear larger.

Chamaecyparis obtusa 'Nana Gracilis'

Enkianthus campanulatus: Layered growth habit resembles a Japanese pagoda. Salmon pink hanging, bell-shaped blooms in spring and richly coloured fall foliage.

Alternative shrubs to consider

Chaenomeles speciosa 'Moerloosei'
Enkianthus campanulatus
Hydrangea paniculata 'Kyushu'
Hydrangea serrata 'Bluebird'
Magnolia stellata 'Water Lily'
Rhododendron 'Blue Danube'
Rhododendron 'Daviesii'

Chaenomeles speciosa **'Moerloosei':** Grow free-standing or against a wall. Delicate salmon pink–flushed blooms in spring are followed by aromatic golden fruits in fall.

Pieris japonica 'Katsura'

Osmanthus heterophyllus 'Goshiki'

Expanding the scheme

Gardeners are most likely to use the Japanese style in a small garden, so I have chosen three additional shrubs that would be suitable in a limited space. Planting distance between shrubs and container size is the same as in the basic combination.

Textural conifer *Chamaecyparis obtusa* 'Nana Gracilis' has tightly packed waves of deep green foliage reminiscent of crushed green velvet or felted coral. Its compact growth conveys maturity and Japanese charm. I particularly like it in a shallow container, where it resembles a bonsai tree.

Pieris japonica 'Katsura' is perhaps the most arresting pieris, with its beaded sprays of pink flowers in spring and mahogany plumes of new leaves. The lacquered appearance of the foliage and gentle curve of each leaf reminds me of the elegant rooflines of Japan.

Maybe it is partly the name of *Osmanthus heterophyllus* 'Goshiki' that makes it seem appropriate for this scheme. But there is no doubt that its changing appearance, green-and-cream variegation, and coppery new leaves add to the scheme in every season.

Cornus kousa 'Satomi'

In a large garden

If space allows, the two larger shrubs at the top of my list are *Cornus kousa* 'Satomi' and *Acer palmatum* 'Bloodgood'. Both grow to much larger proportions and need to be spaced at least 1.5m (5 ft.) apart, or you could grow them in large pots 45cm (18 in.) in diameter or more.

Cornus kousa 'Satomi' is one of the smaller flowering dogwoods, with spreading branches and beautifully poised blooms with salmon pink bracts in early summer. A shrub in full flower resembles the flowing fabric of a kimono.

Although I have already included one maple, the larger-growing *Acer palmatum* 'Bloodgood' would add height. This plant features deep wine-purple foliage that colours brilliantly in fall. This dramatic hue adds depth to the scheme and accentuates the more delicate subjects.

Acer palmatum 'Bloodgood'

Liriope muscari

Fritillaria meleagris

The basic combination

Bulbs & perennials

A few groups of low evergreen perennials and bulbs would add interest to the scheme, particularly where the shrubs are planted in the open ground and surrounded by gravel.

Liriope muscari, lily turf, is a grass-like evergreen perennial with deep green foliage and spikes of purple-blue flowers in fall. It is at its best in shade and works well under maples.

Lovely *Fritillaria meleagris,* snake's head fritillary, is a charming bulb to add for spring, especially if the soil is cool and damp. The checkered purple or white flowers resemble lanterns.

The Exotic Garden in Norwich, England, is an oasis of lush foliage and brilliant blooms in the heart of the city.

Tropical

A focus on foliage, with large, colorful leaves carried aloft on strong stems

The word *tropical* makes me think of big leaves, lush vegetation, and a larger-than-life look to the planting. I imagine a Rousseau painting with defined lines; almost abstract with a three-dimensional quality. This is a strong and bold style. There are no soft, fluffy shapes, pretty flowers, or delicate leaves here.

I feel the shade of tall overhead trees, their straight trunks towering skyward in search of the light. I see flashes of colour darting among the heavy green and exotic birds flying from limb to limb of the trees above. The atmosphere is humid and damp, without a hint of hot, dry, and sunny in the shade of the forest.

The vegetation feels luxuriant and transports me to distant lands, where day and night are similar in length and seasons are the same. This is a piece of paradise, perhaps a leafy retreat from the familiarity of the surrounding landscape; a refreshing cocktail of deepest green with shots of colour.

In reality, deciduous and hardy shrubs are adapted to different climatic conditions, but with a careful selection you can create a tropical vision for the warmer summer months. Maintain the interest during the winter with broad-leaved evergreens and phormiums.

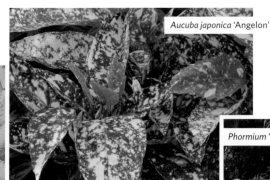

Aucuba japonica 'Angelon'

Melianthus major

Phormium 'Yellow Wave'

The basic combination

The shrubs chosen for the basic combination are comparatively large in order to achieve the lush, tropical feel that the scheme demands. You can contain both the aucuba and melianthus with selective pruning. All the shrubs will grow on any reasonably well-drained soil; plant at least 90cm (3 ft.) apart. If planting these shrubs in containers, choose pots at least 40cm (15 in.) in diameter.

The first shrub in this style of planting is wonderfully architectural *Melianthus major*. It forms a clump of upright, sometimes sprawling, stems carrying magnificent blue-green leaves that unfurl with great mystery, shedding quicksilver raindrops from their sharply toothed margins. In a cold winter it may be knocked back to the ground, but it will rise like a phoenix the following spring.

Phormiums are not truly shrubs, but are used as such in gardens. Here I chose striking *Phormium* 'Yellow Wave' for its broadly arching, pale yellow, green-edged leaves. The colour and texture are the perfect contrast to the melianthus. With some sun, mature phormiums produce striking, almost black, inflorescences.

Few plants are as effective in shade as spotted laurels. *Aucuba japonica* 'Angelon' is a wonderful form with deep green shining leaves heavily splashed with bright gold. It has a lush, tropical feel in shade and brings dappled sunshine to the shadiest corner.

Where would this scheme work?
This scheme would be ideal in a small, sheltered, urban garden where surrounding buildings create the same shade that tropical trees do. It would also work in a larger garden with trees, where the surrounding planting can shelter the tropical glade. Although all the shrubs are reasonably hardy, this scheme does not work in an open, exposed situation.

Expanding the scheme

You could substitute the fatsia for the aucuba in the basic combination, and the leycesteria for the melianthus. All have the potential to grow large without pruning. I do not recommend the clerodendrum for pots. Plant all shrubs at least 90cm (3 ft.) apart in the ground.

Fatsia japonica, Japanese fatsia or false castor oil plant, is one of my first choices for a tropical planting scheme. It has large, hand-like, leathery evergreen leaves. In winter, striking creamy white flower heads add an unseasonal touch of the tropics to the scheme. The shadier the position, the shinier and darker green the leaves.

Leycesteria formosa Golden Lanterns has a gentle habit and soft golden leaves that become lime green in shade. In late summer, ruby clusters hang from the branches like exotic lanterns. For a golden-leaved plant, it has a naturalistic quality missing from many other coloured-foliage shrubs, and it is a wonderful contrast to the fatsia.

Clerodendrum bungei is a surprising hardy shrub with upright stems and curious shiny, rounded leaves. In fall, clusters of pink flowers appear at the stem tips, each surrounded by a rigid collar of glossy foliage. These blooms clash wonderfully with the yellow leaves, adding shots of tropical colour.

Alternative shrubs to consider
Astelia 'Silver Shadow'
Aucuba japonica 'Rozannie'
Euonymus japonicus 'Chollipo'
×*Fatshedera lizei* 'Annemieke'
Paulownia tomentosa
Phormium cookianum subsp. *hookeri* 'Tricolor'
Pittosporum tobira
Rhus typhina Tiger Eyes

Rhus typhina* Tiger Eyes: A dwarf sumach with flamboyant golden leaves and red-brown velvet seed clusters. The fall colour is spectacular in a sunny spot.

Astelia* 'Silver Shadow': The striking sword-shaped leaves of astelia enjoy a shaded situation, where they reflect any shafts of sunlight that reach them. It is good in a pot, and you could substitute it for the phormium in the basic combination.

Fatsia japonica

Clerodendrum bungei

Leycesteria formosa Golden Lanterns

Catalpa bignoniodes 'Aurea'

Cotinus 'Grace'

In a large garden

Catalpa bignoniodes 'Aurea', golden Indian bean tree or southern catalpa, is usually thought of as a tree, but it makes a wonderful shrub if you prune it hard in winter. Few hardy shrubs have such as impact as this one, which has remarkably large, velvety, golden, heart-shaped leaves. It boldly conveys the impression of a rain forest, as its leaves create the impression of warm, tropical sunshine.

Contrasting magnificently with the large golden foliage of the catalpa, the warm coppery leaves of *Cotinus* 'Grace' possess a magical translucency when the sun shines through them. As summer progresses, the red tones of the foliage pick up the colour of the ruby lanterns of the leycesteria. Vigorous upright stems make this a perfect shrub for the back of the scheme.

Aeonium arboretum 'Atropurpureum'

Hemerocallis fulva 'Kwanso'

Houttuynia cordata 'Chameleon'

The basic combination

Bulbs & perennials

You can add spring and summer bulbs to this scheme to extend the season and add shots of summer colour. Consider orange lily–flowering tulips for spring and crocosmias, cannas, callas, and bright single dahlias for summer.

Houttuynia cordata 'Chameleon' is one of the most colourful herbaceous perennials grown for its foliage. Short, suckering stems produce heart-shaped leaves glowing in shades of green, gold, and salmon pink. It grows well in shade or sun and it loves damp soil.

The daylily may normally grace the herbaceous border, but in this scheme the more flamboyant varieties add an exotic note. Double orange-flowered *Hemerocallis fulva* 'Kwanso' blooms for several weeks, and the broad, strap-like leaves contrast well with the other foliage forms.

Adding tender plants on a seasonal basis lends an even more tropical feel to this style. The purple-black succulent rosettes of *Aeonium arboretum* 'Atropurpureum' are an arresting sight in a reasonably sunny situation. Grow it in a pot and move it indoors as the nights grow colder.

Urban contemporary

A chic scheme for modern town garden in sun or shade

The urban garden is a precious outdoor space. It is usually secluded, even if buildings and other vegetation surround it. The urban garden offers a refuge from the buzz of the city and may be a valuable additional living space, an outdoor room to enjoy in fine weather. The planting scheme is crucial, as it brings living colour and texture into the space but also must fit the style of the building and the décor. A modern interior needs a contemporary garden that offers more than the traditional trimmed box shapes and bedding-filled window box.

Small urban gardens are often in the shade for much of the day, as surrounding buildings allow the sun to penetrate only when it is directly overhead in summer. In some cases the planting area may be permanently shaded, even if there is daylight. Shade is often seen as a challenge, as we cannot always grow the plants we like. For most gardeners, a garden means grass and brightly coloured flowers; shade often equals foliage, texture, and more subtle blooms.

The plants you use in an urban garden need to work hard to earn their keep. They must have more than one season of interest and ideally need to look good, but never boring, throughout the year.

A small contemporary garden at the Royal Horticultural Society's Chelsea Flower Show. Clean lines, sleek slate, and neat planting create a pleasing outdoor space.

The basic combination

FOR SUN OR PARTIAL SHADE

Coprosma 'Lemon and Lime' is a kaleidoscope of colour with neat, highly polished leaves in bright green, lime yellow, and orange. It is a citrus cocktail that demands attention, particularly when partnered with a coloured pot. Although not the hardiest of characters, it delivers year-round colour.

In contrast, *Pittosporum tobira* 'Nanum' forms a dome of shining dark green. The leaves are larger than those of the coprosma, and the regular growth pattern contrasts so the two shrubs work well together.

Challenging the rounded forms of the coprosma and pittosporum, dwarf *Phormium* Back in Black offers sharp purple-black leaves that are gently arched toward the tips. Both colour and form are a bold contrast to the other two shrubs.

Phormium Back in Black

Pittosporum tobira 'Nanum'

Coprosma 'Lemon and Lime'

Where would this scheme work?

This scheme would work in the smallest of gardens, where a contemporary style suits the design of the property. Although created for an urban situation it would work anywhere, particularly in small gardens attached to newly built properties. It would also be suitable for a courtyard or balcony.

Because most urban gardens are small and often paved, with little or no bed space, I have included two basic combination schemes, rather than one scheme with larger additions. One combination is designed for a situation that gets at least four hours of direct sun a day for most of the year. The other is intended for a garden that is in shade most of the time. All subjects are suitable to grow in pots filled with loam-based compost. Choose containers at least 35cm (14 in.) in diameter.

In a larger garden

FOR SUN OR PARTIAL SHADE

These picks would work well if you have a little more room or just want something taller. You could substitute the phormium for the phormium in the basic combination for sun or partial shade if you want something lighter and brighter. The euonymus will also grow happily in much heavier shade.

With gently arched green-and-cream-striped leaves, *Phormium cookianum* subsp. *hookeri* 'Cream Delight' is a striking plant that looks stunning in a contemporary container, perhaps a black stone pot or something tall and glazed.

Euonymus japonicus 'Green Rocket' is a real contrast, as it forms a column of deep green rounded leaves on vertical stems. It adds height with its vertical lines but takes up so little room it will fit into the narrowest space. I would use it rising above the coloured leaves of the coprosma.

Phormium cookianum subsp. *hookeri* 'Cream Delight'

Euonymus japonicus 'Green Rocket'

Alternative shrubs to consider for the urban contemporary garden

Fatsia japonica: The large, shiny, exotic leaves of fatsia are stunning in any contemporary setting. A single specimen in a large pot could be the only statement you need in a small, shaded courtyard.

Aucuba japonica 'Rozannie': Aucubas are not used enough as container plants for shade. The simple dark green foliage of 'Rozannie' is wonderfully reflective, and you might get red berries too.

The basic combination

FOR SUN OR PARTIAL SHADE

Heuchera 'Lime Marmalade'

Ophiopogon planiscarpus 'Nigrescens'

Narcissus 'Hawera'

Bulbs & perennials

FOR SUN OR PARTIAL SHADE

These plants would be ideal in pots positioned alongside those in the basic combination. In the open ground you could plant the heuchera and ophiopogon in groups of three and the narcissus in drifts of ten to fifteen bulbs.

Heuchera 'Lime Marmalade' forms a clump of waved lime green leaves. It picks up the variegation of the coprosma and creates a striking contrast with the narrow dark leaves of the phormium.

The tufted, black, grass-like leaves of *Ophiopogon planiscarpus* 'Nigrescens' bring dark foliage to ground level and are perfect for underplanting. When left to spread this plant makes excellent non-invasive ground-cover, but also allows the fine green leaves and pretty soft yellow flowers of *Narcissus* 'Hawera' to poke through and add another dimension in spring.

Astelia nervosa 'Westland'

Euonymus japonicus 'Microphyllus Variegatus'

Viburnum davidii

The basic combination

FOR SHADE

The viburnum and euonymus are also suitable for an open, sunny position. The astelia is more successful when grown in shade.

Gardeners underestimate *Astelia nervosa* 'Westland'. Its elegant spiky leaves are soft pewter-stained purple. It grows with great elegance and finesse without the problem of ugly, faded foliage. It shines in the shade and contrasts with the deep green broad leaves of other shrubs. Spotlight it at night for stunning shadows.

Viburnum davidii has broader, darker leaves than any other shrub in this combination. Each shining green leaf has deep parallel veins and a dark red stem. It is one of the easiest evergreen shrubs to grow and it will thrive in the shadiest corner.

In contrast, *Euonymus japonicus* 'Microphyllus Variegatus' has small, narrow, deep green leaves delicately edged with white. It is a totally different shape and texture than the other two shrubs, and its small, bright leaves will sparkle against the deep green foliage of the viburnum.

Hedera helix 'Erecta'

In a larger garden

FOR SHADE

Where space permits, you could add the following shrubs. You can also substitute them for any of the subjects in the basic combination for shade. The hedera will grow in sun as well as shade. The pieris needs lime-free soil or compost when grown in a pot.

Hedera helix 'Erecta' is quite unlike any other ivy, with its almost upright stems and regularly arranged dark green, angular leaves. It has an abstract, sculptural quality that sits well in contemporary settings.

Pieris japonica 'Carnaval' is grown for its small variegated leaves rather than its small spring flowers. This soft combination of green, cream, and pink is at its best with bold dark green leaves or the pewter-purple spiky foliage of the astelia, which reflects its pink notes.

Pieris japonica 'Carnaval'

Chionodoxa forbesii 'Alba'

FOR SHADE

Bulbs & perennials

Helleborus ×*hybridus*

These plants can be grown in pots grouped with the shrubs. It is best to remove the leaves of the hellebore, although almost evergreen, in winter just before flowering to prevent the spread of leaf-spot diseases.

Helleborus ×*hybridus* Hillier hybrids slate form has almost black single flowers with cream stamens. In large gardens, the flowers can disappear despite their up-close beauty. When shown off against these shrubs in a small garden, they provide a late winter and early spring highlight.

Heucherella 'Tapestry' is a lovely evergreen perennial with intricately patterned sage green, brown, and chestnut patterned leaves. Fine stems of small pinkish flowers appear in summer, but these are of minor interest compared to the leaves.

Chionodoxa forbesii 'Alba' is a delightful little bulb that flowers in very early spring and produces starry, upward-smiling blooms of pure white against bright green leaves.

Heucherella 'Tapestry'

Urban traditional

Traditional style based on foliage, featuring variations on the usual sweet bay and boxwood planting

Trimmed and trained boxwood and sweet bay in a traditional town courtyard setting create a living extension of the stone fabric of the building.

In traditional urban gardens, planting tends to be very green and somewhat formal. Trimmed evergreens form neat lines in window boxes and balconies, often in partnership with bright, temporary colour. In courtyards, ivies cling to the walls and a palette of dark green occupies the limited soil space and a few pots and containers. The surrounding buildings offer warmth and protection, but they also steal light.

Doorways are framed with *Laurus nobilis*, true laurel or common bay, while windows are underlined with *Buxus sempervirens*, trimmed box, and trails of ivy. Box balls, cones, and spirals dominate the court-yards, balconies, and light wells in cities throughout the temperate regions. To make selection even easier, these plants are readily available in nurseries, garden centres, and even furniture stores.

There are plenty of walls to lend support to climb-ers and wall shrubs, but ivy enjoys the shade and copes with the dry conditions that walls impose more than any other plant. Ivy tends to dominate in traditional urban gardens, and you should value its glossy, reflec-tive foliage that contrasts well with the small leaves of other evergreens.

In this scheme I want to preserve the sophisticated, restrained colour palette, but add a lighter note with cream variegations and a few flowers. I avoid the trimmed and trained; there is enough to do without the challenge of topiary. I include some more architectural subjects, but ones with softer character that sit well in a traditional setting. This combination of green and cream is softer than green alone or green and white, and sits well in a more traditional environment.

I have avoided plain green box, which has chal-lenges related to nutrient deficiency and disease. I have highlighted the alternatives instead.

The basic combination

My first choice is *Pittosporum tenuifolium* 'Golf Ball', a mound of small, shining, soft green leaves on fine dark stems. It provides structure without weight and reflects the light playfully, especially when the foliage is wet.

Variegated box, *Buxus sempervirens* 'Elegantissima', is a delightful contrast with its tiny leaves of darkest green edged with rich cream. The overall effect is light and bright, but totally different from the shiny dome of the pittosporum. This box is more resistant to disease if left untrimmed. Although compact, it has a frothy, pretty personality; it is definitely not a boring evergreen.

Phormium provides a total contrast in foliage form and texture. *Phormium* 'Alison Blackman' may seem a rather contemporary choice, but its colours are traditional and sophisticated. It is deep olive green and cream with hints of copper in low light, and these shades are particularly lovely with warm terra-cotta.

Phormium 'Alison Blackman'

Buxus sempervirens 'Elegantissima'

Pittosporum tenuifolium 'Golf Ball'

Where would this scheme work?

This scheme would work in any small garden in the town or country where you want an understated, subtle planting scheme based on foliage. It would sit well alongside traditional or modern properties, but will look best in the enclosed environment of a garden surrounded by walls, fences, or other buildings.

Because small urban gardens can have areas that get some sun and areas in permanent shade, I have divided the scheme into two parts. In many cases the plants are interchangeable and you could grow them in either situation. Urban gardens rarely have much open ground, and some properties have only paved areas or balconies. All shrubs are suitable for growing in pots using loam-based compost. Traditional containers are a good choice in most gardens, so all these plants work well with the warm tones of terra-cotta pots.

Prunus lusitanica 'Myrtifolia'

In a larger garden

FOR SUN OR PARTIAL SHADE

Both shrubs thrive in sun or shade. They will make excellent individual larger specimens, or you can incorporate them with the basic combination. You can prune both to control shape and size.

Euonymus japonicus 'Bravo' is one of the finest variegated shrubs, with eye-catching cream-and-dark-green variegated leaves. The shining foliage will light up the garden in winter and summer, providing far more impact than a few frail flowers.

Small-leaved *Prunus lusitanica* 'Myrtifolia', Portugal laurel, is a brilliant foil for the brighter foliage of other subjects. This subject is slow to grow and is a long-term shrub for the smallest space. Sprays of white flowers add an element of surprise in spring.

Euonymus japonicus 'Bravo'

Alternative shrubs to consider for the urban traditional garden
Lonicera nitida 'Maigrun'
Sarcococca confusa

Lonicera nitida **'Maigrun':** Often used as a landscape shrub for shady situations and planting under trees. It is also a good choice for containers in a shady spot, or for filling a dark corner in the open ground. Its fresh green leaves and slender branches are refreshingly lightening against heavier foliage.

Sarcococca confusa: If you have any open ground space in shade, this shrub is a must for this scheme. Its dark green shining leaves are highly reflective, and it offers the bonus of very fragrant flowers in later winter. This may not be the showiest plant in the garden, but its scent will delight. Do not grow sarcococca in a pot, as it does not like containers.

Narcissus 'Jack Snipe'

Hosta (Tardiana Group) 'June'

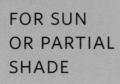

Primula 'Francisca'

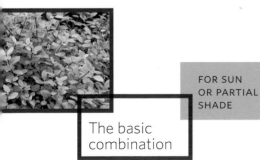

FOR SUN
OR PARTIAL
SHADE

The basic
combination

FOR SUN
OR PARTIAL
SHADE

Bulbs & perennials

Hostas make excellent subjects for pots from the time the new shoots emerge in spring until fall, when the leaves colour and die down. *Hosta* (Tardiana Group) 'June' is one of the best, with soft creamy yellow leaves broadly edged with blue-green.

I have had wonderful results with lovely green *Primula* 'Francisca' in pots year after year. It flowers from midspring right through to early summer, and the blooms are wonderfully pleated and ruffled. Move the containers into shade during summer.

Grow a pot or two of *Narcissus* 'Jack Snipe' to add early spring colour to the scheme. This lovely variety lasts well and is remarkably weather resistant.

Euonymus japonicus 'Microphyllus Aureovariegatus'

Skimmia ×confusa 'Kew Green'

Ilex crenata 'Convexa'

The basic combination

FOR SHADE

My first choice for shade is *Skimmia ×confusa* 'Kew Green', both for its apple green leaves and green winter buds and its fragrant creamy spring flowers. The perfume is pure lily-of-the-valley and will fill an enclosed space in the cool spring air.

To maintain the green-and-cream scheme throughout the year, I would partner the skimmia with *Euonymus japonicus* 'Microphyllus Aureovariegatus'. This compact little shrub is bright, cheerful, and a real survivor, coping well with shade and some neglect.

Ilex crenata 'Convexa' is an excellent alternative to box and has somewhat similar foliage but a looser habit. It grows slowly, needs little attention, and carries the dark green foliage into the shade.

Camellia ×williamsii 'Jury's Yellow'

FOR SHADE

In a larger garden

Camellias love the sheltered situation of a small, enclosed garden away from the morning sun, which can shatter frozen buds. *Camellia ×williamsii* 'Jury's Yellow' is one of the best for its compact growth, shining leaves, and clotted cream flowers. In early spring it will bring this green-and-cream scheme to life.

Although the variegation is whiter than the other subjects, I would choose *Fatsia japonica* 'Variegata' for its large, shiny, bold leaves. It is a stunning contrast to the small-leaved shrubs in this scheme, and it maintains the colour theme throughout the year.

Fatsia japonica 'Variegata'

FOR SHADE

Bulbs & perennials

Ferns, such as *Polystichum setiferum* Plumosomultilobum Group, thrive in the shade and still air of enclosed spaces. They make wonderful subjects for pots, and their feathery foliage is a pleasing contrast to the solid, stiffer leaves of evergreen shrubs.

Walls offer the opportunity to add vertical interest. Ivies love the shade and light up walls with their shining leaves. *Hedera colchica* 'Dentata Variegata' has magnificent large leaves of bright green, soft green, and rich cream; for best results, position plain evergreens in front of it.

Aegopodium podagraria 'Variegatum', variegated ground elder, works very well in a pot. It does not seed like the green form, so have no fears of invasion. It will fill a container with its green-and-cream foliage and lacy flowers from spring to fall.

Aegopodium podagraria 'Variegatum'

Polystichum setiferum Plumosomultilobum Group

Hedera colchica 'Dentata Variegata'

PLANT DIRECTORY

This section includes a selection of hard-working, beautiful shrubs that I use in my own garden and recommend to others. Growing conditions have such an impact on a plant's dimensions that it is difficult to specify height and spread. I have estimated the height and spread (h × s) of each shrub in this directory after a minimum of five years. These figures are based on the time of planting an average-size container-grown plant.

Size definitions
Dwarf: Height up to 60cm (2 ft.)
Small: Height up to 90cm (3 ft.)
Medium: Height up to 1.8m (6 ft.)
Large: Height more than 2.1m (7 ft.)

Most shrubs described as *large* can grow bigger than their listed dimensions. If size is a limiting factor, consider that the ultimate height and spread of a medium or large shrub could be one-third or more than stated, but the plant could take several more years to reach that size. You can usually control the height and spread with selective pruning, and I have included any necessary advice.

I also offer uses and possible planting partners, including other shrubs and perennials. Although these are just suggestions, I hope they give you some ideas on how these shrubs can work in your garden.

Abelia ×grandiflora

Abelia 'Edward Goucher'

Abelia ×grandiflora 'Kaleidoscope'

Abelia

Evergreen abelias are excellent shrubs for their shining leaves on light, arching stems, as well as their fall flowers. They are easy to grow in full sun, and may need eventual pruning to control their size or rejuvenate old plants. Prune in spring by cutting back some older stems by two-thirds or more into the lower part of the shrub. This maintains the plant's graceful arching habit.

Abelia 'Edward Goucher'
1.2M × 1.5M (4 FT. × 5 FT.)

A medium shrub, similar in appearance to *Abelia ×grandiflora* but with bright green foliage tinged bronze at the tips of the shoots. It produces lightly fragrant lilac-pink flowers freely throughout summer and fall. This is a good planting partner for fall-flowering perennials such as asters, echinaceas, and sedums. It also a good choice for smaller gardens.

Abelia ×grandiflora
2.1M × 2.4M (7 FT. × 8 FT.)

A vigorous shrub with arching stems carrying small, neat, glossy evergreen leaves. The funnel-shaped flowers are white tinged with pale pink, and they start to appear from midsummer and continue throughout fall. They are lightly fragrant and attractive to bees.

The pink calyces persist after the flowers have fallen. A good planting partner for the pale blue flowers of deciduous *Ceanothus ×delileanus* 'Gloire de Versailles'.

Abelia ×grandiflora 'Kaleidoscope'
90CM × 1.2M (3 FT. × 4 FT.)

A bright, eye-catching abelia with shining gold-and-green variegated leaves flushed with orange; the colour becomes deeper and more intense in fall as shades of red appear. The flowers are pale lilac-pink and sprinkled over the plant. 'Kaleidoscope' thrives in an open position; it grows quickly but never gets too large. Plant beneath the light, frond-like leaves of *Nandina domestica*.

Abelia parvifolia 'Bumblebee'
90CM × 1.2M (3 FT. × 4 FT.)

A small shrub with medium green leaves and bronze new shoots in spring. It is more compact and bushy than most other abelias, and produces large lilac flowers in late summer and fall that are very attractive to bees and pollinating insects. A good choice for the front of a border with *Spiraea japonica* varieties.

Abelia parvifolia 'Bumblebee'

Acer palmatum 'Jerre Schwartz'

Acer palmatum 'Beni-maiko'

Acer palmatum 'Katsura'

Acer palmatum

Japanese maples are perhaps the most beautiful foliage shrubs. They vary in size from small, light-framed shrubs to robust small trees. Whichever category of woody plants you consider them to be, they are the most useful deciduous foliage shrubs for containers, specimen planting, and mixed borders.

Japanese maples are easy to grow on any reasonable soil with adequate moisture; dry conditions at the roots cause the delicate leaves to go brown and shrivel at the tips. Contrary to popular belief, they do not require acid soil, but the fall colour is usually better in neutral to acid conditions. Some of the delicate variegated varieties prefer shade; others are happy in sun. Japanese maples do not like cold winds and exposure, particularly when the leaves are unfurling early in the season.

Japanese maples require no pruning, and it is best to avoid the practice apart from occasional tidying to remove any dead or damaged branches. Pruning to control size can cause fungal and bacterial disease to enter the branches and lead to die back. If you must prune, do so when the plants are in leaf; pruning in winter is risky. It is always better to choose a maple of the right size and stature in the first place rather than try to control its growth.

Japanese maples make excellent long-term subjects for pots if you plant them in loam-based compost. Growing in containers also naturally restricts their size.

Acer palmatum 'Beni-maiko'
1.2M × 1.2M (4 FT. × 4 FT.)

A small, bushy maple with slender stems and delicate leaves of beautiful colouring. The new foliage is strawberry coloured in spring, becoming softer red, then soft green flushed with red later in the season. This variety is at its best in semi-shade, but in a position where rays of sunlight will shine through its leaves.

Acer palmatum 'Jerre Schwartz'
1.2M × 90CM (4 FT. × 3 FT.)

An upright small Japanese maple with pink new leaves that become bronze-green as they mature and turn vibrant red before they fall. 'Jerre Schwartz' is a compact growing variety, ideal for a pot alongside Leucothoe Lovita.

Acer palmatum 'Katsura'
1.5M × 1.2M (5 FT. × 4 FT.)

A very attractive maple with small lime green lobed leaves that are pale orange when young. The leaves turn yellow and rich orange in fall. A good choice for the small garden and pretty planted with dwarf rhododendrons and Japanese azaleas, where its delicate leaves will lighten and contrast with their heavier foliage.

Acer palmatum RED-LEAVED VARIETIES

The red-leaved Japanese maples are wonderful foliage shrubs that fit into gardens of all sizes. Despite the dark hue of their leaves, they add depth without weight to a planting scheme, and provide colour for many months of the year. The leaves are exquisite from the time they emerge in early spring, like bright fishing flies along the branches, through the delicate wafting canopy of summer to the fiery shades of fall. As a red-leaved Japanese maple matures, it develops an attractive branch silhouette of dark twigs that can be a feature in the winter garden.

The dark foliage of red-leaved maples is a great mixer with other foliage shrubs. It is particularly striking with golden-foliage subjects such as *Spiraea japonica* 'Firelight', *Leycesteria formosa* Golden Lanterns, and *Cornus alba* 'Gouchaultii'. A red-leaved maple also makes a bold statement in a pot. It can add light height in the foreground of a garden vista, and it can also be the basis of stunning combinations with flower bulbs and seasonal bedding plants.

Contrary to popular belief, red-leaved varieties need an open, reasonably sunny position for good foliage colour. In shady situations, the red or wine colour of their leaves becomes a muddy shade of green-brown.

A fine specimen of *Acer palmatum* 'Fireglow' glows in a deep red pot on this terrace, surrounded by pots of heuchera and red-orange tulips that echo the colour of its spring foliage.

Acer palmatum 'Fireglow'

Acer palmatum var. *dissectum* 'Crimson Queen'

Acer palmatum 'Bloodgood'

Acer palmatum 'Shaina'

Acer palmatum 'Bloodgood'
3M × 1.8M (10 FT. × 6 FT.)

The most popular purple-leaved variety; a vigorous plant that is at its best in an open position. This robust shrub will cope with more exposure than other varieties, and it is more drought resistant. Upright at first, 'Bloodgood' becomes spreading as it matures and will develop into a wonderful small tree, with a height and spread of 5m × 4m (16 ft. × 13 ft.) or more, but you can restrict its growth in a pot. It works well as a feature plant in the centre of an island bed, where the foliage will create a dramatic canopy to the rest of the planting.

Acer palmatum var. *dissectum* 'Crimson Queen'
1.2M × 1.5M (4 FT. × 5 FT.)

A Dissectum Group maple with finely cut, feathery foliage of deep red-purple in a reasonably sunny position. Japanese maples in this group normally develop a broad, spreading dome shape with foliage to ground level. They do not mix well with other shrubs but are ideal alongside water or paved areas. You can train them as standards from an early age, but it is better to buy one ready trained if you are looking for a standard form.

Acer palmatum 'Fireglow'
3M × 1.8M (10 FT. × 6 FT.)

Usually referred to as a sport of 'Bloodgood', 'Fireglow' is a little less vigorous in habit, with lighter wine-coloured foliage and stunning red fall colour. It is a better choice than 'Bloodgood' for a large pot, where it will develop an elegant arched habit.

Acer palmatum 'Shaina'
1.5M × 1.2M (5 FT. × 4 FT.)

This is a compact maple with elegant leaves with narrow, gently curled, dark red leaflets; it is lighter in colour when young. Its dense, leafy habit and petite growth habit make it an excellent choice for a small space or a pot. It is robust and weather resistant and will tolerate some wind.

Acer palmatum 'Sango-kaku'

Astelia nervosa 'Westland'

Astelia 'Silver Shadow'

Acer palmatum 'Sango-kaku'
3M × 1.8M (10 FT. × 6 FT.)

This maple, formerly known as *Acer palmatum* 'Senkaki', is best known for its coral red stems that are such a feature in winter. The leaves are small and light green, turning butter yellow in fall. The habit is upright when young and becomes broader as the plant matures. *Acer palmatum* 'Sango-kaku' can eventually develop into a large spreading tree, but average garden growing conditions will restrict its size. It needs good soil with plenty of organic matter to thrive, and it dislikes drought. In poor, dry ground the stems are liable to die back. It is a lovely maple for the winter patio or rising out of evergreen groundcover.

Astelia

Astelias are really evergreen herbaceous perennials, but they fill the role of shrubs alongside phormiums and cordylines. Their silvery, metallic, sword-shaped leaves are a contrast to broad-leaved shrubs, and unlike most silver-foliage plants they thrive in shade. They grow on most well-drained soils, and although they are often recommended as drought tolerant they appreciate sufficient moisture. They are not the hardiest garden plants, but they overwinter happily in sheltered gardens in milder areas. They are excellent in pots, and their architectural character makes them ideal in contemporary schemes. You don't have to prune astelias; just remove any dead or damaged leaves.

Astelia nervosa 'Westland'
90CM × 90CM (3 FT. × 3 FT.)

A tough astelia with slender, gently curved, spiky leaves. The foliage is pewter coloured and wonderfully lustrous, becoming quite purple toward the ribs of the leaves in winter. Excellent in a pot underplanted with black ophiopogon or rising out of purple heucheras and ajugas.

Astelia 'Silver Shadow'
75CM × 75CM (30 IN. × 30 IN.)

This hybrid astelia has a reputation for being hardier than others and resistant to disease. The sword-shaped leaves are bright yellow-green overlaid with bright silver. Grow it with the soft, silvery foliage of *Carex comans* 'Frosted Curls' or against the dark leaves of *Viburnum davidii*.

Aucuba

Aucubas, the spotted laurels, are excellent evergreen shrubs for shade. Many have attractively spotted and blotched leaves, and female forms produce red berries. The young growth can be susceptible to frost damage, but black, shrivelled growth at the ends of the branches is usually a result of drought, so avoid very dry conditions. You can control size by pruning in spring: cut back the shoots to just above any leaf node or pair of leaves. You can also do this on older plants to rejuvenate them or to encourage more compact growth.

Aucuba japonica 'Rozannie'

Aucuba japonica 'Angelon'

Aucuba japonica f. *longifolia* 'Salicifolia'

Aucuba japonica 'Angelon'
1.8M × 1.5M (6 FT. × 5 FT.)

'Angelon' is one of the best gold-variegated aucubas, with dark green leaves heavily blotched with gold. It does not produce berries, but the leaves are showy throughout the year and are best partnered with plain evergreens. If you plant it in a shady corner, it will light up the space and attract attention.

Aucuba japonica 'Rozannie'
90CM × 90CM (3 FT. × 3 FT.)

A small, compact aucuba with very glossy, broad, dark green leaves with toothed margins. This female form freely produces large red berries that ripen from midsummer onward. 'Rozannie' is a very attractive plant for a shady situation and a good foil for gold- or white-variegated evergreens.

Aucuba japonica f. longifolia 'Salicifolia'
1.8M × 1.5M (6 FT. × 5 FT.)

A lovely evergreen with narrow deep green leaves on sea green stems. This female form produces red fruits that are well displayed among the shining green leaves. This aucuba is a nice alternative to heavier plain evergreen shrubs.

Ballotta

Ballottas are sun-loving shrubs that also adore dry situations. They are ideal for the gravel garden, or to plant alongside paved areas. Prune in spring; cut back to encourage new growth, which should make a rounded mound of foliage by midsummer.

Ballotta pseudodictamnus
60CM × 60CM (2 FT. × 2 FT.)

Upright stems on Grecian horehound form a mound with small, rounded, very woolly grey leaves. Mauve-pink flowers appear between the leaves in midsummer. This soft, textural shrub is a pleasing contrast alongside purple sage and Convolvulus cneorum by the patio or in a dry border at the base of a sunny wall.

Berberis

Although not always considered the most glamorous shrubs, berberis, with thorny stems and evergreen or deciduous leaves, are some of the most useful and adaptable garden plants. They are tough, easy to grow, and tolerant, thriving on most soils in sun or semishade. They cope with very dry conditions. The deciduous ones are extremely hardy, and nearly all survive the vagaries of climate.

Ballotta pseudodictamnus

Berberis darwinii 'Compacta'

Berberis darwinii

Berberis ×stenophylla 'Etna'

You do not need to prune berberis, but you may do so to control size and shape. Evergreen *Berberis darwinii* can be clipped to form a hedge; do this right after flowering. Remove any floppy or unruly shoots from fastigiate berberis, such as 'Helmond Pillar', to preserve shape. You can prune other varieties after flowering, or tackle the deciduous ones in winter when the leaves have fallen. To prune an older plant, cut out some of the oldest and tallest shoots by two-thirds or more, back into the heart of the shrub.

Berberis darwinii
3M × 1.8M (10 FT. × 6 FT.)

Darwin's barberry is an excellent evergreen shrub with very small, dark green, holly-like leaves crowded on densely branched stems. The growth is upright, bushy, and vigorous when the plant gets going, although it can be quite slow in the first year or two. The flowers appear in spring in drooping clusters: they are deep orange, sometimes with a hint of red, and produced over several weeks. The contrast of the deep green foliage and bright orange flowers is striking and spectacular, particularly when underplanted with blue muscari or myosotis.

Berberis darwinii 'Compacta'
1.2M × 90CM (4 FT. × 3 FT.)

The compact form of *Berberis darwinii* is a much better choice for the smaller garden. It is also shade tolerant and one of the more successful shrubs to establish under trees.

Berberis ×stenophylla 'Etna'
1.2M × 1.2M (4 FT. × 4 FT.)

Golden barberry is a medium-size shrub with arching stems and small, narrow, dark green leaves. The stems are extremely thorny, but the growth habit is attractive where space allows. The stems are wreathed in deep yellow-orange flowers in late spring. 'Etna' is a better choice for most gardens because of its smaller stature. The leaves are narrow and dark green, but shinier than those of the species. The flowers are the colour of blood oranges, and they smother the branches in late spring. The light, airy habit of this shrub allows it to mix easily with other plants; grow it with bronze carex and anything blue.

Berberis thunbergii f. *atropurpurea* 'Helmond Pillar'

Berberis thunbergii f. *atropurpurea* 'Rose Glow'

Berberis thunbergii f. *atropurpurea* 'Admiration'

Berberis thunbergii f. *atropurpurea* 'Helmond Pillar'

1.8M × 90CM (6 FT. × 3 FT.)

This variety of Japanese barberry is an upright shrub with vertical stems forms a narrow column when young and becomes broader with age, but retains its columnar form. The deep purple foliage turns flame red in fall. Use this shrub as a strong focal point in a planting scheme. This plant may be regarded as invasive in parts of the United States.

Berberis thunbergii f. *atropurpurea* 'Admiration'

60CM × 60CM (2 FT. × 2 FT.)

This very useful and colourful dwarf Japanese barberry is an excellent choice for a narrow border, a gravel garden, or a pot. The stiff, thorny stems form a dense rounded bush. The leaves appear red-orange in early spring, turning to wine red as they mature, and eventually narrowly edged with gold. In fall the foliage turns to flame before falling, leaving small red fruits on the branches. This is a lovely shrub for a terra-cotta or red-brown glazed pot. This plant may be regarded as invasive in parts of the United States.

Berberis thunbergii f. *atropurpurea* 'Rose Glow'

1.2M × 1.2M (4 FT. × 4 FT.)

One of the most versatile foliage shrubs, with upright arching stems carrying deep purple-red leaves suffused with salmon pink at the tips of the shoots. The colour is at its best in an open, sunny position where it will colour brilliantly to flame red in fall. Small red fruits often remain on the stems when the leaves have fallen. The small, creamy flowers appear in late spring, but are insignificant in comparison to the foliage. *Berberis thunbergii* 'Harlequin' is very similar, but with smaller leaves and somewhat pinker new growth. This variety is increasingly grown as an alternative to 'Rose Glow', and the varieties are often confused. Plant 'Rose Glow' alongside the silver weeping pear *Pyrus salicifolia* 'Pendula' for contrast. This plant may be regarded as invasive in parts of the United States.

Brachyglottis

Formerly known as senecio, brachyglottis are grown for their weather-resistant grey felted leaves. They are tough, tolerant plants that cope with any soil conditions except for waterlogged sites. They respond well to rough treatment and poor pruning, so they are often used in amenity planting. The plant hails from New Zealand, and while it does not tolerate extreme cold, it is unaffected by wind and salt-laden air and thus ideal for coastal gardens.

Brachyglottis (Dunedin Group) 'Sunshine'

Buddleja 'Lochinch'

Buddleja davidii 'Griffin Blue'

Brachyglottis (Dunedin Group) 'Sunshine'
90CM × 1.2M (3 FT. × 4 FT.)

This is the widely grown, familiar form with grey felted stems and silvery grey leaves that become greener on the upper surface as they mature. The clusters of grey buds appear in late spring, opening to bright yellow daisy flowers in summer. Prune when the plants are in bud. The flowers are a hard, acid colour, and usually unpopular, so cutting back before they open has two benefits. Plant on dry, sunny banks with cistus.

Buddleja

Buddlejas are valuable for their late-summer flowers, their fragrance, and most of all their attraction of butterflies—hence the common name butterfly bush. The varieties with long flower panicles come in a range of colours from white through pink and lilac to deep purple and red. However, some come with round flower clusters that can be orange or cream. I always choose the lilac, purple, and red varieties for their fragrance and their colours, which suit the late summer garden.

Most of the familiar buddlejas are easy to grow, thriving just about anywhere in full sun. They are particularly useful on poor, dry soil. Although the flowering season is not long, it comes when many other flowering shrubs are over. You can extend the season by removing the first flowers as they fade, which allows more to develop to their full potential.

Buddlejas are brittle, woody plants that soon become leggy and ungainly if you do not prune. Cut back hard to 90cm (3 ft.) or less above ground level in late winter, which ensures vigorous arching growth and flowers where you can see them.

Buddleja davidii 'Griffin Blue'
1.8M × 1.5M (6 FT. × 5 FT.)

This is an excellent variety of the common buddleja, with vigorous, arching growth, large panicles of deep blue flowers, and grey-green leaves. It is a wonderful contrast to the soft golden leaves of *Cornus alba* 'Aurea'. This plant may be regarded as invasive in parts of the United States.

Buddleja 'Lochinch'
1.8M × 1.5M (6 FT. × 5 FT.)

A lovely buddleja with bushy, compact growth and upright grey stems carrying silver-backed, soft green leaves that give the whole shrub a silver-grey appearance. The flowers are carried in broad upright panicles; they are pale lilac-blue, each with an orange eye, and sweetly fragrant. 'Lochinch' is a colour that goes with anything and is a good planting partner for *Philadelphus maculatus* 'Sweet Clare' to extend the season of interest.

Buddleja 'Miss Ruby'

Buddleja Nanho Blue

Buxus sempervirens 'Suffruticosa'

Buxus sempervirens 'Elegantissima'

Buddleja 'Miss Ruby'
1.8M × 1.5M (6 FT. × 5 FT.)

A stunning, more recently introduced buddleja with large, fragrant panicles of red flowers and green leaves. This would be a good choice to plant with *Sambucus nigra* f. *porphyrophylla* 'Eva'.

Buddleja Nanho Blue
1.2M × 1.2M (4 FT. × 4 FT.)

A number of Nanho buddleja varieties have a smaller habit than most buddlejas and are more suited to the smaller garden. They have small, narrow grey-green leaves and slender panicles of fragrant flowers. 'Nanho Blue' sports medium blue fragrant flowers on greyish stems. It is behind silver-foliage shrubs and lavenders.

Buxus

Most gardeners think of *Buxus sempervirens*, boxwood or common box, as a hedging plant or a subject for topiary. This hardy evergreen shrub, with compact growth and small, closely packed leaves, responds well to trimming and has been formally shaped and trained in gardens for centuries. It is also useful when grown naturally as an evergreen shrub that, in time, can reach over 3m (10 ft.) in height with a similar spread. It is particularly useful in shade and on dry soils, but it resents waterlogging at the roots.

Box is trimmed in midsummer to allow it time to produce a new flush of growth that can ripen before winter frosts. Plain green forms need regular feeding with a slow-release fertilizer. They are particularly susceptible to potash deficiency, which causes bronzing of the foliage, especially in winter. This is easily rectified with a high-potash liquid feed like tomato fertilizer.

In certain areas box blight has been a problem. The disease causes die back and defoliation after the growth at the ends of the shoots becomes brown and papery. Cut out affected growth, treat with a fungicide, apply a slow-release fertilizer, and keep the shrub watered. Plants usually recover unless the attack is severe.

Buxus sempervirens 'Elegantissima'
60CM × 60CM (2 FT. × 2 FT.)

The variegated box is a lovely shrub with small, cream-edged, deep green leaves. It is excellent in containers and in small beds and borders, where its light but compact habit looks good throughout the year. It does not suffer from the same foliage discolouration that green-leaved varieties often exhibit. Grow it in a pot alongside *Camellia japonica* 'Jury's Yellow'.

Buxus sempervirens 'Suffruticosa'
30CM × 30CM (1 FT. × 1 FT.)

The dwarf form of box is generally used for low hedges in knot gardens and parterres. It is slow growing and ideal in the small garden or in pots and containers. You can lightly trim to maintain a neat, rounded shape, and it is useful as evergreen structure in narrow borders.

Callicarpa var. giraldii 'Profusion'

Calluna vulgaris 'Joy Vanstone'

Calluna vulgaris 'Robert Chapman'

Callicarpa

Beautyberries are interesting deciduous shrubs grown for their wonderful fall foliage colour and clusters of small purple berries that last through winter. They are best in an open position with adequate direct sunlight, and they produce more fruit when planted in groups of three or more. Prune to control size in late winter, after the berries.

Callicarpa var. *giraldii* 'Profusion'
1.5M × 1.2M (5 FT. × 4 FT.)
The most popular variety grown for its bronze new leaves, pink and gold fall foliage, and shining purple berries. The shrub freely produces fruits in large clusters following small, inconspicuous pink flowers in summer. Carried on straight stems, the metallic berries have a molecular appearance and are stunning against the purple-black winter foliage of *Pittosporum tenuifolium* 'Tom Thumb'.

Calluna

Garden designers often overlook the hardy heathers, which are some of the most useful dwarf shrubs for neutral to acid soils. Those gardening on alkaline soils should choose *Erica carnea* or *Erica ×darleyensis* instead.

Ericas and callunas are excellent for groundcover in sun or semi-shade. Although both grow in shady situations, foliage colour and flowering is better with some sun. Both tolerate exposed, cold and damp sites.

Most callunas flower from midsummer to fall.

Some have flowers that do not open; these are called bud-blooming heathers, and are useful in pots and containers for seasonal fall and winter interest. Many of the good garden varieties make excellent cut flowers and are often fragrant.

Some of the most useful callunas have attractive winter foliage colour or brightly coloured new growth tips in spring. To keep plants compact and well branched, trim after flowering if they bloom early in the season, or early the following spring if they flower in fall or have colourful foliage. It is not essential to do this every year.

There are a great many cultivars from which to choose. I would select those with interesting foliage for creative planting. Plant summer- and fall-flowering heathers at the front of beds and borders with dwarf rhododendrons and evergreen and deciduous azaleas. In semi-shade combine them with leucothoe and pachysandra. They also work well with evergreen perennials, such as liriope and ophiopogon, and compact grasses and sedges.

Calluna vulgaris 'Joy Vanstone'
45CM × 45CM (18 IN. × 18 IN.)
Deep golden foliage becomes orange in winter. Bright mauve-pink flowers.

Calluna vulgaris 'Robert Chapman'
45CM × 30CM (18 IN. × 1 FT.)
Gold summer foliage becomes orange in fall, then red and orange in winter. Light purple flowers.

Calluna vulgaris 'Silver Queen'

Camellia ×williamsii 'Jury's Yellow'

Calluna vulgaris 'Spring Torch'

Calluna vulgaris 'Silver Queen'
45CM × 45CM (18 IN. × 18 IN.)

This very pretty heather, with soft silver-grey foliage and pretty silver-mauve flowers, mixes well with any other colour.

Calluna vulgaris 'Spring Torch'
45CM × 45CM (18 IN. × 18 IN.)

Strong growing variety with dark green foliage producing cream and orange tips to the shoots in spring. White flowers in late summer. A colourful heather that mixes well with other shrubs.

Camellia

Camellias are magnificent evergreen shrubs that produce exquisite blooms for late winter through spring, according to variety and situation. They vary in habit and eventual size, from loose, open shrubs to upright and compact specimens. On neutral to acid soil, under protection and light shade of trees, some can make massive mounded shrubs up to 5m (16 ft.) in height with a similar spread. The more compact and upright varieties are useful subjects for pots and containers, especially in shaded situations. Camellias flower more freely in open sunny situations, but avoid the early morning sun of eastern aspects in the Northern Hemisphere.

Most camellia varieties are free flowering, but some produce large blooms in exotic shades of pink and red. These can look out of place in a garden setting, so be sure to position them carefully. I have included only two of my favourites here, both of which I find easy to combine with other shrubs.

Camellias require no regular pruning, but you can selectively shape immediately after flowering.

Camellia ×williamsii 'Jury's Yellow'
1.5M × 90CM (5 FT. × 3 FT.)

This is a compact, upright growing camellia with excellent dark green foliage. It flowers freely, producing abundant blooms with larger outer petals and masses of gently waved petals in the centre of each bloom. The colour is that of clotted cream, and pleasing and easy to combine in a planting scheme. 'Jury's Yellow' is an excellent choice for a pot or a small courtyard garden.

Camellia ×williamsii 'St Ewe'
1.5M × 1.2M (5 FT. × 4 FT.)

Dark green foliage and a lighter, open habit make this variety easy to combine with other shrubs. The flowers are single and not too large, with pink petals cupped around golden stamens; it is a lovely camellia to cut. Grow it in the shade of *Pittosporum* 'Garnettii'.

Ceanothus 'Concha'

Ceanothus ×delileanus 'Gloire de Versailles'

Camellia ×williamsii 'St Ewe'

Catalpa bignoniodes 'Aurea'

Catalpa

Indian bean trees or southern catalpas are normally grown as trees, and they have large, heart-shaped velvety leaves carried on spreading, antler-like branches. Mature trees produce spikes of foxglove-like flowers in summer.

Catalpa bignoniodes 'Aurea'
3M × 2.4M (10 FT. × 8 FT.)
This catalpa makes a wonderful large shrub if cut back hard to 90cm (3 ft.) or less in winter. It then produces strong upright stems with magnificently large, velvety golden yellow leaves from early summer through fall. When grown in this way it rarely flowers, but few shrubs produce such stunning, luxuriant leaves.

Ceanothus

California lilacs are valued for their stunning blue flower heads, which can transform a shrub into a fluffy, bright blue haze in spring or fall. The evergreen varieties, which can be grown against walls or as free-standing shrubs, are the most popular. However, the deciduous varieties and the prostrate spreading types are also extremely valuable.

Most evergreen ceanothus resent pruning, so you should avoid it. If necessary, prune right after flowering, as little as possible, and only into wood carrying leaves. There are exceptions, but most do not shoot from bare wood. Prune deciduous ceanothus in late winter.

Evergreen ceanothus are not long-lived shrubs. Although they grow quickly at first, the average lifespan is around ten years. It is always worth planting a replacement after seven or eight.

Ceanothus 'Concha'
3M × 2.4M (10 FT. × 8 FT.)
A stunning evergreen ceanothus with neat dark green leaves on strong ascending, arching stems. The deeply hued flowers are carried in tight clusters in late spring and early summer, transforming the whole plant into an explosion of blue. A show-stealer in any garden; stunning with the deep orange flowers of *Berberis darwinii*.

Ceanothus ×delileanus 'Gloire de Versailles'
1.8M × 90CM (6 FT. × 3 FT.)
A deciduous ceanothus of light, open habit. Open clusters of soft blue flowers appear in summer and again in fall, often almost continuously. 'Gloire de Versailles' is small and light enough to grow with roses or herbaceous perennials, and delightful with any colour, especially pale yellow. Grow it with *Potentilla fruticosa* 'Primrose Beauty' for a three-month display of flowers.

Ceanothus thyrsiflorus var. repens

Ceratostigma willmottianum

Ceanothus thyrsiflorus 'Skylark'

Ceanothus thyrsiflorus var. *repens*
90CM × 1.8M (3 FT. × 6 FT.)

This ceanothus, often planted as a groundcover shrub, has horizontal arching stems and shining dark green leaves. It is initially prostrate, then eventually forms a low, spreading mound smothered with pale blue fluffy flower heads in early summer. It is very useful on a bank or in the foreground in a large bed; do not underestimate its spread. It makes a good contrast to low-spreading golden-foliage junipers.

Ceanothus thyrsiflorus 'Skylark'
3M × 2.4M (10 FT. × 8 FT.)

A large evergreen ceanothus with shining bright green foliage and upright stems that grow quickly to considerable height. The plant produces blue flowers later than other varieties, extending the season from early to midsummer. A good screening shrub or for structure in the middle of a large bed. Lovely planted with vigorous dark red shrub roses such as 'Zigeunerknabe' ('Gipsy Boy') or 'William Lobb'.

Ceratostigma

These small shrubs, often referred to as Chinese plumbagos, combine well with other shrubs or perennials. They enjoy an open, sunny position on any well-drained soil. The stems often die back to ground level in winter, but it is best to cut back hard in late winter regardless of whether they do.

Ceratostigma willmottianum
90CM × 90CM (3 FT. × 3 FT.)

Red-brown stems carry small deep green leaves that colour rich shades of gold and red-orange in fall. These make a lovely combination with the blue plumbago-like flowers that are produced in small clusters. Late-flying butterflies enjoy the nectar of the blossoms.

Ceratostigma willmottianum Forest Blue
90CM × 90CM (3 FT. × 3 FT.)

The popular selection of this shrub has a more compact habit and branched stems that carry more flowers. The fall foliage colour is not as reliable. Good in a sunny border with *Potentilla fruticosa* 'Abbotswood'.

Cercis

The best-known cercis, *Cercis siliquastrum*, is a small tree, although many see it as a multi-stemmed specimen shrub. All species, including this one, are characterized by their rounded, heart-shaped leaves and pea-like flowers produced on the stems in spring. In some cases the flowers are the main feature; in all instances the foliage is just as important. Prune selectively in winter to control size and spread.

Cercis canadensis 'Forest Pansy'

Cercis chinensis 'Avondale'

Ceratostigma willmottianum Forest Blue

Chaenomeles speciosa 'Moorloosei'

Cercis canadensis 'Forest Pansy'

3M × 3M (10 FT. × 10 FT.)

A variety of eastern redbud with exquisite, velvety, red-purple leaves that resemble pansy blooms hanging from the branches. The young leaves are shining and dark red as they emerge with a jewel-like quality. The tiny purple flowers are insignificant and not a feature, but the fall leaf colour is spectacular as gold and flame shades invade the red-purple foliage. You can grow this variety as a standard tree, but it is usually a large, broadly spreading shrub that can reach much larger proportions as it matures. Superb when planted with deciduous azaleas such as *Rhododendron* 'Irene Koster'.

Cercis chinensis 'Avondale'

1.8M × 1.5M (6 FT. × 5 FT.)

Chinese redbud is a medium-size shrub with upright stems and large, heart-shaped, bright green leaves that turn rich gold in fall. In spring, showy purple-pink, pea-like flowers crowd the branches before the leaves emerge. The effect is quite spectacular, especially alongside the fresh purple foliage of Japanese maples.

Chaenomeles

Ornamental quinces are usually grown as wall shrubs and are particularly useful for shaded situations. They flower early and bloom on the bare branches; this makes them lovely for cutting and for minimalist planting schemes, such as Japanese. The brightly coloured red and orange varieties are more suited to walls, whereas pale flowering cultivars combine with other shrubs more easily.

Chaenomeles tolerate most soils and are easy to grow, and you can grow them as free-standing specimens, although their habit can be sprawling and untidy if you do not cut back and shape immediately after flowering. This practice also encourages more flowers the following year.

Chaenomeles speciosa 'Moorloosei'

1.8M × 90CM (6 FT. × 3 FT.)

Common flowering quince freely produces exquisite apple-blossom flowers in large clusters in early spring. This variety is lovely and probably the most useful in planting schemes. A heavenly colour if underplanted with blue pulmonarias.

Chamaecyparis

The word *conifer* strikes a note of horror with some gardeners, but chamaecyparis are conifers that offer a seemingly endless variety of shapes, sizes, textures, and foliage colours. Certainly some are only suited to being grown as stand-alone specimens, and some associate best with their own kind. However, many mix well with broad-leaved shrubs and perennials, providing year-round structure, colour, and interest in a planting scheme. I have included only one. It is a favourite for its unusual form and texture, but there are many others that are worth exploring.

Choisya

Mexican orange is one of the most popular shrubs. It has many of the qualities we look for in a long-term garden plant: it sports evergreen, glossy foliage that looks good throughout the year; it has a dense, leafy habit; and it responds well to pruning to control its size. It is easy to grow on any well-drained soil, in sun or shade, and it is generally free of pests and diseases. It flowers in late spring and again in fall, producing fragrant white flowers with golden stamens in clusters all over the shrub. Choisya is related to citrus, so its foliage of choisya is strongly aromatic, pleasing to

some but not to others, and generally unpalatable to deer and rabbits.

You can improve older choisya plants by pruning out the older shoots and cutting back into the plant to encourage new growth from lower on the stems. This method also works to reduce overall size. Although choisyas are hardy, cold winter weather often damages the tips of the shoots, as the upward-facing leaves hold on to moisture that freezes and damages them. If you cut these out in spring, the shrub quickly recovers.

Choisya ×dewitteana 'Aztec Gold'

Choisya ×dewitteana 'Aztec Pearl'

Choisya ×dewitteana 'Aztec Gold'

1.5M × 1.5M (5 FT. × 5 FT.)

A more recently introduced golden-foliage choisya. It flowers more freely than *Choisya ternata* 'Sundance', producing similar clusters of flowers to its parent 'Aztec Pearl'. It has the fine, waxy, weather-resistant foliage of 'Aztec Pearl'; bright golden yellow at the ends of the shoots and bright green deep in the heart of the plant. This makes 'Aztec Gold' easier to associate with other plants, especially gold-and-green variegations.

Choisya ×dewitteana 'Aztec Pearl'

1.8M × 1.5M (6 FT. × 5 FT.)

A lovely hybrid choisya with longer, narrower leaflets and an altogether lighter, more airy habit. The flower buds are pink opening to fragrant white single flowers in large, loose clusters. 'Aztec Pearl' prefers a sunny position and is exceptionally free flowering; a mature shrub is often smothered in bloom right to the ground. It will grow in some shade, but its habit is looser and flowers fewer. A good planting partner for *Philadelphus* 'Belle Etoile' to extend the season.

The fragrant flowers of *Choisya ternata* appear in spring and fall. They are rich in nectar, and bees and butterflies appreciate them.

Choisya ×dewitteana 'White Dazzler'

Choisya ternata 'Sundance'

Choisya ternata

Choisya ×dewitteana 'White Dazzler'
90CM × 90CM (3 FT. × 3 FT.)

An altogether smaller and more compact choisya. The shrub's habit is dense and rounded, with smaller leaves than 'Aztec Pearl' and narrower dark green leaflets. The shrub is heavily studded with compact clusters of pure white flowers in spring and late summer. 'White Dazzler' is a good choice for a small garden or a large patio container.

Choisya ternata
1.5M × 1.5M (5 FT. × 5 FT.)

This widely grown variety has bright green foliage, and each leaf consists of three leaflets. It grows well in shade, but more freely produces fragrant white flowers in a sunny position. A basic in any green-and-white planting scheme and a good partner for *Cornus alba* 'Elegantissima'.

Choisya ternata 'Sundance'
1.5M × 1.5M (5 FT. × 5 FT.)

The widely grown golden foliage form of *Choisya ternata* has been very popular since its introduction. It has the same size and spread, and its shining bright gold leaves command attention wherever it is planted. In shade the foliage takes on a more subtle shade of lime, making a pleasing contrast to darker evergreens. Flowers are similar to those of *Choisya ternata* but are few in number and a secondary feature of the plant. Lighten it in shade with *Lonicera nitida* 'Baggesen's Gold'.

Cistus ×hybridus

Cistus ×cyprius var. ellipticus 'Elma'

Chamaecyparis obtusa 'Nana Gracilis'

Cistus ×dansereuari 'Decumbens'

Chamaecyparis obtusa 'Nana Gracilis'
90CM × 90CM (3 FT. × 3 FT.)

Hinoki false cypress is a slow-growing conifer with flattened sprays of green foliage that twist and turn, creating a coral-like effect. A very beautiful foliage shrub with the appearance of crushed green velvet; a contrasting texture to that of broad-leaved evergreen shrubs. Grow it in gravel with a few well-placed stones and creeping thymes and sedums.

Cistus

Sun roses are excellent plants for hot, dry, sunny conditions. Although they withstand moderate frost, they are not a good choice for cold gardens and heavy soil. They thrive on alkaline soils and are excellent for seaside gardens. They flower in midsummer and some continue intermittently through to fall. Their single open flowers with prominent stamens are attractive to bees and pollinating insects.

Cistus are short-lived shrubs, usually with a lifespan of around ten years in ideal growing conditions. They do not like being moved once established, so replacement is always the best option. Most resent pruning when mature, but light pruning when the plants are young promotes branching and bushy growth.

Cistus ×cyprius var. ellipticus 'Elma'
1.2M × 1.2M (4 FT. × 4 FT.)

A lovely cistus with dark green, shiny, resinous, willow-shaped leaves on a vigorous shrub of upright habit. The large, pure white, silky blooms have golden stamens and are gloriously displayed against the emerald leaves. 'Elma' is not the hardiest cistus, but is perfect against a sunny wall or fence with *Lavandula angustifolia* 'Hidcote'.

Cistus ×dansereuari 'Decumbens'
60CM × 1.2M (2 FT. × 4 FT.)

A low-spreading cistus with narrow, dark green, sticky leaves. The flowers are large, white, and upward facing, with deep red blotches toward the base of the petals. Lovely for a sunny bank, or surrounded by pebbles and gravel with *Helianthemum* 'Rhodanthe Carneum' and creeping sedums.

Cistus ×hybridus
90CM × 90CM (3 FT. × 3 FT.)

One of the hardiest cistus, with medium green foliage and a domed habit. The shrub freely produces white flowers with golden stamens in midsummer, with a few flowers later in the season. You can prune this cistus in early spring to control its size, but never cut back to the bare wood. Good on a dry bank with *Ceanothus thyrsiflorus* var. *repens*.

Cistus ×pulverulentus 'Sunset'

Clerodendrum bungei

Cistus obtusifolius 'Thrive'

Cistus ×purpureus

Clerodendrum trichotomum var. fargessi 'Carnival'

Cistus obtusifolius 'Thrive'
60CM × 60CM (2 FT. × 2 FT.)

A neat, compact cistus with small dark green leaves and a domed habit. The small white, golden-eyed flowers are freely produced all over the shrub in midsummer and continue in some quantity through to fall. You can lightly trim in early spring to promote a neater habit and remove the flower stalks left from the previous year. Works well in a cloud bed with *Hebe albicans* and *Hebe pinguifolia* 'Sutherlandii'.

Cistus ×pulverulentus 'Sunset'
60CM × 60CM (2 FT. × 2 FT.)

A dwarf shrub of open habit with upright stems carrying soft, felty, soft green leaves packed closely on the stems. The brilliant cerise flowers, which have bright golden eyes, appear from midsummer onward. This is a good shrub to plant with silver-foliage shrubs and purple sage.

Cistus ×purpureus
90CM × 90CM (3 FT. × 3 FT.)

With a more open habit than many, *Cistus ×purpureus* has narrow, waxy leaves on dark stems. The habit is loose but upright and the large, rosy red flowers with golden stamens are well spaced. The tissue paper petals have deep maroon central blotches and a poppy-like character. A good choice for a sunny border with *Weigela florida* 'Foliis Purpureis'.

Clerodendrum

Clerodendrums are a variable group of shrubs, valuable for their late summer and fall flowers and their attractive foliage. Most have a strikingly architectural habit, either with upright stems or a tree-like canopy.

Clerodendrum bungei
1.5M × 1.5M (5 FT. × 5 FT.)

This suckering shrub, known in the United States as glory flower, produces a clump of upright stems with large, rounded, dark green, shiny leaves. In fall, clusters of deep pink flowers appear at the end of the shoots. A good choice for large gardens alongside bamboos and mature hydrangeas.

Clerodendrum trichotomum var. *fargessi* 'Carnival'
1.5M × 1.5M (5 FT. × 5 FT.)

Harlequin glorybower, as it is referred to in the United States, is an attractive foliage shrub with the bonus of late-summer flowers. The leaves of 'Carnival' are soft teal and green, edged with creamy white; they have a brighter colour when they first appear in late spring. The white flowers shine from purple calyces and are carried in loose clusters above the leaves. The foliage smells of rubber when brushed, and deer and rabbits avoid the shrub. An attractive partner for *Hydrangea arborescens* 'Annabelle'.

Convolvulus cneorum

Coprosma 'Lemon and Lime'

Cordyline australis 'Torbay Dazzler'

Cordyline 'Southern Splendour'

Convolvulus

Convolvulus are generally thought of as trailing and climbing plants; they are annuals or perennials and rarely considered shrubs. They have unusual funnel-shaped flowers and in some regions are normally recognized as weeds.

Convolvulus cneorum
60CM × 60CM (2 FT. × 2 FT.)

Shrubby convolvulus has small, narrow, silky, silver leaves carried on silver stems on a short, bushy plant. The flowers are trumpet shaped, pure white, flushed yellow deep in the trumpet, and deep brown-pink—and somewhat striped on the reverse. A good shrub for full sun on well-drained soil or in a pot. Not the hardiest of subjects, but surprisingly frost resistant on dry soil. Prune at an early age to encourage branching. Plant with *Cistus obtusifolius* 'Thrive'.

Coprosma

Coprosmas are small, compact shrubs with small, shining, evergreen leaves in a fantastic array of colours and variegations. They are best in a sunny situation on well-drained soil. They are ideal as container shrubs, so you can move them indoors or into a sheltered spot in winter. They are not hardy and will need winter protection in all but the mildest areas. Prune lightly in spring to remove any winter damage and encourage bushy growth.

Coprosma 'Lemon and Lime'
60CM × 45CM (2 FT. × 18 IN.)

A bright and cheerful small shrub with shining waxy leaves variegated in shades of bright green and lime yellow, often tinted with bright orange in full sun, especially in fall and winter. Few shrubs pack such foliage colour into a small plant. Stunning in a citrus-coloured pot planted alongside lime green heucheras.

Cordyline

Cabbage palms are popular for their architectural form and spiky leaves. As young plants they are ideal in containers; when mature they make statuesque shrubs or exotic small trees. Those with coloured leaves are the most useful in planting schemes as a more formal alternative to phormiums. They are reasonably hardy, but severe frost will damage them.

Cordyline australis 'Torbay Dazzler'
3M × 90CM (10 FT. × 3 FT.)

One of the most striking varieties, with green-and-cream striped leaves. It is a smaller plant than the red or green forms, and most useful in a patio pot or as a focal point in a bed of low-mounded shrubs such as dwarf boxwood and hebes.

Cornus alba 'Elegantissima'

Cornus alba 'Aurea'

Cornus alba 'Gouchaultii'

Cordyline 'Southern Splendour'
1.5M × 90CM (5 FT. × 3 FT.)

One of a number of pink cordylines with exotic pink-and-green, softly striped leaves. It is not as hardy as other dark red– and green-leaved varieties but is a striking plant for a container in a sheltered, sunny situation. Combines well with purple-leaved heucheras and black ophiopogon.

Cornus

Cornus, also known as red-barked or red twig dogwoods, includes a vast range of valuable garden shrubs grown for their foliage, flowers, and winter stems. Most are easy to grow and reliable, and they have become staples in our garden plant palette. I have arranged them according to their principal attributes for ease of selection.

CORNUS FOR FOLIAGE

These dogwoods are grown mainly for their coloured or variegated leaves, although some also have the benefit of flowers, fruits, and coloured winter stems. These are some of the most valuable garden shrubs, and I use them extensively in planting schemes. They are all easy to grow on most soils in sun or shade.

Cornus alba 'Aurea'
2.1M × 1.5M (7 FT. × 5 FT.)

A red-barked variety with dark red stems and soft golden leaves. The foliage is a brighter yellow in a sunny position, and it does not scorch. As with other varieties of red-barked dogwood that are grown mainly for their winter stems, it is best to cut back hard in late winter every two years. This underrated shrub thrives in most soil conditions; it is one of the most reliable deciduous shrubs with golden foliage. Striking planted with *Berberis thunbergii* f. *atropurpurea* 'Helmond Pillar'.

Cornus alba 'Elegantissima'
2.1M × 1.5M (7 FT. × 5 FT.)

Another red-barked dogwood with dark red stems. The soft leaves are heavily mottled and irregularly edged with white. It is surprisingly vigorous, and unless pruned it will form a very large, sprawling shrub with long, flexible stems. Cut back hard every two years to maintain a manageable size. It is a good choice against a dark background of evergreen screening shrubs.

Cornus alba 'Gouchaultii'
1.5M × 90CM (5 FT. × 3 FT.)

A medium-size shrub with dark red stems and gold-and-green variegated leaves tinged with red-pink. The variegation is subtle and pleasing. Cut back every two or three years to maintain size. Lovely planted with dark red–flowering persicaria on a moist site.

Cornus alternifolia 'Argentea'

Cornus controversa 'Variegata'

Cornus mas 'Variegata'

Cornus alba 'Sibirica Variegata'

Cornus alba 'Sibirica Variegata'
90CM × 90CM (3 FT. × 3 FT.)

This is the most valuable red-barked dogwood for any garden. It remains small and fairly compact and requires no pruning. The dark red stems carry green-and-creamy-white-variegated leaves with a tinge of red-pink. The fall colour is rich pink with a hit of mauve and gold. Shining blue-white berry clusters often appear in late summer. This is an excellent shrub to mix with perennials and roses, but is also lovely with *Pittosporum tenuifolium* 'Tom Thumb' or *Berberis thunbergii* f. *atropurpurea* 'Rose Glow'.

Cornus alternifolia 'Argentea'
1.5M × 1.2M (5 FT. × 4 FT.)

The variegated form of pagoda dogwood is perhaps the most refined and sophisticated of variegated shrubs. The dark stems and horizontal branches create a frothy, layered effect with the small, soft, green-and-white variegated leaves. Left to grow naturally, the shrub will become quite dense as it matures, although never heavy in appearance. To maintain a lighter and more open habit, thin out the number of vertical shoots at an early age. An essential ingredient in any light, ethereal, green-and-white scheme, and a lovely specimen in a small garden.

Cornus controversa 'Variegata'
3M × 2.4M (10 FT. × 8 FT.)

Where space allows, wedding cake tree is a more dramatic alternative to *Cornus alternifolia* 'Argentea'. The stems are red and the green leaves are broadly edged with silver-white, appearing to hang on the branches as the season progresses. The shrub appears to be awkward and spreading when young, until a lead shoot takes over and the main stem gains height. Pruning is unnecessary and may threaten the beautiful form of this shrub. The layered branches and abundant silver-white foliage of a more mature specimen make this one of the most stunning woody garden plants. Grow it as a solitary specimen or alongside *Cotinus* 'Grace'.

Cornus mas 'Variegata'
1.5M × 90CM (5 FT. × 3 FT.)

The variegated form of the cornelian cherry is a slow-growing shrub with striking white-margined leaves and red fruits in fall. You do not have to prune, but if you choose to, do it in winter to influence shape. The small yellow flowers on the branches in late winter are not showy but are an added bonus. This shrub's clean and crisp variegation gives it a sparkling, fresh appearance, shown to advantage against a dark background. A good partner for *Osmanthus delavayi*.

Cornus 'Eddie's White Wonder'

Cornus sericea 'Hedgerows Gold'

Cornus florida f. rubra

Cornus kousa var. chinensis

Cornus sericea 'Hedgerows Gold'
2.1M × 1.5M (7 FT. × 5 FT.)

A vigorous suckering shrub, known as redosier dogwood, with dark red stems and large, yellow-gold variegated leaves. The variegation is strong and bold, becoming softer and richer in fall as orange and red tones develop. A useful dogwood where you want impact quickly; best cut back hard every two to three years. It is useful to lighten a hedge or screen of heavy laurels, and will compete in terms of colour and vigour.

CORNUS FOR FLOWERS

Flowering dogwoods are arresting shrubs, and some eventually develop into small trees. The true flowers are insignificant, carried as tight globular structures surrounded by showy coloured bracts of great elegance and beauty. The dove-like blooms appear in early summer, beautifully poised on the horizontally sweeping branches.

These cornus prefer neutral to acid soils that are rich in organic matter, but they are more tolerant than many gardeners imagine. I have seen them growing well on dry, sandy soils and on alkaline soils enriched with compost. Most require a little patience, as they never look their best as young plants.

It's best to avoid pruning, but if necessary to control size, do it right after flowering.

Some varieties of flowering dogwood have variegated foliage. These plants can be rather inelegant in habit, and the variegation may detract from the simple beauty of the blooms.

Cornus 'Eddie's White Wonder'
3M × 1.5M (10 FT. × 5 FT.)

A compact and upright shrub with large, pure white, gently waved bracts in late spring and spectacular red-orange fall foliage colour. A good alternative to a more traditional flowering tree in a small garden.

Cornus florida f. rubra
3M × 1.5M (10 FT. × 5 FT.)

A lovely form of flowering dogwood, with rosy pink waved bracts and spectacular red-orange fall foliage colour. Mature shrubs have a conical pagoda shape with interesting, informally layered branches. A lovely specimen shrub to underplant with *Erica carnea* and *Erica ×darleyensis*.

Cornus kousa var. chinensis
2.1M × 1.5M (7 FT. × 5 FT.)

This beautiful Chinese dogwood grows to form a loose shrub with spreading branches. The creamy white blooms are carried on upright stalks in late spring and early summer. In a good year, the branches may be sheets of perfect flowers. The blooms are often followed by strawberry-like fruits in fall, when the foliage colour can be rich bronze and red. This cornus is meant for neutral to acid soil.

Cornus FOR WINTER STEMS

These are the dogwoods grown principally for their winter stems. Others may have the benefit of colourful winter stems, but these are planted mainly for that quality. Although often recommended for moist soils, these cornus are tolerant and grow well in all but the driest conditions. *Cornus alba* varieties thrive on heavy, wet soils and are particularly effective planted near water. Cornus grown for their winter stems are always more effective when underplanted with evergreen groundcover that thrives in the shade of their foliage in summer and shows off the stems to advantage in winter. This may involve removing the fallen cornus leaves in early winter.

To encourage vigorous growth and fine upright stems, prune hard in early spring, cutting back to 10cm (4 in.) above ground level. Plants respond with vigorous shoots that grow quickly and light up the garden the following winter. Sizes listed assume hard pruning at least every other year.

The long, wand-like stems of most cornus are flexible, and you can cut and make them into wreaths or garlands for decoration. The cut stems also look effective in a glass vase, where they remain in good condition for several weeks.

In large gardens these cornus are particularly effective grown in large groups or drifts, particularly where two or more varieties can be grown alongside each other. The winter colour effect can be stunning. You will need to protect cornus from deer and rabbits if they are problematic in your area.

The winter stems of dogwoods make a spectacular display around the white bark of Himalayan birches. *Cornus sericea* 'Flaviramea' in the foreground against *Cornus sanguinea* 'Midwinter Fire', with *Cornus alba* 'Sibirica' in the background.

Cornus alba 'Kesselringei'

Cornus sanguinea 'Anny's Winter Orange'

Cornus alba 'Sibirica'

Cornus sanguinea 'Magic Flame'

Cornus sanguinea 'Midwinter Fire'

Cornus sericea 'Flaviramea'

Cornus alba 'Kesselringei'
1.5M × 75CM (5 FT. × 30 IN.)

This black-stemmed dogwood, with plain green leaves, is popular for its dark purple-black, upright stems that provide a stunning contrast to other more brightly coloured dogwoods. It is also effective when planted with white-barked birches and underplanted with a bright carex or variegated hedera.

Cornus alba 'Sibirica'
1.5M × 90CM (5 FT. × 3 FT.)

This red-barked dogwood is perhaps the most popular shrub grown for its winter stems, with glowing red winter bark on the vigorous upright shoots. The leaves are plain dark green throughout summer, but turn to rich red in fall. In a good year the fall foliage is as much of a feature as the winter stems. Plant against dark green mahonias to show off the stems.

Cornus sanguinea 'Anny's Winter Orange'
1.2M × 90CM (4 FT. × 3 FT.)

A newer introduction than 'Midwinter Fire', with plain green summer foliage and rich orange stems in winter. The habit is perhaps broader spreading and the fall colour is rich gold flushed with pale orange. These varieties are particularly effective with bronze carex and alongside the mahogany bark of *Prunus serrula*.

Cornus sanguinea 'Magic Flame'
1.2M × 90CM (4 FT. × 3 FT.)

An alternative to 'Midwinter Fire' with a similar habit and similar winter stem colour. The fall foliage colour is intense and can be bright gold or red.

Cornus sanguinea 'Midwinter Fire'
1.2M × 90CM (4 FT. × 3 FT.)

This variety of bloodtwig dogwood, sometimes sold as 'Winter Flame', lives up to its name. The branched stems are orange-gold at the base and red-orange at the tips of the shoots. The summer foliage colour is light yellow-green and the fall hue rich gold tinged with orange. It grows well on wet or dry soil, and is a good subject for a pot for a season or two. Even a single plant in the garden is an outstanding feature on cloudy days.

Cornus sericea 'Flaviramea'
1.5M × 90CM (5 FT. × 3 FT.)

A suckering golden twig dogwood with olive green stems that appear green-gold in winter. Plain green leaves in summer and unremarkable fall colour may make this an unappealing planting proposition, but in large gardens it is effective when mass planted, particularly on damp soil.

Cornus kousa 'Satomi'

Coronilla valentina subsp. *glauca* 'Citrinus'

Cornus kousa 'Gold Star'

Cornus 'Porlock'

Cornus kousa 'Gold Star'

1.8M × 1.2M (6 FT. × 4 FT.)

A variegated form with dark green leaves that are rich gold in the centre. The creamy white bracts appear in early summer and are well displayed against the simple variegation. In fall the leaves turn purple, with red in the centre. This is a good cornus for light dappled shade where flowers and foliage are shown off to advantage. Lovely alongside *Leycesteria formosa* Golden Lanterns.

Cornus kousa 'Satomi'

1.5M × 1.5M (5 FT. × 5 FT.)

A beautiful cornus with spreading branches and soft salmon pink bracts that have a richer colour in an open, sunny position. The best variety for the smaller garden or under the dappled shade of trees, as long as the soil is moist enough. The foliage turns rich red in fall. Underplant with *Alchemilla mollis* for its frothy lime green flowers.

Cornus 'Porlock'

3M × 2.4M (10 FT. × 8 FT.)

A wonderful flowering hybrid dogwood with arching branches and semi-evergreen foliage. The creamy white bracts, produced in early summer, turn to white and then pink before falling. These are followed by red hanging fruits in fall. These fruits are often referred to as edible, but are best left to the birds. You can successfully grow this cornus in a large pot in a small garden or courtyard.

Coronilla

Scrambling shrubs of the pea family with sprawling, almost climbing stems and small vetch-like leaves. They enjoy a warm, sunny position and are a good choice for the base of a wall. Their greatest attributes are their long flowering season and tolerance of poor soils.

Lightly prune after the first flush of spring flowers to encourage bushy growth.

Coronilla valentina subsp. *glauca* 'Citrinus'

90CM × 90CM (3 FT. × 3 FT.)

False senna is a lovely shrub with blue-grey leaves and soft, pale yellow flowers in small clusters. The blooms start to appear in late winter, reach a peak in midspring, and continue intermittently throughout the year. Pretty planted with a blue-flowered rosemary or the soft purple blooms of *Erysimum* 'Bowles's Mauve'.

Cotinus

Smoke trees are so named because of their smoke-like fluffy flower heads. However, their greatest attribute is undoubtedly their foliage, as their rounded leaves have a different shape than most other shrubs. Those with colourful summer foliage and stunning fall colour are the most valuable.

Cotinus are easy to grow, mostly vigorous shrubs for any reasonably fertile soil that is not too dry. Prune in late winter to control size. You can carry out hard pruning on overgrown shrubs to rejuvenate them; this practice results in vigorous upright stems.

Cotinus coggygria Golden Spirit

Cotinus 'Grace'

Cotoneaster atropurpureus 'Variegatus'

Cotinus coggygria 'Royal Purple'

Cotinus coggygria Golden Spirit
1.5M × 1.5M (5 FT. × 5 FT.)

A reasonably compact cotinus with soft golden yellow foliage that is yellow-green in semi-shade. It does not scorch in sun and turns pale orange in fall before the leaves drop. An eye-catching focal point in a planting scheme alongside a garden feature and a lively partner for *Hydrangea arborescens* 'Annabelle'.

Cotinus coggygria 'Royal Purple'
2.1M × 2.1M (7 FT. × 7 FT.)

The most popular variety, with deep wine-purple leaves turning red-orange in fall. This strong-growing shrub can reach much larger proportions in time. It has a pleasing, loose habit and is a good foundation for a large island bed with pink shrub roses and silver foliage. Stunning planted with the deep red fall blooms of dahlias and crocosmias.

Cotinus 'Grace'
3M × 1.8M (10 FT. × 6 FT.)

A vigorous cotinus with strong upright stems carrying large, rounded leaves of red-brown colouring. The fluffy flower heads are loose and open, and they hang like clouds around the stems in late summer. The long-lasting fall foliage colour is spectacular glowing red. Position this shrub where the sun will shine through the leaves, especially in fall.

Cotoneaster

Cotoneasters include deciduous, semi-evergreen, and evergreen varieties. These plants are easy to grow on most soils, and gardeners have used many as basic garden shrubs for years. They are mostly grown for their fall berries, which wild birds enjoy, but their small, single, usually white spring flowers are attractive to bees and pollinating insects. Their flowers and fruit make them popular as shrubs to attract wildlife. Some have the benefit of good fall foliage colour.

If you have to prune to control size and shape, do so after the berries disappear in late winter.

Cotoneaster atropurpureus 'Variegatus'
60CM × 90CM (2 FT. × 3 FT.)

Also known as *Cotoneaster horizontalis* 'Variegatus', this is a low-growing shrub with spreading herringbone branches and tiny green-and-white variegated leaves. Mini white spring flowers are followed by shining red berries. The foliage colours rich pink and red in fall to spectacular effect. Good as part of a green-and-white groundcover scheme or if planted at the base of a wall.

Cotoneaster frigidus 'Cornubia'

Cotoneaster dammeri

Daphne bholua 'Jacqueline Postill'

Cotoneaster franchetii

Cotoneaster dammeri
15CM × 90CM (6 IN. × 3 FT.)

This may not be the showiest shrub, but it is a useful plant to have in your palette. Long, trailing stems hug the ground carrying small shining deep green evergreen leaves. The tiny white flowers produce large, round, red, shiny berries in fall. *Cotoneaster dammeri* is a useful groundcover shrub on banks and to cover the ground beneath mature shrubs. Grow it with variegated forms of *Vinca minor*.

Cotoneaster franchetii
1.8M × 1.5M (6 FT. × 5 FT.)

This is the most useful cotoneaster for its light, arching branches and pretty soft green, semi-evergreen leaves, which are heavily felted on the undersides and give the whole plant a silvery appearance. Small white flowers lead to large orange berries that last through fall into winter. Cut out a few of the older branches each year to maintain the open habit. A good choice for country gardens and naturalistic schemes.

Cotoneaster frigidus 'Cornubia'
3M × 4M (10 FT. × 13 FT.)

A vigorous, spreading, semi-evergreen shrub with willow-like leaves and clusters of white flowers in spring. In fall, these are replaced with large, showy clusters of shiny red berries that birds appreciate in early winter. A good transitional shrub for a country garden or as an alternative to a spreading, screening tree in a large space. It has the potential to grow considerably larger in time.

Daphne

Many gardeners consider daphnes to be some of the most desirable shrubs, and they are prized for their deliciously fragrant flowers. Some are difficult to propagate, hence their reputation as challenging to grow. Most, including *Daphne odora*, are not long-lived plants, and their performance usually declines after a few years. They do not thrive in pots, but grow well on alkaline soils and tolerate acid ones. It's best to avoid pruning, but if necessary, do it right after flowering. At the same time, remove declining branches that fail to come into leaf.

Daphne bholua 'Jacqueline Postill'
1.8M × 90CM (6 FT. × 3 FT.)

Grow this daphne for its fragrance. An upright shrub with flexible tan stems and pointed deep green leaves. It is evergreen in mild locations and may shed some of its leaves on colder sites. It is quite happy on any well-drained soil in sun or partial shade. In late winter, the deep pink-purple buds open to clusters of lilac-white flowers that are purple on the reverse. The fragrance is sweet, strong, and powerful, and it will fill the garden. Plant near the house where you can enjoy the perfume in all types of weather.

Deutzia ×hybrida 'Strawberry Fields'

Daphne odora 'Aureomarginata'

Daphne odora 'Rebecca'

Deutzia pulchra

Daphne odora 'Aureomarginata'
75CM × 75CM (30 IN. × 30 IN.)

The most widely grown daphne forms a low-mounded shrub with narrow evergreen leaves that are finely edged with gold. Purple flower buds open to fragrant mauve-and-purple flowers in late winter. Size of specimens varies considerably. Foliage colour and growth is usually better in partial shade. Lovely when planted with *Cyclamen coum* and black ophiopogon.

Daphne odora 'Rebecca'
75CM × 75CM (30 IN. × 30 IN.)

A stunning form of *Daphne odora* with broad gold margins to the leaves, carried in bold rosettes on regularly branched stems. In late winter clusters of mauve-pink, sweetly fragrant flowers appear in the centres of the rosettes. 'Rebecca' is a small compact shrub that is surprisingly vigorous considering its variegation. It is at its best in partial shade in a sheltered situation. Plant alongside other gold variegations and *Vinca minor* 'La Grave', with its early sky blue flowers.

Deutzia

Deutzias are hardy, tolerant, easy to grow, deciduous shrubs that would be more widely planted if the flowers were fragrant. Even though they lack scent, they are free flowing, and in winter the bare stems are not unattractive with their tan-coloured peeling bark. Deutzias are particularly good on poor, dry soil. Prune after annual flowering, leaving the emerging shoots to develop a graceful arching habit that will be garlanded with blooms the following season.

Deutzia ×*hybrida* 'Strawberry Fields'
1.8M × 1.5M (6 FT. × 5 FT.)

Medium green foliage is carried on strong, upright, arching stems. Sprays of open, starry, mauve-pink flowers, etched with white, garland the branches in midsummer. Plant it alongside *Cotinus coggygria* 'Royal Purple' or *Physocarpus opulifolius* 'Diablo'.

Deutzia pulchra
1.8M × 1.8M (6 FT. × 6 FT.)

The loveliest white deutzia, with dark green leaves and sprays of pure white flowers in early to midsummer. Each tiny flower is a slender bell, like an elfin hat filled with golden stamens. Lovely in a green-and-white scheme with *Choisya ternata* and *Cornus alba* 'Elegantissima'.

Elaeagnus

These evergreen and deciduous shrubs are grown for their ornamental foliage; most also produce tiny fragrant flowers. They grow on most soils in sun or semi-shade and tolerate wind and salt-laden air. Variegated evergreen elaeagnus tend to revert, so cut out plain shoots as they appear. Prune deciduous types in winter, evergreens in early spring.

Elaeagnus ×ebbingei

Elaeagnus 'Quicksilver'

Elaeagnus ×ebbingei 'Viveleg'

Enkianthus campanulatus

Elaeagnus ×ebbingei
3M × 3M (10 FT. × 10 FT.)

A strong-growing evergreen shrub with arching branches and deep green leaves that are silver on the reverse. Tiny fragrant flowers appear in the leaf axils in early fall. A solid background and screening shrub with the potential to grow to very large proportions. Good in exposed and coastal conditions, and makes an excellent hedge.

Elaeagnus ×ebbingei 'Viveleg'
1.5M × 1.5M (5 FT. × 5 FT.)

An excellent evergreen shrub with deep green leaves broadly edged with gold. Left unpruned it has a light, open habit and the foliage is good for cutting. It does not revert as readily as the widely planted *Elaeagnus pungens* 'Maculata', and it has a more cheerful colour. It is an excellent choice for a sunny position in a scheme with other gold-variegated foliage shrubs.

Elaeagnus 'Quicksilver'
3M × 2.4M (10 FT. × 8 FT.)

Oleaster is a deciduous shrub with willow-like leaves of silky silver-grey on arching branches, weeping at the ends. Tiny creamy flowers appear in midsummer and fill the garden with their sweet, heavy fragrance. Although shrubs produce suckers, this is rarely a problem. This is the best large silver-foliage shrub, and a wonderful background for pastel roses and perennials. Stunning planted alongside *Cotinus coggygria* 'Royal Purple' with a deep purple clematis growing through its branches.

Enkianthus

Enkianthus are some of the most beautiful ericaceous subjects, with exquisite, small, lantern-like flowers and outstanding fall leaf colour. They like acid soil rich in organic matter, and are suited to open woodland settings. Avoid pruning, which is unnecessary and liable to spoil the plant's shape.

Enkianthus campanulatus
2.4M × 90CM (8 FT. × 3 FT.)

Also called redvein enkianthus, and the easiest variety to grow. Upright stems branch regularly to twigs crowned with whorls of medium green leaves. The copper–salmon pink flowers appear in late spring; close inspection reveals intricate patterning and great detail on every tiny lantern. The leaves colour rich shades of gold, orange, and red in fall. You can grow it in a large pot filled with lime-free, loam-based compost. Lovely underplanted with bronze carex.

Erica ×darleyensis 'Lena'

Erica carnea 'Aztec Gold'

Erica carnea 'Myretoun Ruby'

Erica carnea 'Foxhollow'

Erica ×darleyensis 'White Perfection'

Erica

Among the many species and cultivars of erica, the most useful are the dwarf shrubs *Erica carnea* and *Erica ×darleyensis*, the winter-flowering heathers. Both make excellent groundcover subjects, have attractive evergreen foliage, and flower in winter and early spring. They are also more versatile because they tolerate lime; they will grow on most soils except shallow chalk. Both grow in sun or semi-shade and are useful under the light canopy of birches, although they flower more freely when given a reasonable amount of direct sunlight. *Erica carnea* varieties are generally lower growing than *Erica ×darleyensis* hybrids. Both types, especially the taller-growing varieties of *Erica ×darleyensis*, are excellent for cutting. They also make excellent subjects for winter container planting. To promote branched bushy plants and plenty of new growth, clip over with shears after flowering. This practice is essential where you use these shrubs as groundcover.

Plant winter-flowering heathers at the front of beds and borders with bergenias, *Euonymus fortunei* varieties, heucheras, and dwarf hebes.

Erica carnea 'Aztec Gold'
20CM × 30CM (8 IN. × 1 FT.)
A low-growing mat of bright gold foliage turning bronze and orange in winter, with light pink flowers.

Erica carnea 'Foxhollow'
20CM × 30CM (8 IN. × 1 FT.)
Low-growing shrub with yellow-green foliage, rich gold tinged with orange in winter; pale pink flowers produced in early spring.

Erica carnea 'Myretoun Ruby'
20CM × 30CM (8 IN. × 1 FT.)
Deep green foliage and dark pink flowers in early spring; regarded as one of the best varieties.

Erica ×darleyensis 'Lena'
45CM × 60CM (18 IN. × 2 FT.)
Dark bronze-green foliage and magenta flowers with prominent dark brown stamens.

Erica ×darleyensis 'White Perfection'
45CM × 60CM (18 IN. × 2 FT.)
A strong-growing winter shrub with bright green foliage and white flowers.

Erysimum 'Bowles's Mauve'

Escallonia 'Apple Blossom'

Eucryphia ×nymansensis 'Nymansay'

Escallonia 'Iveyi'

Erysimum

Perennial wallflowers are short-lived shrubs. They grow quickly and have a long flowering period, but last for only two or three years. They need a sunny position on well-drained soil. Pruning involves cutting off the flower spikes as they fade. The plants rarely rejuvenate if cut back. They are easily propagated from cuttings, so if you take cuttings annually anytime in spring and summer, you can replace the shrub.

Erysimum 'Bowles's Mauve'
60CM × 60CM (2 FT. × 2 FT.)
Long, dark, green, narrow leaves in whorls and tall spikes of light purple flowers from early spring through to winter. This is one of the longest-flowering small shrubs for a sunny spot, and ideal for seaside gardens. Plant it with silver-foliage shrubs such as santolina and helichrysum, or alliums.

Escallonia

Escallonias are evergreen shrubs with small, tough, dark green leaves and stiff branching stems. They grow well in open, sunny situations, and they tolerate wind and salt spray but dislike extreme cold. The larger-growing varieties make excellent hedging and screening shrubs. Most flower freely in summer, even when trimmed as hedges. Clip in early spring before growth commences or after flowering in midsummer, if cutting out flowered shoots from shrubs left to grow naturally.

Escallonia 'Apple Blossom'
1.2M × 1.2M (4 FT. × 4 FT.)
A slow-growing escallonia with small shining leaves and large clusters of pink-and-white flowers in early to mid summer. 'Apple Blossom' is a useful evergreen flowering shrub for a mixed border with blue geraniums and deep pink shrub roses.

Escallonia 'Iveyi'
1.8M × 1.5M (6 FT. × 5 FT.)
An upright shrub with shining dark green waved leaves and large, loose clusters of pure white flowers in summer. Not as hardy as some of the smaller-leaved varieties, but more successful in semi-shade than other escallonias. A lovely shrub for any green-and-white scheme, especially with white variegated foliage; underplant with *Euonymus fortunei* 'Emerald Gaiety'.

Eucryphia

These evergreen summer-flowering shrubs and small trees for moist, acid soils are some of the most ravishing shrubs when in full bloom. Most are upright and narrow in habit, so not greedy on space, but they eventually grow tall. For best results, plant where the roots are shaded. Prune only to remove dead or damaged shoots.

Euonymus alatus

Euonymus fortunei 'Emerald Gaiety'

Euonymus europaeus 'Red Cascade'

Eucryphia ×*nymansensis* 'Nymansay'
3M × 90CM (10 FT. × 3 FT.)

The most widely grown eucryphia, and one of the easiest. Its dense column of dark green leaves can make a strong focal point amidst the light shade of surrounding trees. In late summer the branches are festooned with large, single white, cup-shaped flowers, each with a pincushion of stamens. A stunning specimen shrub for a lightly shaded garden; good with white-barked birches.

Euonymus

Many different euonymus are grown in our gardens as free-standing shrubs, groundcover subjects, container plants, and even climbers. The evergreen ones are popular for their colourful variegations and foliage effects, and they are also easy to grow, as they thrive on most soils. Evergreen euonymus are particularly valuable in shade, and they tolerate atmospheric pollution and the salt-laden air of coastal gardens. *Euonymus fortunei* are usually lax, sprawling subjects that will grow as short evergreen climbers against walls and fences.

Gardeners cultivate deciduous varieties of euonymus for their fall foliage colour and attractive fruits. Their natural, open habit makes them ideal for country gardens and naturalistic planting. If you must prune, do so in winter, after fruits have fallen, to control shape and size.

Euonymus alatus
1.2M × 1.2M (4 FT. × 4 FT.)

Winged euonymus is slow-growing shrub with stiff, spreading branches with curious winged bark. The small, light green leaves are pretty through summer, and clusters of tiny yellowish flowers appear in spring. The fall colour is truly spectacular, as the leaves turn vibrant shades of red-pink. This plant has become naturalized in parts of the United States and threatens native species, so it is not grown in gardens. This is not an issue in the United Kingdom. It is a good planting companion for summer-flowering perennials, such as hemerocallis, to add structure and fall interest.

Euonymus europaeus 'Red Cascade'
3M × 1.8M (10 FT. × 6 FT.)

An open, arching shrub, known as spindle tree or European euonymus, with slender branches and narrow green leaves turning rich red in fall. The deep red-pink seed capsules hang all along the branches in fall, splitting open to reveal bright orange seeds. A lovely shrub for a paddock or wild garden planted with *Viburnum opulus*.

Euonymus fortunei 'Emerald Gaiety'
60CM × 90CM (2 FT. × 3 FT.)

With the same growth habit as 'Emerald 'n' Gold', this euonymus also makes a good short climber against a shady wall or fence. The small, dark and soft green-and-white variegated leaves flush pink in winter in a light position. Excellent for shrubby groundcover under trees with *Sarcococca confusa*.

Euonymus japonicus
UPRIGHT EVERGREEN VARIETIES

Japanese euonymus varieties are bushy shrubs of upright habit; their thick leathery leaves are resistant to sun, wind, atmospheric pollution, and sea air. The variegated forms with larger leaves are colourful subjects and some of the showiest evergreen shrubs. The small-leaved varieties are compact and ideal for small gardens, narrow borders, and containers. They resemble box and can be used as an alternative, particularly in containers.

All *Euonymus japonicus* varieties succeed in shady situations and are ideal for urban gardens. The variegated forms are an ideal way to introduce colour into the planting in shaded situations. Choose either a yellow or white variegation to lead the colour scheme in a planting combination, but avoid mixing, as they do not sit happily together.

If necessary, prune evergreen euonymus in spring before growth commences. Cut out any plain green shoots as they appear; if left to develop, they may well take over.

Euonymus japonicus 'Green Rocket'

Euonymus japonicus 'Chollipo'

Euonymus japonicus 'Microphyllus Variegatus'

Euonymus japonicus 'Bravo'

Euonymus japonicus 'Microphyllus Aureovariegatus'

Euonymus japonicus 'Microphyllus Pulchellus'

Euonymus japonicus 'Bravo'
1.5M × 1.2M (5 FT. × 4 FT.)
A lovely variety with broad cream margins to the green-and-cream variegated shining leaves. The stems are upright, and you can easily prune to create a broad column of striking foliage. It is a good planting partner with cream- or white-flowered evergreens. Excellent with *Pittosporum tobira* in a sheltered garden.

Euonymus japonicus 'Chollipo'
1.5M × 1.2M (5 FT. × 4 FT.)
Similar in habit to 'Bravo', but with leaves that are dark green in the centre, broadly margined, and variegated with creamy gold. It has altogether more pleasing colour than the widely planted *Euonymus japonicus* 'Ovatus Aureus', and mixes well with other gold-and-green variegations and is effective against plain evergreens. A good choice with yellow- and purple-leaved phormiums.

Euonymus japonicus 'Green Rocket'
90CM × 30CM (3 FT. × 1 FT.)
A fastigiate variety with very upright stems regularly packed with rounded, dark green, shining leaves. This plant is striking and architectural in character, and an excellent choice for a pot or a narrow border in a small garden. Underplant with a white variegated vinca, such as *Vinca minor* 'Ralph Shugert', for a pleasing combination in shade.

Euonymus japonicus 'Microphyllus Aureovariegatus'
60CM × 45CM (2 FT. × 18 IN.)
Like 'Microphyllus Pulchellus', but with dark green leaves edged with soft gold. Good alongside the dark green foliage of *Ilex crenata* 'Convexa'; both are excellent in pots.

Euonymus japonicus 'Microphyllus Pulchellus'
60CM × 45CM (2 FT. × 18 IN.)
Small, glossy green leaves, suffused with gold, crowded onto upright stems on a neat, compact shrub. The green-gold foliage of this euonymus is a good partner for the gold-and-green variegation of *Euonymus fortunei* 'Emerald 'n' Gold' in a shady spot.

Euonymus japonicus 'Microphyllus Variegatus'
60CM × 45CM (2 FT. × 18 IN.)
Like 'Microphyllus Pulchellus', but with dark green leaves edged with white. Good when planted with *Pachysandra terminalis* 'Variegata' in a narrow border.

Euonymus fortunei 'Emerald 'n' Gold'

Exochorda macrantha 'The Bride'

Euonymus fortunei 'Silver Queen'

×Fatshedera lizei 'Annemieke'

Euonymus fortunei 'Emerald 'n' Gold'
60CM × 90CM (2 FT. × 3 FT.)

Small, rich gold, and dark green variegated leaves; bushy but loose habit. The foliage becomes lighter, often flushed pink in winter. Good for planting beneath trees with dark evergreens, or with golden-leaved spiraeas for a bright and cheery combination in sun or semi-shade.

Euonymus fortunei 'Silver Queen'
60CM × 90CM (2 FT. × 3 FT.)

The best of the *Euonymus fortunei* varieties, but a little slower in growth. New leaves are creamy white, maturing to green-and-cream variegations. Tiny white flowers usually develop into creamy seed capsules in fall. Spreading, bushy habit, but also an excellent short climber. Lovely planted alongside *Choisya ternata* or *Magnolia stellata*.

Exochorda

These beautiful deciduous shrubs, with graceful arching branches and soft green leaves, are grown for their delicate white flowers, which appear in late spring. Exochordas grow on most soils, but the foliage yellows on shallow chalk. Prune right after flowering, removing some of the shoots that have flowered.

Exochorda macrantha 'The Bride'
1.5M × 1.5M (5 FT. × 5 FT.)

Pearlbush is a densely weeping mound of pale green leaves. The open double flowers are carried in short sprays all over the shrub in late spring; they are pure white with tissue-paper petals. When in bloom, 'The Bride' has a dazzling frothy character; it is stunning against a dark purple berberis or alongside a blue spring-flowering *Ceanothus* 'Concha'.

×*Fatshedera*

A hybrid between hedera and fatsia, with evergreen foliage resembling small fatsia leaves. You can grow this shrub against a wall or fence, or allow it to sprawl naturally in a shady position. Prune in early spring only if necessary to control spread and habit.

×*Fatshedera lizei* 'Annemieke'
90CM × 1.2M (3 FT. × 4 FT.)

A shrub with leathery leaves, dark green boldly marked with lime green in the centres, carried on semi-upright stems. The size and spread vary according to location, but tree ivy will thrive in any shaded spot. A good choice for town gardens and under the canopy of trees. Grows well with any variegated ivy planted for groundcover.

Fatsia japonica 'Variegata'

Fuchsia 'Genii'

Fatsia japonica

Forsythia ×intermedia

Fatsia

Fatsias are exotic-looking shrubs that thrive in any type of soil. Only two forms of one species of fatsia are widely grown in gardens. Cut back leggy plants hard in spring to stimulate new growth and rejuvenate.

Fatsia japonica
1.8M × 1.5M (6 FT. × 5 FT.)

Often referred to as castor oil plant, which it resembles, *Fatsia japonica* has large, glossy, green-lobed leaves. Its exotic appearance and shining foliage create a tropical effect in a shady corner or a pot. It makes a good choice for a town courtyard garden or a shaded balcony. Striking white flower heads appear at the end of the stems in winter, occasionally followed by black berries. In a large space grow it alongside black- or golden-stemmed bamboo.

Fatsia japonica 'Variegata'
1.5M × 1.2M (5 FT. × 4 FT.)

The variegated form is usually smaller in stature, but with the same large, shining, dark green leaves, boldly tipped with creamy white. It also produces structured flower heads in winter. Grow it as part of a green-and-white scheme with *Euonymus fortunei* 'Silver Queen' and *Viburnum davidii*.

Forsythia

These are tough, hardy, and easy to grow shrubs known for their profuse golden yellow flowers in early spring. They may be common and widely planted, but they are also versatile and useful as background and screening shrubs. You can prune them, control them, or trim them as hedging plants. The stems of buds are also excellent for cutting for flower arranging. For a natural habit, prune right after flowering, removing some of the flowered stems.

Forsythia ×intermedia
2.4M × 1.8M (8 FT. × 6 FT.)

There are many cultivars of *Forsythia ×intermedia*, and all have golden yellow flowers. *Forsythia ×intermedia* Weekend is a free flowering, more compact form. *Forsythia ×intermedia* Goldrausch flowers from the ground to the tip of the plant. It is hard to distinguish between all these cultivars, as flower colour and foliage are similar. You can easily rejuvenate old plants with hard pruning. Plant forsythia against a background of dark evergreens for a shot of spring sunshine.

Fuchsia

Although many fuchsias are grown as summer container plants, the hardiest varieties make wonderful shrubs in milder and coastal areas. In colder places they may die back to ground level in winter and shoot from the base in spring, which limits their size considerably. Fuchsias flower for a long period from early

Griselinia littoralis 'Variegata'

Fuchsia 'Riccartonii'

Fuchsia 'Hawkshead'

Fuchsia 'Tom West'

summer through fall, when their beautiful pendant flowers hang from arching branches. They are particularly useful because they will grow and flower in sun or shade. Prune, if necessary, in late winter; cut back dead stems to ground level at the same time.

Fuchsia 'Genii'
60CM × 30CM (2 FT. × 1 FT.)
A small fuchsia with upright reddish stems and yellow-green leaves. The flowers are red and purple, plumper than those of 'Riccartonii'. Attractive planted as a group in semi-shade with *Leycesteria formosa* Golden Lanterns.

Fuchsia 'Hawkshead'
1.2m × 90cm (4 ft. × 3 ft.)
A lovely form with upright stems, medium green leaves, and delicate green-tinged flowers. Pleasing in semi-shade against dark green foliage and with white variegated shrubs such as *Cornus alba* 'Elegantissima'.

Fuchsia 'Riccartonii'
1.8M × 1.2M (6 FT. × 4 FT.)
A tall, slender shrub with reddish young stems, dark green leaves, and red-and-purple flowers. This variety is widely grown as a hedging plant in mild districts, especially near the sea. Grow it with *Brachyglottis* (Dunedin Group) 'Sunshine'.

Fuchsia 'Tom West'
30CM × 30CM (1 FT. × 1 FT.)
'Tom West', an excellent choice for a pot, is a low shrub with arching branches and pale green leaves edged with creamy pink. The leaves at the tips of the shoots are bronze and pink, and the flowers red and purple; it is an altogether colourful plant. Grow it in a pot alongside purple heucheras or black ophiopogon.

Griselinia

An interesting foliage shrub with rounded glossy leaves on seaweed green stems. *Griselinia littoralis* is often grown as a hedging or screening shrub and is excellent for coastal gardens. Griselinia dislikes cold, exposed situations and shallow chalk soils. Prune in spring to control size and shape.

Griselinia littoralis 'Variegata'
2.4M × 1.8M (8 FT. × 6 FT.)
Upright stems carry apple green leaves edged and sometimes streaked with creamy white. The variegation of this form of New Zealand broadleaf is soft but striking. The growth is shorter and usually more compact than *Griselinia littoralis*, so this variegated form makes a very attractive hedge. This shrub is a good companion for *Pittosporum tobira* in a sheltered garden, as the cream flowers of the pittosporum pick up the cream in the leaves of the griselinia.

Hamamelis

Witch hazels are beautiful, elegant shrubs with fragrant winter flowers and wonderful fall foliage colour. They are usually at their best in late winter, as their delicate, ribbon-petalled flowers are remarkably resistant to frost and snow. They are easy to grow on well-drained, fertile soil that is rich in organic matter, and they prefer neutral to acid conditions. Avoid shallow, alkaline, or very dry soil. They are happy in sun or semi-shade, and suit woodland gardens and rural settings. They can be successful in large containers of lime-free, loam-based compost for several years.

Witch hazels make excellent specimen shrubs, and are impressive as free-standing specimens in grass. Eventually they can grow much larger than stated here, so give them space to develop and attain their natural shape and spread, and avoid pruning. They are normally grafted plants, so remove suckers as they appear.

The common name comes early British settlers, who used branches of the North American species *Hamamelis virginiana* as water-divining rods. They had the same magic properties as branches of hazel used at home, so the plant gained the moniker "witch hazel."

Plant yellow-flowered varieties against a dark background, such as a large evergreen shrub. Orange- and red-flowered witch hazels are best positioned where the morning or afternoon sun will light the blooms. Make sure you choose a scented variety with good fall leaf colour.

All witch hazels make wonderful planting companions for cornus grown for their winter stems. *Cornus sanguinea* 'Midwinter Fire', 'Anny's Winter Orange', and 'Magic Flame' all have wonderful fall leaf colour, so they make a spectacular show in the garden with witch hazels in fall and again in late winter. Like cornus, hamamelis are enhanced with evergreen underplanting of hedera, vinca, or carex.

The fragile, fiery petals of a witch hazel unfurl on the bare stems in midwinter against a glowing backdrop of red-barked dogwoods.

Hamamelis ×intermedia 'Aurora'

Hamamelis ×intermedia 'Orange Peel'

Hamamelis ×intermedia 'Pallida'

Hamamelis ×intermedia 'Robert'

Hamamelis ×intermedia 'Aurora'

1.8M × 1.2M (6 FT. × 4 FT.)

An upright witch hazel with large, very fragrant, bronze-yellow flowers that are red at the base of the petals and pale toward the tips. Wonderful fall leaf colour in shades of orange, gold, and red. Good alongside the strong green foliage of *Mahonia japonica*, often developing orange and red highlights in an open position.

Hamamelis ×intermedia 'Orange Peel'

1.8M × 1.2M (6 FT. × 4 FT.)

Upright when young, 'Orange Peel' becomes more spreading when more than ten years old. The flowers are deep orange and sweetly scented. In fall, the leaves colour richly in shades of yellow, orange, and red. Striking rising above *Uncinia rubra* and a pink or orange phormium.

Hamamelis ×intermedia 'Pallida'

1.5M × 1.8M (5 FT. × 6 FT.)

The most popular witch hazel, with pale yellow flowers freely produced on spreading branches; their fragrance is strong and sweet. Clear golden yellow fall leaf colour. Adds another dimension to a dark green or gold spotted aucuba in semi-shade.

Hamamelis ×intermedia 'Robert'

1.8M × 1.2M (6 FT. × 4 FT.)

An early flowering witch hazel that opens in midwinter. The growth habit is upright when young, becoming broader as the shrub ages. The large flowers are rich copper-red-orange and sweetly scented; somewhat reminiscent of the heart of a ripe peach. The fall leaf colour is yellow to red-orange. Underplant with *Nandina domestica* 'Fire Power' for its red and orange winter foliage colour.

Hebe 'Caledonia'

Hebe 'Frozen Flame'

Hebe 'Emerald Gem'

Hebe albicans

Hebe

Really useful evergreen shrubs that grow on most well-drained soils, providing they are not too dry. These natives of New Zealand dislike hot, dry conditions, although the small-leaved compact varieties are far more tolerant. The large-leaved hebes are not as hardy and often succumb to fungal diseases inland in the United Kingdom, so I rarely use them. The small-leaved hebes are good in pots, in small gardens, in gravel, and at the front of beds and borders. They all flower in summer, and the dense spikes of single flowers are attractive to bees and butterflies.

Prune only on older plants to rejuvenate, and do so in spring; cut back to where new shoots are emerging lower in the shrub.

Hebe albicans
60CM × 75CM (2 FT. × 30 IN.)

A dense hebe with small, rigid, blue-green leaves packed on stiff stems. Clear white flowers in small spikes appear in summer. This is one of the hardiest hebes; ideal as a low-evergreen structure shrub alongside silver-foliage shrubs and lavenders.

Hebe 'Caledonia'
60CM × 60CM (2 FT. × 2 FT.)

A rounded shrub with narrow dark green leaves, flushed red-purple at the tips of the shoots. Slender spikes of violet flowers from late spring right through to fall. *Hebe* 'Pascal' is similar and a good alternative. An excellent shrub to add evergreen interest and contrasting foliage alongside *Spiraea japonica* 'Firelight'.

Hebe 'Emerald Gem'
60CM × 60CM (2 FT. × 2 FT.)

Also known as *Hebe* 'Green Globe'. A bright green compact hebe with tiny apple green leaves on upright stems. White flowers in tiny spikes appear at the tips of the shoots in summer, like downy feathers resting on the firm foliage. A good choice for a low cloud bed of clipped evergreens in gravel; this one needs no attention.

Hebe 'Frozen Flame'
75CM × 90CM (30 IN. × 3 FT.)

A very hardy hebe with soft grey-green and white irregularly variegated foliage that turns intense purple and pink in winter and spring. Spikes of pretty blue flowers appear in midsummer. A good choice for a patio container alongside purple heucheras and violas.

Hebe 'Midsummer Beauty'
90CM × 90CM (3 FT. × 3 FT.)

A hardier, larger-leaved hebe with narrow deep green leaves, flushed red on the undersides. Long lilac-pink sprays of flowers throughout summer are attractive to butterflies. Lovely planted in a sheltered garden with the pink-tinged variegated leaves of *Pittosporum tenuifolium* 'Elizabeth'.

Hebe pinguifolia 'Sutherlandii'

Hedera helix 'Erecta'

Hebe 'Midsummer Beauty'

Hebe 'Red Edge'

Helianthemum 'Rhodanthe Carneum'

Hebe pinguifolia 'Sutherlandii'
60CM × 60CM (2 FT. × 2 FT.)

Similar in habit to 'Emerald Gem', but with grey-green foliage crowded on upright stems tipped with white flowers in summer. Excellent as a grey-green alternative to trimmed box balls, or in a sunny border with helianthemums.

Hebe 'Red Edge'
75CM × 75CM (30 IN. × 30 IN.)

Ever-popular hebe forming a dense mound of upright stems with rigid grey-green leaves that colour purple-red in winter at the tips of the shoots. Short spikes of small white flowers appear in summer. 'Red Edge' is a very useful shrub, and a good planting companion for *Berberis thunbergii* f. *atropurpurea* 'Rose Glow'.

Hedera

Gardeners have a love-hate relationship with ivy. Its self-clinging stems threaten brickwork, and the more vigorous forms have a habit of getting out of hand. But hederas are excellent in shade, they grow on any soil, and they tolerate atmospheric pollution and the worst growing conditions. You can easily prune to control size and spread, ideally in spring. Some shrubby forms make interesting and architectural evergreen shrubs.

Hedera helix 'Erecta'
75CM × 90CM (30 IN. × 3 FT.)

Slow-growing and dense shrub with upright growth and pointed but waved, stiff, dark green leaves regularly arranged up the stems; as they grow taller they lean and then grow again vertically. Excellent for a pot or a shady corner with ferns, or the architectural *Astelia chathamica* 'Silver Spear'. *Hedera helix* may be regarded as invasive in parts of the United States.

Helianthemum

Helianthemums, often called rock roses, are dwarf evergreen shrubs that thrive in hot, sunny situations on dry and well-drained soil, especially chalk. They are ideal at the edges of paths and paved areas, and thrive when planted in gravel, where they form spreading mats studded with colourful flowers in summer. They are easy to grow and good for small situations, containers, and coastal gardens. They dislike shade and damp soil.

Prune after flowering, cutting back to below the flower stems to keep the plants compact. You can hard prune old plants with straggly growth at the same time.

Helianthemum 'Rhodanthe Carneum'
20CM × 30CM (8 IN. × 1 FT.)

One of the most popular helianthemums, often sold as 'Wisley Pink', with small silver-grey leaves and soft pink tissue-paper flowers. Each open bloom has a conspicuous eye of golden stamens. Lovely planted alongside the shining silver foliage of *Convolvulus cneorum* or in front of lavenders.

Hibiscus syriacus 'Hamabo'

Hydrangea arborescens Invincibell Spirit

Helichrysum italicum 'Korma'

Hydrangea arborescens 'Annabelle'

Helichrysum

The silver-leaved shrubby varieties of helichrysum are useful dwarf shrubs that love the warm, sunny, situations that most silver-foliage subjects appreciate. They are good on dry and well-drained soils and thrive in pots on the patio. They mix well with other sun lovers and maintain winter interest with their evergreen foliage. These are short-lived shrubs, so you will need to replace them after three or four seasons.

In most cases the flowers are undesirable, so pruning means cutting back in early summer as the flower buds are produced. If you want to retain the blooms, prune after flowering.

Helichrysum italicum 'Korma'
30CM × 30CM (1 FT. × 1 FT.)

A very aromatic form of curry plant with fine, narrow, silver leaves that shine in summer and winter. This light, airy shrub is ideal planted with dianthus and lavenders, and it is an excellent choice for hiding unsightly allium foliage. Particularly good with *Allium cristophii*.

Hibiscus

Hardy hibiscus are not as showy and flamboyant as the tropical types, but they are wonderful flowering shrubs that produce a magnificent display late in the season. They need full sun and a good summer to perform at their best. The upright grey twigs are rather late to come into leaf, so take this into account

when positioning them. They grow well on most well-drained soils.

Pruning is rarely necessary, but if necessary, do so in winter to control size and shape.

Hibiscus syriacus 'Hamabo'
2.4M × 1.5M (8 FT. × 5 FT.)

A lovely hibiscus with an upright, bushy habit and fresh dark green foliage. In the United States it is known as rose-of-sharon, but that name refers to a different plant entirely in the United Kingdom. 'Hamabo' is one of the most reliable varieties, producing abundant pale pink, deep red-eyed flowers. The blooms are large and open, rather than the poor shrivelled flowers that some hibiscus produce in cooler areas. Superb planted alongside *Cotinus coggygria* 'Royal Purple'.

Hydrangea

Hydrangeas are wonderful shrubs for their summer and fall flowers. Although hydrangea conjures images of the large mophead and lacecap varieties, many other beautiful types fit in with different situations and planting schemes. You can grow hydrangeas easily on most soils, but they dislike dry conditions at the roots, even though many are happy under the light shade of trees.

Prune *Hydrangea macrophylla* and *Hydrangea serrata* varieties in early spring. Remove old flower heads and cut back the stems to the first pair of fat buds behind last season's flower. You can cut back some of the older, darker stems of mature plants to allow new

Hydrangea aspera Kawakamii Group

Hydrangea macrophylla 'Mariesii Perfecta'

Hydrangea serrata 'Bluebird'

Hydrangea macrophylla 'Ayesha'

shoots to develop. Prune *Hydrangea arborescens* and *Hydrangea involucrata* varieties in early spring. Cut back to a low pair of healthy buds between 20cm (8 in.) and 30cm (1 ft.) above ground level. Do this every year. *Hydrangea aspera* requires little or no pruning.

Some *Hydrangea macrophylla* and *Hydrangea serrata* varieties turn from pink and red to blue on acid soil. You can also achieve this colour change in pots by using lime-free soil and hydrangea colourant. White hydrangeas do not change colour according to soil type, but they may blush pink in the sun.

Hydrangea arborescens 'Annabelle'
75CM × 75CM (30 IN. × 30 IN.)

A lovely hydrangea with slender upright stems, soft green leaves, and large heads of crowded florets. It is green to start, turning cream and then pure white. The heavy flower heads can make the stems flop, so plant among shrubs that will lend support. Beautiful under the light shade of trees with lime green alchemilla, ferns, and tellima.

Hydrangea arborescens Invincibell Spirit
75CM × 75CM (30 IN. × 30 IN.)

Slender upright stems carry loose heads of crushed strawberry pink florets. The flower heads remain upright and are not as heavy as those of 'Annabelle'. It is a good planting companion for nepeta, blue salvias, and purple-sage, and also useful to extend the season of shrub roses.

Hydrangea aspera Kawakamii Group
1.5M × 1.8M (5 FT. × 6 FT.)

Large velvety green leaves are carried on spreading branches. The lacecap flower heads are exquisitely beautiful in late fall. Warm pink buds open to deep violet-blue fertile florets in the centre; large, sterile white-pink, sparkling florets surround them. Stunning with the fall tints of Japanese maples in a semi-shaded situation.

Hydrangea macrophylla 'Ayesha'
1.2M × 1.2M (4 FT. × 4 FT.)

A most unusual mophead hydrangea with large glossy green leaves and compact heads of thick-petalled, lilac-like flowers. The blooms are lilac-pink on alkaline soil and soft blue on acid soil, and they have a slight fragrance. Makes a subtle planting combination with *Abelia ×grandiflora*.

Hydrangea macrophylla 'Mariesii Perfecta'
1.5M × 1.5M (5 FT. × 5 FT.)

A classic, vigorous, lacecap hydrangea; at its best in light shade. The tiny fertile florets are always blue, surrounded by large mauve-pink sterile florets that become bright blue on acid soil. A lovely shrub under white-barked birches.

Hydrangea serrata 'Bluebird'
90CM × 7CM (3 FT. × 30 IN.)

A small, slender, lacecap hydrangea with upright stems and small, pointed, deep green leaves flushed with wine-red. The dainty flower heads are purple-pink on alkaline soils and bright blue on acid. Good in sun or in the semi-shade with bold perennials such as pentemons and sedums.

Hydrangea paniculata
LATE-SUMMER FLOWERING SHRUBS

Varieties of *Hydrangea paniculata* are invaluable shrubs for their spectacular late summer and fall flowers. They produce a stunning display when many other hydrangeas are past their peak. Upright or arching stems carry conical heads of florets that resemble lilac.

You can use *Hydrangea paniculata* at the back of a border of herbaceous perennials and roses to prolong the season. If conditions are not too dry, it grows well under the light shade of trees. The hardy shrub grows easily on most well-drained, fertile soils. The blooms are useful for cutting for floral decoration. They last well if cut when mature, and some varieties lend themselves to drying.

Hydrangea paniculata flowers late in summer and fall, so you should prune in late winter. The plant responds to hard pruning. If you cut back annually to between 30cm (1 ft.) and 60cm (2 ft.), it produces strong, upright shoots and holds its flowers high. Cut out any thin and weak stems at the same time. Older plants of more vigorous varieties can be cut back each year to around 90cm (3 ft.).

Hydrangea paniculata is often trained as a standard, and it looks stunning, if somewhat fragile, when grown this way. It makes a striking subject for a large pot in a courtyard or paved area close to the house. Although it is deciduous, the faded flowers of most varieties remain attractive through winter.

Hydrangea paniculata 'Floribunda'

Hydrangea paniculata 'Kyushu'

Hydrangea paniculata 'Floribunda'
2.4M × 1.8M (8 FT. × 6 FT.)
Upright stems carry tall sprays of large pure white florets that blush pink and green with age. An old, established variety excellent in semi-shade with *Choisya ternata*.

Hydrangea paniculata 'Kyushu'
1.5M × 1.2M (5 FT. × 4 FT.)
Upright in habit, with ascending stems carrying lacy flower heads with large sterile florets and small fertile ones. Dark green shiny foliage. Makes a frothy combination with *Cornus alternifolia* 'Argentea'.

The lacy flowerheads of *Hydrangea paniculata* contrast with the large, bold leaves of *Paulownia tomentosa* behind.

Hydrangea paniculata 'Limelight'

Hydrangea paniculata Vanille Fraise

Hydrangea paniculata 'Unique'

Hydrangea paniculata 'Limelight'
1.5M × 1.2M (5 FT. × 4 FT.)
An upright variety with solid, densely packed heads of lime green florets that turn white, then blush pink, in a sunny position. Plant this shrub for the green stage of the flowers, which lasts a long time. A good choice as part of a green-and-cream planting scheme with *Griselinia littoralis* 'Variegata' or *Euonymus japonicus* 'Bravo'.

Hydrangea paniculata Vanille Fraise
1.8M × 1.5M (6 FT. × 5 FT.)
A beautiful variety with large flower heads that turn from white to strawberry pink and then light red in sun. The flowers can weigh down the arching stems. For a mouthwatering combination, underplant with *Berberis thunbergii* f. *atropurpurea* 'Rose Glow'.

Hydrangea paniculata 'Unique'
2.4M × 1.8M (8 FT. × 6 FT.)
A vigorous variety with strong stems and huge flower heads that turn from white to deep pink flushed with green, then fade to parchment and remain attractive through winter. You can also cut and dry at any stage when they are mature. 'Unique' makes a good specimen shrub, or you can grow it as an alternative to a small tree.

Ilex aquifolium 'Pyramidalis'

Ilex crenata 'Convexa'

Ilex aquifolium 'Argenteo Marginata'

Ilex aquifolium 'Elegantissima'

Ilex

There are many species of holly, both evergreen and deciduous. The evergreens are normally grown in gardens as wonderful structure shrubs and sometimes small trees. The larger-leaved hollies, including varieties of the British native *Ilex aquifolium*, are not hardy enough for colder regions; the smaller-leaved, tougher *Ilex ×meserveae* is used instead.

The larger hollies are often rather sparse in growth when young, becoming fuller and more beautiful as they mature. They are evergreen shrubs to plant for future. Prune to control size and spread in early spring, before new growth commences.

Ilex aquifolium 'Argenteo Marginata'
2.1M × 1.2M (7 FT. × 4 FT.)

The broad-leaved silver holly has deep green shining leaves with broad, creamy white edges and pink-tinged young shoots. It is a female variety that produces a good crop of red berries in the presence of a male pollinator. Plant with *Choisya ternata* or *Pittosporum tobira* in semi-shade.

Ilex aquifolium 'Elegantissima'
2.1M × 1.2M (7 FT. × 4 FT.)

Broad, dark green, spiny leaves boldly edged with creamy white on green stems. The new growth is flushed pink. This is a male holly, so it produces no berries. It is a good choice in any green-and-white scheme in town or country, and a good pollination partner for either of the other two *Ilex aquifolium* varieties listed here.

Ilex aquifolium 'Pyramidalis'
2.1M × 1.2M (7 FT. × 4 FT.)

An excellent, plain green–leaved holly with green stems and slightly spiny deep green leaves. It is narrow and conical when young, becoming broader with age. This is a self-fertile holly that fruits freely, producing masses of red berries even without another holly to pollinate it. Plant it with a light, variegated evergreen such as *Pittosporum tenuifolium* 'Elizabeth'.

Ilex crenata 'Convexa'
60CM × 60CM (2 FT. × 2 FT.)

This small evergreen shrub is easily mistaken for a variety of box. It has small, shining, dark green, convex leaves with a very rounded appearance. It often produces neat, round, black berries in fall; these persist for months on the plant. It is slow growing, dense, and bushy, ideal for the small garden, in gravel, in a narrow border, or alongside steps or a patio. It makes a superb slow hedge. Grow it in pots instead of box; it does not suffer from the bronzing of the foliage that often affects *Buxus sempervirens*, especially in winter.

Kolkwitzia amabilis

Laurus nobilis

Lavatera ×clementii 'Mary Hope'

Kolkwitzia

Kolkwitzia is closely related to abelia, and its arching stems make a gracefully mounded shrub that produces a wonderful display of flowers in early summer. Prune after flowering, cutting back some of the stems that have flowered to where new shoots are appearing low down on the plant.

Kolkwitzia amabilis
1.5M × 1.2M (5 FT. × 4 FT.)
Beauty bush is a lovely shrub with soft green leaves flushed pinkish-red at the stalks. In late spring the stems become garlands of small pink trumpet-shaped flowers with golden throats; in a good year the whole shrub will appear as a mound of flowers. Lovely in a country garden setting, especially alongside the new foliage of a purple-leaved sambucus.

Laurus

Laurels are large evergreen shrubs or small trees with leathery, drought-resistant leaves. They grow on all well-drained soils, but although hardy they can be susceptible to frost damage in severely cold weather. Small greenish flowers appear in early spring, but these are insignificant; laurels are grown for their structure and foliage. Prune in early spring, just before new growth commences.

Laurus nobilis
2.1M × 1.2M (7 FT. × 4 FT.)
True laurel or common bay is the species grown as an ornamental in gardens and for the culinary use of its leaves. It has also been used since ancient times to create crowns and garlands for decorating heroes. If left untrained, it forms upright stems when young, with matte green aromatic leaves. It grows to form a large, conical shrub, but responds well to clipping and training. It grows well in pots and containers and is an excellent choice for coastal gardens. A lightly clipped conical bay makes a strong focal point amidst lavender and silver-foliage subjects.

Lavatera

The shrubby mallows are fast-growing, but often short-lived, shrubs with upright stems and hollyhock-like flowers throughout summer and fall. They grow on any well-drained soil and are excellent in coastal gardens. They are not a good choice for heavy, wet soils or cold situations.

The plants can get tall and sprawling during the growing season, so it is necessary to cut back some of the flowered stems to prevent collapse. Prune in early spring, cutting back all stems by one-half to two-thirds, or even lower, to encourage new growth from the base.

Lavatera ×clementii 'Mary Hope'
1.2M × 90CM (4 FT. × 3 FT.)
A compact lavatera with pink-white, tissue paper flowers with deep pink eyes. It is similar to the previously popular variety 'Barnsley', which frequently reverts and is taller and less stable. Lovely planted with dark red penstemons or annuals such as cosmos and nigella.

Lavandula

Lavenders are the most widely grown and best-loved aromatic shrubs. They have so many uses in gardens, and they grow on most well-drained soils in sunny, open positions. They are particularly at home alongside gravel and paving and are a good choice for coastal gardens. They dislike heavy, wet soils; shade; and stagnant, damp air, and they do not survive long in these conditions. The fragrance of their leaves and flowers is distinctive and calming, and they are a natural choice in sensory planting schemes. The varieties of *Lavandula angustifolia*, English lavender, have a sweet fragrance, whereas those of *Lavandula stoechas*, Spanish lavender, have more menthol and eucalyptus aroma.

Prune lavenders immediately after flowering, cutting back to just below the flower stems. If you cut back into bare wood they rarely rejuvenate. It is best to replace old, woody lavenders, rather than to attempt rejuvenation.

Lavenders are often planted in front of herbaceous perennials. Although they look good with herbaceous geraniums, achilleas, nepeta, and other perennials, they dislike being smothered. Leave enough space and support any lax perennial plants. Lavenders are frequently planted alongside roses, which they associate well with. However, lavenders dislike the rich, fertile soil that roses need, so allow enough space between them and keep manure away from the lavenders.

The silver leaves and deep blue flowers of lavender soften the base of a large stone pot in a dry, sunny position.

Lavandula angustifolia 'Hidcote'

Lavandula angustifolia 'Imperial Gem'

Lavandula stoechas subsp. sampaioana 'Purple Emperor'

Lavandula pedunculata subsp. pedunculata

Lavandula angustifolia **'Hidcote'**

60CM × 60CM (2 FT. × 2 FT.)

The finest lavender. It has narrow, silver-green leaves and dense spikes of violet-blue flowers in summer. The fragrant blooms are attractive to bees and butterflies and retain their colour and fragrance when cut and dried. This lavender is compact and long lived in the right growing conditions; it is best for a low hedge and excellent for softening pathways and paving. Plant anywhere—in front of roses, in mixed borders, in pots and cloud beds. The plant is so versatile it is impossible to suggest the perfect planting partner.

Lavandula angustifolia **'Imperial Gem'**

60CM × 60CM (2 FT. × 2 FT.)

Similar in appearance to 'Hidcote', but with more silver foliage and deep purple-blue flowers in summer. 'Imperial Gem' is another hardy shrub with a compact habit. The flowers are also excellent for cutting and drying, as they retain their colour and fragrance. To keep them at their best, cut in peak condition and hang upside-down in bunches in a warm, airy room.

Lavandula pedunculata **subsp.** *pedunculata*

60CM × 60CM (2 FT. × 2 FT.)

A variety of French lavender with soft grey-green foliage, upright stems, and compact flower spikes winged with long petals, hence the name butterfly lavender. It is less hardy than *Lavandula angustifolia* and needs a warm, sunny, sheltered position. It is a good choice for pots that you can shelter from winter wet. Lovely planted with silver-foliage shrubs, and a good choice for narrow beds and borders.

Lavandula stoechas **subsp.** *sampaioana* **'Purple Emperor'**

60CM × 45CM (2 FT. × 18 IN.)

A superb form of Spanish lavender with soft green, aromatic leaves carried on upright stems. It needs a warm, sunny, sheltered spot and may require winter protection. The flower stalks rise above the foliage, carrying compact flower heads of soft red-purple. These are crowned with upright purple wings and appear from early summer. A lovely lavender for a pot alongside a short, dark phormium such as *Phormium* Back in Black.

Leucothoe Lovita

Leucothoe keiskei 'Royal Ruby'

Leptospermum scoparium 'Red Damask'

Leycesteria formosa Golden Lanterns

Leptospermum

Leptospermums grown in gardens are usually varieties of *Leptospermum scoparium*, common manuka or tea tree. These are tender shrubs with many fine, dark stems and tiny dark green, narrow leaves. In some mild coastal gardens they can make quite tall, airy shrubs, but in most situations they need a sunny, sheltered position and possibly winter protection. They require well-drained neutral to acid soil and can be grown in pots of lime-free, loam-based compost.

Prune only after flowering, when the plants are young, to promote bushy, well-branched plants.

Leptospermum scoparium 'Red Damask'
1.2M × 90CM (4 FT. × 3 FT.)

A compact variety with very dark stems and dark, red-tinted foliage. The large double flowers crowd the stems in early summer, creating an extravagant, velvety effect. Spectacular planted alongside a bright blue ceanothus or any shrub with silver foliage.

Leucothoe

Leucothoes are attractive, mostly low-growing, evergreen shrubs that need shade and acid soil to succeed. However, the compact forms are ideal in containers of lime-free, loam-based compost. In the open ground they make excellent groundcover in humus-rich, moist soil under trees. They provide year-round interest with their glossy green foliage that turns red in winter. They produce small, insignificant flowers; their main feature is their wonderful foliage. They require no pruning and have a compact, suckering habit similar to sarcococca.

Leucothoe keiskei 'Royal Ruby'
45CM × 60CM (18 IN. × 2 FT.)

A lovely leucothoe with arching shoots and elegant, long, pointed leaves of deep green turning ruby red in winter. Plant it in a pot alongside purple heucheras and *Helleborus niger*.

Leucothoe Lovita
45CM × 45CM (18 IN. × 18 IN.)

A compact shrub with flexible stems and neat, shiny, dark green leaves that turn deep purple-red in winter, especially toward the tips of the shoots. Grow it in a pot alongside *Skimmia japonica* 'Rubella' and purple ajugas.

Leycesteria

Fast-growing, hollow-stemmed shrubs that thrive in semi-shade and grow on any soils, including damp sites. The species *Leycesteria formosa* is naturalized in parts of Britain, but it is still a useful garden shrub for its green stems and hanging clusters of purple fruits surrounded by purple-red bracts. The ripe berries of late summer and fall are attractive to birds, especially pheasants, hence the common name pheasant berry.

Prune in winter, cutting out some of the old stems to the base and clearing side shoots from the young green stems. This practice will make the stems look good alongside red-barked dogwoods.

Leycesteria formosa Golden Lanterns
1.8M × 1.5M (6 FT. × 5 FT.)

A lovely form with bright green, upright, arching stems and soft golden leaves that become more lime yellow in shade. Starting in midsummer, pendant flower

Lonicera nitida 'Baggesen's Gold'

Ligustrum ovalifolium 'Aureum'

Lonicera nitida 'Maigrun'

clusters hang from the branches like lanterns. These consist of layers of deep red bracts that are a striking contrast to the golden leaves. Golden Lanterns is a striking planting partner for purple-foliage shrubs in a sunny position and is useful with green-and-gold variegated leaves in semi-shade.

Ligustrum

There are both evergreen and deciduous varieties of privet. All grow on a wide variety of soils, and they are generally tough, tolerant shrubs. Most produce characteristically fragrant flowers and poisonous black berries. The common privet was so widely grown as a hedging plant it may have earned privets a poor reputation as ornamental shrubs.

Prune evergreen varieties in spring, just before growth commences. You can trim and shape, but if you grow them for foliage, prune selectively to promote an open, loose habit.

Ligustrum ovalifolium 'Aureum'
2.4M × 1.8M (8 FT. × 6 FT.)

Golden privet, frequently used as a hedging plant, is often overlooked as a light evergreen that grows well on any soil in any situation. If left to grow naturally, it has an airy, open habit with upright stems and medium-size gold–and–soft-green variegated leaves. It works well alongside the bold leaves of phormium, fatsia, and yellow-variegated and green-leaved cornus. This plant may be regarded as invasive in parts of the United States.

Lonicera

Lonicera usually conjures images of climbing honeysuckles, but there are many shrubby varieties, both evergreen and deciduous, some of which are widely used in gardens and general landscape planting. These are hardy, easy to grow shrubs that tolerate all soils, shade, and atmospheric pollution.

Prune the evergreen varieties in spring, before growth commences. You can trim to shape or for hedging. Selective pruning of the longest shoots maintains an open, natural habit.

Lonicera nitida 'Baggesen's Gold'
1.5M × 1.5M (5 FT. × 5 FT.)

Arching stems with straight twigs carry tiny golden leaves that become greener as light levels fall in winter. The colour of the foliage is softer when grown in shade. If left to grow, it forms a light, spreading shrub that softens more solid evergreens. You can keep it much smaller with pruning, and it responds well to trimming as a hedge. Plant in shade with bold gold-and-green variegated evergreens such as aucuba, euonymus, and elaeagnus.

Lonicera nitida 'Maigrun'
75CM × 90CM (30 IN. × 3 FT.)

A low, horizontally branched shrub with fine, straight twigs carrying small, narrow, bright green leaves. It may not be the showiest shrub, but it is brilliant in shade and really useful under trees where other shrubs will not grow. Plant it with *Euonymus fortunei* 'Emerald Gaiety' for a cool, green-and-white, shade-loving planting solution.

Magnolia

Magnolias are some of the best-loved and most spectacular flowering shrubs and trees. Many reach giant proportions. Magnolias grow well on heavy, fertile soil, and the deciduous varieties love clay. Some dislike alkaline soils, but may succeed if there is good soil depth and the soil is well conditioned. They like good drainage and respond to feeding.

Deciduous magnolias flower in spring, so frost and wind can damage their exotic, delicate blossoms. The smaller-flowered varieties are more weather resistant. *Magnolia grandiflora*, which is evergreen, flowers in summer, but can take a few years to produce its waxy, lemon-scented blooms.

Prune deciduous magnolias after flowering, but only if absolutely necessary. To control size, carefully cut back selected branches right into the shrub, where the wound will go unnoticed. If you cut branches halfway, they produce ugly, straight twigs and rob the shrubs of their naturally elegant habit.

Prune evergreen magnolias in early spring, before growth commences. *Magnolia grandiflora* is often trained as a large wall shrub, so you may have to establish some strong support to enable young shoots to be tied in as they grow.

Magnolia 'Elizabeth'

The graceful branches of *Magnolia* ×*soulangeana* carry elegantly poised blooms that are a delight in the spring garden.

Magnolia stellata 'Water Lily'

Magnolia ×*soulangeana*

Magnolia ×*loebneri* 'Leonard Messel'

Magnolia grandiflora

Magnolia 'Susan'

Magnolia 'Elizabeth'
1.5M × 1.2M (5 FT. × 4 FT.)

An unusual magnolia with fresh green leaves and beautiful primrose yellow, fragrant flowers in midspring. It remains compact and upright as it matures, and is striking planted against a background of dark evergreens or underplanted with blue pulmonarias.

Magnolia grandiflora
3M × 1.8M (10 FT. × 6 FT.)

The evergreen magnolia is a magnificent foliage shrub with large, shining green leaves, often with russet velvet undersides. The summer flowers are large, waxy, creamy white, and deliciously lemon scented. I would plant this magnolia for its foliage. *Magnolia grandiflora* 'Victoria' is a very hardy variety with dark green leaves that are rich brown beneath. 'Gallissoniere' is also excellent and has a compact conical habit. Either makes a dramatic subject for a large pot in a sheltered, sunny spot; you will have to do some pruning to keep the shape compact.

Magnolia ×*loebneri* 'Leonard Messel'
2.4M × 1.2M (8 FT. × 4 FT.)

A strong-growing, upright shrub with slender branches that is easy to grow on any soil. The fragrant, narrow-petalled flowers are lilac-pink and emerge from silky buds in midspring. A good choice for a mixed border of other shrubs, roses, and perennials.

Magnolia ×*soulangeana*
3M × 1.8M (10 FT. × 6 FT.)

This is the most popular magnolia, and it will ultimately achieve larger and more spreading proportions than stated here. It is not usually recommended for chalk soils, but it seems to thrive wherever it is planted. The large, tulip-shaped flowers are blush-white, flushed purple-pink at the base of the petals. Grow it as a stand-alone specimen to show off its elegant habit and give it space to spread.

Magnolia stellata 'Water Lily'
1.5M × 1.2M (5 FT. × 4 FT.)

The best magnolia for smaller gardens. A slow-growing shrub with spreading, layered branches and small medium green leaves. The brilliant white starry flowers open from early spring. Silky grey buds adorn the branches and catch the light throughout winter. Underplant with bright blue muscari and blue-flowering *Vinca minor*.

Magnolia 'Susan'
1.8M × 1.2M (6 FT. × 4 FT.)

Upright sweeping branches and neat foliage make this shrub easy to accommodate in the average garden. The flowers are not the largest and they have few petals, but their colour is vibrant and eye catching. The slender buds are brilliant red-purple, purple-pink on the inside of the petals, and are elegantly poised on the branches. Grow it alongside an orange-flowered berberis for a risky but striking combination.

Mahonia japonica

Melianthus major

Lonicera pileata 'Lemon Beauty'

Mahonia ×media 'Winter Sun'

Lonicera pileata 'Lemon Beauty'
75CM × 75CM (30 IN. × 30 IN.)

A low evergreen shrub with horizontal branches and small, narrow, dark green leaves edged with pale yellow. It is not the most robust plant, and it grows best in semi-shade in a fairly sheltered situation.

Mahonia

Mahonias are bold evergreen shrubs that grow well on any soil in sun or shade. They have architectural foliage and winter flowers. The spiny leaves are carried in whorls on upright stems, the dainty flowers in sprays at the tips of the branches. There are low-growing groundcover types, but I have only included the larger shrubby mahonias here. This plant may be regarded as invasive in parts of the United States.

Prune in spring after flowering, cutting back to just above any whorl of leaves; although no growth buds are visible, the plants soon produce plentiful new shoots. Hard pruning will rejuvenate old, leggy plants.

Mahonia japonica
1.5M × 1.2M (5 FT. × 4 FT.)

Ascending branches carry medium to dark green leaves that will often colour in fall and winter in an open, sunny position and on poor soil. The pale yellow flowers are carried in lax sprays in late winter; they are wonderfully fragrant with the perfume of lily-of-the-valley. An excellent shrub for shade with *Lonicera nitida* 'Baggesen's Gold'.

Mahonia ×*media* 'Winter Sun'
1.8M × 1.2M (6 FT. × 4 FT.)

Upright stems carry spiny dark green leaves. The stems are topped with clusters of upright spikes of fragrant yellow flowers in early winter. One of the most scented of the early flowering mahonias. Plant in a shady corner with *Aucuba japonica* 'Angelon'.

Melianthus

Melianthus are tender evergreen shrubs that are often herbaceous in cold areas. They are grown for their bold architectural foliage, but just a few degrees of frost can kill leaves and stems. They grow on most well-drained soils and are at their best in a warm, sunny position. If pruning is necessary, cut back to just a few centimetres above the ground in early spring.

Melianthus major
1.8M × 1.5M (6 FT. × 5 FT.)

Honey flower is a stunning architectural shrub with large blue-green leaves and deeply pleated and toothed leaflets that give an exotic effect. Curious spikes of red-brown flowers appear at the tips of the stems in a good summer. Stunning with deep red and purple dahlias, cannas, and tropical bedding subjects.

Myrtus

Most of the evergreen shrubs previously classified as myrtles have now been reclassified; the common myrtle and its varieties remain as *Myrtus*. They are not the hardiest shrubs, but they are excellent for sunny, sheltered situations and milder coastal gardens. Do any pruning in spring to remove dead and damaged wood and control shape.

Myrtus communis

Nandina domestica 'Fire Power'

Nandina domestica

Osmanthus ×burkwoodii

Myrtus communis
1.5M × 1.2M (5 FT. × 4 FT.)

A beautiful, aromatic, evergreen shrub with shining bright green leaves on tan-coloured stems. The single white flowers filled with fine cream stamens are produced in late summer, and these are followed by blue-black berries. This is a lovely shrub with a long history in gardens and an important place in folklore. Beautiful planted against a sheltered, sunny wall with ceratostigma, hardy plumbago.

Nandina

Nandinas are evergreen shrubs with large, frond-like leaves and small leaflets; a contrast to heavier, broad-leaved evergreens. They resemble bamboo in their character and movement (hence the common name heavenly bamboo or sacred bamboo), but are curious relations of berberis. When planted in an open position their foliage colours during fall and winter. They grow on any well-drained soil but dislike open, exposed situations that can cause the leaves to fall. Nandinas require no pruning apart from removing damaged or diseased foliage.

Nandina domestica
1.2M × 75CM (4 FT. × 30 IN.)

Heavenly or sacred bamboo has tall, upright stems carrying fine, fern-like leaves with pointed, lustrous leaflets that colour rich shades of orange and red in fall and winter. The leaves have the appearance of delicate side branches on cane-like stems. The tips of the stems carry tiny white flowers in large open sprays in summer; these sometimes develop into small, round, bright red fruits. A lovely shrub for Japanese schemes surrounded by stones, moss, and low groundcover.

Nandina domestica 'Fire Power'
60CM × 45CM (2 FT. × 18 IN.)

A dwarf compact nandina with broader leaflets carried loosely on fine leaf stalks. The leaflets, which pucker and curl, are olive green through summer and make a lovely rustling sound when stirred by the wind. The foliage colours vibrantly in winter. An excellent shrub for a narrow border with ferns, vincas, and ajugas.

Osmanthus

Osmanthus, often mistaken for hollies, are wonderful evergreen shrubs, many of which are ideal in smaller gardens for year-round foliage interest. Some have the bonus of fragrant flowers. They grow on most well-drained soils in sun or light shade.

Osmanthus ×burkwoodii
1.8M × 1.2M (6 FT. × 4 FT.)

Upright at first, then becoming bushy in habit, Burkwood osmanthus is an excellent structure shrub with small, dark green, leathery leaves. It is very hardy and responds well to pruning, and you can use it as a hedge. In spring the stems are smothered with small, white, tubular, wonderfully fragrant flowers. An excellent shrub for the back of a border or alongside the light, airy, green-and-white foliage of *Cornus alternifolia* 'Argentea'.

Osmanthus heterophyllus 'Variegatus'

Osmanthus heterophyllus 'Goshiki'

Osmanthus delavayi

Paulownia tomentosa

Osmanthus delavayi
1.2M × 1.2M (4 FT. × 4 FT.)

Delavay osmanthus is one of the best spring-flowering shrubs. The stiff arching shoots carry small, very dark green leaves that are well spaced on the branches. Pointed buds open to tubular white flowers that are deliciously scented and will perfume the whole garden, both on a warm spring day and a cool evening. Lovely underplanted with the bright blue flowers and green-and-white leaves of *Vinca minor* 'Ralph Shugert'.

Osmanthus heterophyllus 'Goshiki'
90CM × 75CM (3 FT. × 30 IN.)

A very slow-growing osmanthus, sometimes called holly tea olive or holly osmanthus, with small, holly-like leaves of dark green mottled and suffused with honey yellow. The new foliage is bronze and superb against the mature leaves. 'Goshiki' is a solid choice for a pot or a small garden and a good shrub alongside *Phormium* 'Alison Blackman' or *Cordyline australis* 'Torbay Dazzler'.

Osmanthus heterophyllus 'Variegatus'
1.2M × 75CM (4 FT. × 30 IN.)

Rather looser in habit than 'Goshiki', this osmanthus has small, dark green, holly-like leaves with broad, creamy white margins. The whole effect is light and bright, and the shrub can grow much taller with age if you allow it. Good in a shady spot underplanted with *Sarcococca confusa*.

Paulownia

Paulonias are normally grown as trees, like catalpas, and you can hard prune in winter to restrict their size and promote large leaves. This practice will sacrifice any flowers, but it results in magnificent foliage. Paulownias will grow on most soils in sun or partial shade.

Paulownia tomentosa
3M × 90CM (10 FT. × 3 FT.)

Royal paulownia has magnificent large, green, slightly hairy leaves that can be up to 45cm (18 in.) across if you cut back the woody stems to 30cm (1 ft.) above ground in winter. This produces an exotic-looking plant that is a striking addition to any dramatic or tropical scheme. Grow it with cannas and colourful dahlias, or in the corner of a contemporary town garden. This plant may be regarded as invasive in parts of the United States.

Perovskia

Perovskias are aromatic shrubs with finely cut leaves and blue flowers late in summer and fall. They are useful in dry, sunny situations and mix well with other silver-foliage shrubs and lavenders. Prune in late winter, cutting right back to where new shoots are visible toward the base of the plants.

Philadelphus maculatus 'Sweet Clare'

Perovskia 'Blue Spire'

Philadelphus 'Virginal'

Philadelphus 'Belle Etoile'

Perovskia 'Blue Spire'
75CM × 60CM (30 IN. × 2 FT.)

A light, airy plant, also known as Russian sage, with fine silver stems, silver-and-green toothed leaves, and branched spikes of lilac-blue flowers in late summer. The stems sweep upward gracefully and remain as silvery skeletons in the garden through winter. A wonderful see-through subject; grow it at the front of a border and look through it to the planting beyond. Superb planted with grasses and the fine stems and delicate purple flowers of *Verbena bonariensis*.

Philadelphus

No garden should be without a mock orange for the ravishing summer fragrance of its flowers. These deciduous shrubs vary in stature and may not have other seasons of interest, but they are easy to grow on most soils and thrive in alkaline and dry conditions. Philadelphus need an open, sunny position to flower well. Prune after flowering, cutting back some of the flowered stems to where new shoots are developing low down in the shrub.

Philadelphus 'Belle Etoile'
1.8M × 1.2M (6 FT. × 4 FT.)

A beautiful philadelphus with large single blooms of creamy white, stained maroon at the base of the petals. Golden stamens fill the centre of every flower. The fragrance is strong, sweet, and reminiscent of orange blossom. 'Belle Etoile' is one of the best varieties of philadelphus to grow, as it does not get too large. Plant it with a purple cotinus, where its maroon-eyed blooms will be shown to advantage.

Philadelphus maculatus 'Sweet Clare'
1.2M × 1.2M (4 FT. × 4 FT.)

This is the loveliest philadelphus. Very fine arching stems carry tiny grey-green leaves to form a light mound of frothy foliage. Round grey flower buds open all along the stems in early summer to pendant, open, single white flowers, faintly stained maroon at the heart. The fragrance is strong, sweet, and delicious, and will fill the whole garden. This variety needs no regular pruning. Plant against the silver leaves of Elaeagnus 'Quicksilver' if you have space, or with white-flowered shrub roses.

Philadelphus 'Virginal'
3M × 1.8M (10 FT. × 6 FT.)

A large philadelphus with strong, upright stems and broad green leaves. The double white, sweetly scented flowers are carried in clusters in early summer. A good choice for a large garden with the late-flowering *Ceanothus thyrsiflorus* 'Skylark'.

Phormium

New Zealand flax are useful architectural plants that provide spiky form and texture in a planting scheme. If you choose well, they will sit happily with other shrubs and herbaceous perennials. Phormiums grow in any well-drained, fertile soil, but they dislike waterlogged conditions and tolerate drought once established. They are often used in patio containers, and although they grow in sun or semi-shade, their colour is better in full sun. There are a great many varieties that vary in habit, colour, and size. The brightly coloured phormiums are usually smaller than the plain green or purple-leaved varieties. Although reasonably hardy, severe weather can affect or even kill phormiums. The highly coloured varieties with pink and orange leaves are the least hardy.

Phormiums make excellent plants for contemporary schemes and gravel gardens, and they thrive in coastal gardens because they tolerate salty air.

In good summers most varieties produce dramatic flower spikes on mature plants. These rise above the foliage and look good through winter. Once established, phormiums do not respond well to being moved. The only way to reduce their size is to cut off some of the leaves at the base.

Phormium 'Alison Blackman'

Phormium cookianum subsp. *hookeri* 'Cream Delight'

Phormium Back in Black

Phormium 'Alison Blackman'
90CM × 60CM (3 FT. × 2 FT.)
A superb phormium with olive green, bronze, and cream-striped broad, upright leaves. Hardy 'Alison Blackman' is ideal for pots and containers and a good mixer with other shrubs. It makes a striking combination when planted with the light, airy foliage of *Nandina domestica*.

Phormium Back in Black
60CM × 45CM (2 FT. × 18 IN.)
A very small phormium with purple-black narrow leaves that are upright, then arch at the tips. The backs of the leaves have a silky appearance and give a reflective, two-tone effect in sunlight. Good with silver-foliage subjects and a wonderful contrast to the very white variegated *Pittosporum tenuifolium* 'Irene Patterson'.

Phormium cookianum subsp. *hookeri* 'Cream Delight'
90CM × 90CM (3 FT. × 3 FT.)
Smaller in stature and lighter in colour than 'Yellow Wave', 'Cream Delight' has a more upright habit but gracefully arching leaves. The foliage is cream edged and striped with medium green. A good phormium for planting in gravel with lavenders and *Santolina rosmarinifolia* 'Primrose Gem'.

An extravagant planting of phormiums with euonymus and dwarf palms creates a dramatic sub-tropical effect in this coastal garden.

Phormium cookianum subsp. *hookeri* 'Tricolor'

Phormium 'Yellow Wave'

Phormium 'Jester'

Phormium cookianum subsp. *hookeri* 'Tricolor'
1.2M × 1.5M (4 FT. × 5 FT.)

A strong phormium with broad, arching leaves. It is more upright when young and becomes spreading. The leaves are green striped with rich cream and edged with dark red. This is a good phormium for a focal point in planting and to use alongside a bold contemporary sculpture or on the corner of a building.

Phormium 'Jester'
90CM × 90CM (3 FT. × 3 FT.)

A colourful small phormium with slender, arching leaves of deep salmon pink edged with olive green. It is best in a sunny, sheltered position or a pot close to the house.

Phormium 'Yellow Wave'
1.2M × 1.5M (4 FT. × 5 FT.)

Probably the most widely planted phormium, with broad, arching leaves of soft yellow striped with green. It has a spreading habit, so give it plenty of room. A good phormium for semi-shade to lighten dark evergreens; excellent planted alongside the gold-spotted foliage of aucubas or the dark green foliage and yellow flowers of mahonias.

Photinia ×fraseri 'Little Red Robin'

Photinia ×fraseri 'Red Robin'

Photinia ×fraseri Pink Marble

Phlomis italica

Phlomis

Shrubby phlomis thrive in open, sunny situations on dry or well-drained soil. Naturally evergreen and often from Mediterranean climates, many are not very hardy and prefer warm, sheltered gardens. They mix well with cistus, silver-foliage shrubs, helianthemums, and lavenders. The hairy, felty leaves make them undesirable to deer and rabbits, which is an advantage for some gardeners. Cut back in early spring if necessary.

Phlomis italica
75CM × 75CM (30 IN. × 30 IN.)
Balearic Island sage is a suckering shrub with upright, very felty stems carrying silver felted leaves. Mauve-pink flowers appear in the leaf axils and at the tips of the shoots in summer. A very pretty planting partner for *Salvia officinalis* 'Purpurascens'.

Photinia

The evergreen varieties of photinias are mainly grown in gardens. Their main attraction is their bright red or bronze new growth, which you can stimulate with regular trimming. The widely planted *Photinia ×fraseri* varieties, redtip photinias, are some of the best-known evergreen shrubs, and are used for screening, hedging, trimming, and training. They are widely planted in amenity landscape situations in many areas of the world. Photinias are tolerant shrubs that grow on most soils. They respond well to pruning in spring, just before growth commences, and again in late summer to stimulate more new growth before winter. If you

selectively prune a branch to where leaf nodes are close together, it produces a number of shoots from that point. If cut to just above a widely spaced leaf node, only one shoot appears. Keep this in mind when you are pruning to create a bushy plant.

Photinia ×fraseri 'Little Red Robin'
90CM × 90CM (3 FT. × 3 FT.)
A small photinia with very dark green leaves and deep red young growth that holds its colour. The lax branches respond to regular pruning to form a bushy shrub that looks good throughout the year. Grow it in a pot alongside *Berberis thunbergii* 'Admiration'.

Photinia ×fraseri Pink Marble
1.2M × 90CM (4 FT. × 3 FT.)
Variegated leaves of deep green, soft green, and creamy white with bright salmon red new shoots make this a colourful foliage shrub. The growth tends to be lax and sprawling, so it is essential to prune regularly from an early age to encourage branching. Pink Marble is not always the best shrub in the open ground, but it works in a pot on a sunny or partly shaded patio. In the open ground grow it with *Potentilla fruticosa* 'Pink Beauty'.

Photinia ×fraseri 'Red Robin'
3M × 1.8M (10 FT. × 6 FT.)
The most popular photinia has shiny dark green leaves and bright red new growth. It is vigorous and upright in habit and needs control. Even if it is too frequently used in the wrong situations, it is worth planting as a background screening shrub and is striking when trained as a standard.

Physocarpus opulifolius 'Diable d'Or'

Pieris japonica 'Carnaval'

Physocarpus opulifolius 'Diablo'

Physocarpus

Physocarpus are deciduous foliage shrubs that are easy to grow and thrive on any moist or well-drained soil. The upright stems become more arching and spreading as they mature. They quickly make an impact in a planting scheme and are good mixers with other deciduous and evergreen shrubs, roses, and perennials. Prune physocarpus in winter, removing some of the older, darker stems to allow space for the lighter, newer stems to develop.

Physocarpus opulifolius 'Diable d'Or'
1.5M × 1.5M (5 FT. × 5 FT.)
Arching stems carry deep bronze foliage that is lighter and copper-orange at the tips of the shoots. The pinkish flower clusters develop to ruby-like fruit clusters in late summer. This stunning foliage shrub, common nine bark, is wonderful partnered with *Rosa* Lady Emma Hamilton or another orange or salmon pink shrub rose.

Physocarpus opulifolius 'Diablo'
1.8M × 1.2M (6 FT. × 4 FT.)
Upright tan-coloured stems carry dark purple-black leaves. Clusters of white and pink-tinted flowers appear in early summer, and these mature to clusters of dark, rather inconspicuous fruits. The matte dark foliage makes a dramatic, if rather heavy, backdrop for lighter shrubs and perennials; this is a wonderful shrub to contrast with *Elaeagnus* 'Quicksilver' or *Pittosporum* 'Garnettii'.

Pieris

Varieties of pieris, lily-of-the-valley bush, are highly ornamental, evergreen flowering shrubs. Perhaps their most striking feature is new growth, which can be any shade from copper-pink to bright red; this appears in spring and intermittently at other times of the year. It is susceptible to frost damage, so a sheltered spot is desirable. Most pieris produce lovely sprays of lily-of-the-valley flowers in early spring.

Pieris are ericaceous plants and need acid soil. However, they are ideal grown in pots containing lime-free, loam-based compost. In pots and in the open ground they are at their best in semi-shade but will succeed in quite shady situations. Although no pruning is required, you can do so after flowering to control shape and size.

Pieris japonica 'Carnaval'
90CM × 75CM (3 FT. × 30 IN.)
A small, compact shrub with olive green and cream foliage heavily flushed with copper-pink in winter. The new growth is bright red and the small sprays of flowers are white. This colourful subject is good in a pot for a bright splash in a shady corner.

Pinus mugo 'Wintergold'

Pieris japonica 'Katsura'

Pieris japonica 'Little Heath'

Pittosporum tenuifolium

Pieris japonica 'Katsura'
90CM × 75CM (3 FT. × 30 IN.)

Shining olive green leaves make the perfect background for the stunning mahogany-red new growth. Heavy sprays of deep red–stained flowers hang on the tips of the shoots in early spring. A beautiful pieris to grow with deep pink winter-flowering ericas.

Pieris japonica 'Little Heath'
75CM × 75CM (30 IN. × 30 IN.)

A compact pieris with small soft green leaves edged with creamy white; the overall effect is light and pretty. The new growth is copper coloured, and a few small white flowers emerge from pink buds in spring. Although it is shy to flower, it is one of the best foliage shrubs for a pot; grow it alongside *Astelia nervosa* 'Westland'.

Pinus

Most pines make large evergreen trees with drought- and cold-resistant foliage and aromatic, resinous sap. There are shrubby forms that have upright, sweeping branches. They are attractive and architectural in character and a pleasing contrast to broad-leaved evergreen and deciduous shrubs. They need an open, sunny position and good drainage to thrive, and they prefer acid soil. No pruning is required.

Pinus mugo 'Wintergold'
1.5M × 1.5M (5 FT. × 5 FT.)

Mountain pine is small and bushy, with spreading then upright branches and foliage that is olive green through summer, turning rich gold in winter. It is a lovely choice with heathers grown for their winter foliage, low-growing evergreens, or as a specimen among rocks or gravel.

Pittosporum

Although many pittosporums produce small, fragrant flowers, gardeners mainly grow them for their evergreen foliage. They are easy to grow on most well-drained soils, in sun or semi-shade, but they do not like cold conditions and severe frost can kill them. They grow well near the sea and in sheltered town gardens.

Pittosporums generally respond well to pruning to control size and shape, and you can trim the small-leaved varieties to create more regular shapes or even use them for hedging. Do this in spring, before new growth commences.

Pittosporum tenuifolium
3M × 1.5M (10 FT. × 5 FT.)

A large shrub with wavy-edged, shining, medium green leaves on dark stems. It grows quickly to form a bushy column that, although dense, is never heavy in the garden. When mature, you can remove the lower branches to make a small, standard tree.

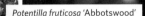

Pittosporum tobira

Pittosporum tobira 'Nanum'

Pittosporum tobira 'Variegatum'

Potentilla fruticosa 'Abbotswood'

Pittosporum tobira
1.5M × 1.2M (5 FT. × 4 FT.)

Japanese pittosporum is a versatile shrub that is widely grown in the Mediterranean region, often for hedging. Leathery, round-tipped leaves are carried in whorls on upright stems. Orange blossom–scented cream flowers appear in clusters at the tips of the shoots in summer. This is a surprisingly hardy pittosporum, ideal for town and coastal gardens. It is excellent in pots and containers, tolerates dry conditions, and does surprisingly well in shade. Plant it with *Euonymus fortunei* 'Silver Queen'.

Pittosporum tobira 'Nanum'
75CM × 75CM (30 IN. × 30 IN.)

A compact form of *Pittosporum tobira* that grows to form a dense, regular mound of leathery green foliage. 'Nanum' is striking when planted in groups as part of a large, contemporary scheme, and also good in pots. Grow it in a cloud bed with trimmed santolina and *Buxus sempervirens*.

Pittosporum tobira 'Variegatum'
1.2M × 90CM (4 FT. × 3 FT.)

Usually a little smaller than *Pittosporum tobira*, the variegated form has soft grey-green leaves edged with creamy white. It is also good in pots for courtyard and balcony, and works well planted alongside *Hebe pinguifolia* 'Sutherlandii'.

Potentilla

The shrubby potentillas are some of the hardiest, easiest to grow deciduous shrubs, as they succeed on any well-drained soil and are very tolerant of dry conditions. They thrive in sun or partial shade and produce single buttercup-like flowers from early summer through to late fall. Few other flowering shrubs have such a long season.

Most varieties form a twiggy rounded shrub that is not beautiful when the leaves fall in the winter. However, pruning is simple: a light clip over with shears in late winter keeps the shrubs in shape and promotes a bushy habit.

Potentillas offer a range of colours, including strong yellows. The softer shades are more appealing and more versatile in planting schemes.

Potentilla fruticosa 'Abbotswood'
60CM × 60CM (2 FT. × 2 FT.)

Shrubby cinquefoil is a small shrub with spreading branches, dark green leaves, and plenty of white flowers with golden stamens. It mixes well with silver-foliage shrubs and lavenders.

Pittosporum tenuifolium
VARIETIES WITH COLOURFUL FOLIAGE

Pittosporum tenuifolium varieties are some of the most attractive and useful evergreen shrubs. Fine, well-branched stems and small, shining leaves result in shrubs with a neat, light habit. All variegated and coloured-foliage forms add year-round interest to any planting scheme in an open, sunny position. You can successfully grow them in large pots. They produce small, brown, sweetly scented flowers in late spring, and although their fragrance is not a showy feature, it is a wonderful and often delightful surprise.

Pittosporums are reasonably hardy but need some shelter. In cold, wet conditions they have a habit of dropping their leaves, although some leaf drop is normal in early spring before they produce a new flush of growth. As they grow, the narrow habit of larger varieties makes them susceptible to wind rock, and you may have to stake on more exposed sites.

You can prune *Pittosporum tenuifolium* varieties to control size, but do not waste the cut foliage, which is wonderful for floral decoration. No flower arranger's garden should be without pittosporum for cutting at any time of the year.

The variegated forms of *Pittosporum tenuifolium* are some of the few shrubs that are light enough in colour and habit to grow with shrub roses. If you plant in the foreground, they also successfully lift heavy evergreen screening shrubs. The light foliage helps to create an illusion of space in a small garden, and their narrow upright habit supports this.

The light, evergreen foliage
of *Pittosporum tenuifolium*
'Elizabeth' adds contrast amidst
the rich red-purple leaves
of cotinus and berberis.

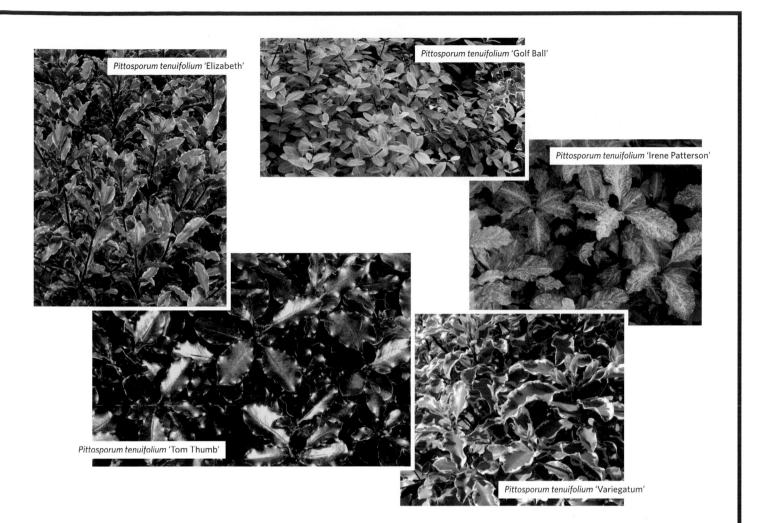

Pittosporum tenuifolium 'Elizabeth'

Pittosporum tenuifolium 'Golf Ball'

Pittosporum tenuifolium 'Irene Patterson'

Pittosporum tenuifolium 'Tom Thumb'

Pittosporum tenuifolium 'Variegatum'

Pittosporum tenuifolium 'Elizabeth'

1.8M × 1.2M (6 FT. × 4 FT.)

A lovely pittosporum with grey-green leaves, edged with white and flushed pink, especially in winter. It has a light, narrow, upright habit, but is more compact than the widely planted *Pittosporum* 'Garnettii'. Excellent for cutting with pink winter heathers, and a delightful planting partner for pink shrub roses.

Pittosporum tenuifolium 'Golf Ball'

90CM × 90CM (3 FT. × 3 FT.)

A low, mound-forming shrub with small, flat green leaves on dark stems. Although the shrub is dense in habit, the outer shoots retain a lightness that makes the effect less solid. An excellent choice for a cloud bed with small-leaved hebes.

Pittosporum tenuifolium 'Irene Patterson'

1.5M × 90CM (5 FT. × 3 FT.)

The lightest and brightest of variegated shrubs, with pale green leaves heavily suffused with creamy white. The new growth is almost pure white, and the overall effect is cool but striking. You can plant this very slow-growing variety in a small, mixed border; it is a good planting partner for *Potentilla fruticosa* 'Abbotswood'.

Pittosporum tenuifolium 'Tom Thumb'

90CM × 75CM (3 FT. × 30 IN.)

One of the few purple-foliage evergreens, 'Tom Thumb' is a striking garden plant in any season. In winter the foliage becomes intense purple-black and the waved leaves shine in the low light. In spring bright green new growth studs the dark shrub. A dramatic backdrop to the colourful winter stems of red-barked dogwoods.

Pittosporum tenuifolium 'Variegatum'

1.8M × 1.2M (6 FT. × 4 FT.)

A dense, bushy pittosporum that makes an excellent light-structure shrub. The leaves are waved, blue-green, and edged with cream. A good choice for a large pot, and a subtly coloured partner to rosemary and purple sage in a sunny border.

Prostanthera cuneata

Prunus incisa 'Kojo-no-mai'

Potentilla fruticosa 'Primrose Beauty'

Potentilla fruticosa 'Tangerine'

Potentilla fruticosa 'Primrose Beauty'
90CM × 90CM (3 FT. × 3 FT.)

This is my favorite potentilla: a bushy shrub with spreading branches, soft grey-green leaves, and pale, primrose yellow flowers. It is an excellent mixer with other shrubs and perennials, even those with pink flowers like *Spiraea japonica* 'Little Princess'.

Potentilla fruticosa 'Tangerine'
60CM × 60CM (2 FT. × 2 FT.)

A small, spreading shrub with medium green foliage and copper-orange flowers. The blooms tend to fade in sun and are a deeper colour in semi-shade. Underplant with a blue-flowered vinca, such as *Vinca minor* 'La Grave'.

Prostanthera

Prostantheras, known as mint bushes, are small shrubs with tiny, sweetly aromatic leaves. They are hardy only in milder areas and may need winter protection. In cold gardens it is best to grow them in pots moved under cover in winter. They like a warm, dry spot and are never at their best on very alkaline soil. You can prune after flowering, but this is rarely necessary.

Prostanthera cuneata
60CM × 60CM (2 FT. × 2 FT.)

The hardiest and most well-known mint bush. The stems are crowded with small crinkled and toothed dark green leaves, which give the plant an almost velvety appearance. Tiny white-and-purple flowers appear in late spring. Grow it in a pot on a sunny patio where you can stroke the foliage and enjoy its fragrance.

Prunus

Plants in the genus *Prunus* come in many forms, from productive and flowering cherries to laurels used for hedging and groundcover. They grow happily on most soils. The deciduous varieties like sun, and the evergreens grow in sun or shade.

Never prune deciduous cherries in winter, as this practice makes them susceptible to disease; cut back in summer, when in full leaf. Prune evergreen varieties in early spring, before growth commences.

Prunus incisa 'Kojo-no-mai'
90CM × 90CM (3 FT. × 3 FT.)

Fuji cherry has elegant, layered branches and zigzag twigs. Pink buds open to white flowers that hang in dainty bunches all along the branches in early spring. It has the added bonus of neat, small, serrated leaves that turn rich shades of orange in fall. It is ideal as a specimen in a rock garden, alongside a terrace, or—better still—in a pot. When grown in a container, it has a bonsai-like appearance and makes a dramatic and beautiful feature on the patio or near the house.

Rhododendron 'Colonel Coen'

Prunus lusitanica

Rhododendron 'Firelight'

Prunus lusitanica 'Myrtifolia'

Prunus lusitanica
3M × 1.8M (10 FT. × 6 FT.)

Portuguese laurel is a very handsome evergreen shrub with neat, dark green, shining leaves on red leaf stalks. Long sprays of fragrant white flowers appear in early summer. If left unpruned, it will develop into a dense, bushy, small tree, but it responds well to pruning and you can shape it as needed. This very hardy evergreen makes a wonderful structure shrub at the back of a border.

Prunus lusitanica 'Myrtifolia'
1.8M × 1.2M (6 FT. × 4 FT.)

This compact form is also slower growing. The narrow leaves are dark green with conspicuous red leaf stalks. It forms a dense, cone-shaped shrub, which you can shape as required. It freely produces white flowers in early summer. Grow it in pots instead of *Laurus nobilis*, as it is more attractive and less susceptible to winter damage.

Rhododendron

Rhododendrons are some of the most spectacular and colourful flowering shrubs. They include not only the large-flowering, hardy, hybrid rhododendrons, but also evergreen and deciduous azaleas, all of which are botanically rhododendrons.

All these plants require reasonably moist, acid soil and prefer sheltered situations in semi-shade. They grow well and look at their best under the light shade of trees, but many are ideal subjects for pots and containers if grown in lime-free, loam-based compost.

Rhododendrons and azaleas do not require regular pruning, but you can prune straggly plants after flowering to stimulate new, vigorous growth. If you do so, it is essential to water and feed to help the plants recover. The large-leaved, hardy hybrid rhododendrons benefit from dead-heading after flowering; carefully break off the seed heads to allow the new growth shoots to develop.

There are a great many varieties from which to choose. Here are just a small selection of my favorites.

Rhododendron 'Colonel Coen'
1.5M × 1.5M (5 FT. × 5 FT.)

An upright, hardy hybrid rhododendron with deep green, stiff, shiny foliage. The rounded heads of jewel-like deep purple flowers spotted with black are a spectacular sight in late spring. Plant against the lime green new leaves of *Cotinus coggygria* Golden Spirit.

Rhododendron 'Firelight'
1.2M × 1.5M (4 FT. × 5 FT.)

A hardy hybrid rhododendron with olive green foliage and an open, spreading habit. The late spring, hose-in-hose flowers are coral–salmon pink, deeper in bud and carried in loose clusters. The warm colour of the flower and its unusual shape make this a very appealing shrub. Grow it in a naturalistic setting, underplanted with bluebells.

Rhododendron
DECIDUOUS AND EVERGREEN AZALEAS

Deciduous azaleas are far more graceful in habit than the evergreen hybrid rhododendrons. Their tan-coloured branches make an open-framed shrub with well-spaced foliage. The spring flowers are elegantly held in loose, well-spaced clusters and are often wonderfully fragrant. Because of their habit deciduous azaleas mix easily with other shrubs and perennials. They also have the benefit of excellent fall leaf colour before the foliage drops to reveal an attractive branch silhouette. For this reason they make good shrubs for large containers in semi-shaded situations, particularly close to the house where their form creates foreground interest and provides the light height that makes any garden vista more interesting.

Deciduous azaleas offer a wide colour range, from strong, vibrant hues to soft, subtle tones. They are often recommended for the woodland garden, and because of their need for moist, acid soil they are underused in smaller gardens and are well worth considering.

Evergreen azaleas have a more compact habit and spreading branches as they mature. Their small leaves give them a lighter character than the evergreen hybrid rhododendrons, and they form a neat, low layer in the planting picture. They are particularly useful in pots and containers and ideal for small gardens. Sadly, they have been rather oversupplied and planted in recent years, so many designers ignore them. They do offer some fantastic, jewel-like colours; the deep red-and-purple "Venetian" colours are particularly valuable.

Rhododendron 'Arabesk'

Rhododendron 'Blue Danube'

Rhododendron 'Daviesii'

Rhododendron 'Arabesk'
60CM × 75CM (2 FT. × 30 IN.)
A very hardy evergreen Japanese azalea with spreading branches and deep green, glossy foliage. The large, open, funnel-shaped flowers are rich red and stunning against the dark leaves. Grow it in a glazed pot on a terrace or doorstep in semi-shade; it is lovely under a red-leaved Japanese maple.

Rhododendron 'Blue Danube'
60CM × 75CM (2 FT. × 30 IN.)
An evergreen azalea with spreading branches and emerald-green leaves. Large violet-blue flowers in late spring give the plant an exotic and striking appearance. Stunning with *Acer palmatum* 'Katsura', a Japanese maple with lime green, orange-flushed young foliage.

Rhododendron 'Daviesii'
1.2M × 90CM (4 FT. × 3 FT.)
One of the most beautiful deciduous azaleas, with large, delicate white flowers, each of which has a golden yellow flare. The fragrance is strong, sweet, and delicious. Lovely planted with the finely cut leaves of *Sambucus nigra* f. *porphyrophylla* 'Eva'.

Evergreen azaleas make excellent shrubs for pots. Here *Rhododendron* 'Arabesk' makes a colourful subject for a rustic ceramic container.

Rhododendron 'Fireball'

Rhododendron 'Irene Koster'

Rhododendron luteum

Rhododendron 'Fireball'
1.2M × 90CM (4 FT. × 3 FT.)
A very open shrub with copper-red young leaves and vibrant red-orange blooms. Each flower is very open, with slightly recurved petals and prominent stamens. Plant with bright blue ceanothus or *Iris sibirica*.

Rhododendron 'Irene Koster'
1.2M × 90CM (4 FT. × 3 FT.)
A very graceful deciduous azalea with slightly spreading branches. The delicate salmon pink blooms with small golden flares are wonderfully fragrant. Lovely under the young purple leaves of *Cercis canadensis* 'Forest Pansy'.

Rhododendron luteum
1.2M × 90CM (4 FT. × 3 FT.)
This is the deciduous azalea to grow for fragrance. The delicate golden yellow flowers have both the appearance and fragrance of honeysuckle. A plant in flower on a warm early summer evening is unmistakable. The fall colour is equally stunning. *Rhododendron luteum* can be rather slow to start to grow, but it is worth the wait.

Rhododendron 'Mrs. T. H. Lowinsky'

Rhododendron 'Horizon Monarch'

Rhododendron 'Nancy Evans'

Rhododendron 'Horizon Monarch'
1.5M × 1.8M (5 FT. × 6 FT.)

An excellent rhododendron that grows to form a large dome-shaped shrub with softly shining, deep green leaves that are olive on the reverse. These are rounded at the tips and carried in bold whorls on tan-coloured stems. The buds are orange as they open, unfurling into waved, creamy yellow blooms carried in large clusters. A lovely variety that mixes well in any colour scheme; plant it with the early rose-purple flowers of *Cercis chinensis* 'Avondale'.

Rhododendron 'Mrs. T. H. Lowinsky'
1.8M × 1.5M (6 FT. × 5 FT.)

A bold, vigorous, hardy hybrid rhododendron with large, flamboyant heads of soft lilac flowers, deeper in colour toward the edge of the petals. Each bloom is marked with a conspicuous copper flare. Plant it under *Betula nigra* or any other tree with copper-coloured bark.

Rhododendron 'Nancy Evans'
60CM × 75CM (2 FT. × 30 IN.)

A compact hybrid rhododendron with neat, dark green foliage, red-orange buds, and creamy, waxy, waved flowers. A superb rhododendron for a pot grouped with caramel-coloured heucheras and the cream-and-green foliage of *Buxus sempervirens* 'Elegantissima'.

Rhus

Rhus typhina, stag's horn sumach, is best known as a tree with felted stems, curious cone-like seed clusters, and wonderful fall colour. It is very easy to grow on any soil. It used to make frequent appearances in gardens, but it has now diminished in popularity because of its suckering habit.

Shrubs often have a spreading habit, but you can safely remove branches in winter to promote more upright growth.

Rhus typhina Tiger Eyes
1.5M × 90CM (5 FT. × 3 FT.)

A very slow-growing compact variety with golden yellow foliage and chestnut brown seed clusters. It has a striking, exotic appearance. In fall the foliage turns vivid orange and makes this one of the showiest plants in any garden. This is also a good shrub to give the effect of a small tree in a tiny garden, or to plant to rise out of a cloud of the feathery grass *Stipa tenuissima*.

Ribes

Flowering currants are survivors. Not only do they tolerate virtually any soil or growing conditions, but they also survive the passage of time. Like forsythia, they have graced gardens since early in the last century. They are mostly vigorous and upright in habit; the drooping flower clusters emerge at the same time the aromatic leaves uncurl in early spring. You can cut as the buds are swelling and use them for floral decoration. They flower most freely in sun or semi-shade.

Rhus typhina Tiger Eyes

Ribes 'White Icicle'

Ribes 'Koja'

Rosa ×alba 'Alba Semiplena'

This plant may be regarded as invasive in parts of the United States.

Prune after flowering, cutting back some of the stems that have flowered to encourage new shoots to grow from the base of the shrubs.

Ribes 'Koja'
1.5M × 1.2M (5 FT. × 4 FT.)
A reliable variety with large, drooping clusters of red flowers on upright branches. Position it against light variegated evergreens, such as *Pittosporum* 'Garnettii', or the early purple foliage of cotinus or physocarpus.

Ribes 'White Icicle'
1.5M × 1.2M (5 FT. × 4 FT.)
A wonderful white-flowering variety with large clusters of flowers on vigorous upright stems. It makes a fresh and pretty planting partner for the lime green *Euphorbia characias*. *Ribes* 'Elkington's White' is similar.

Rosa

Roses abound in gardens throughout the world, and gardeners love them for the shape, colour, texture, and fragrance of their flowers. Many of us focus on rose blooms and their historical cultivation, and we forget that the rose is a flowering shrub. Most roses combine well with other shrubs and contributing to the planting picture through summer and fall. However, some are best planted with their own kind in designated beds, and others are best enjoyed as cut flowers.

Roses are easy to grow, but not all are easy to grow well. Most like a heavy, fertile soil and adequate moisture in the growing season. However, some roses are more tolerant of poor soils and dry, well-drained conditions.

Roses are notorious for being prone to fungal diseases, so it is important to select disease-resistant varieties. Regular feeding with a rose fertilizer in early spring and in midsummer helps prevent disease by encouraging strong growth.

Prune shrub roses in midwinter by cutting back by up to one-third to encourage bushy, branched growth and more flowers.

Rosa ×alba 'Alba Semiplena'
1.8M × 1.5M (6 FT. × 5 FT.)
White rose of York is loose shrub with arching branches and grey-green healthy foliage. The large, open, semi-double flowers appear in early summer; they are wonderfully fragrant and have delicate white petals and golden yellow stamens. The leaves and flowers of the rose reflect the foliage colours of evergreen *Pittosporum tenuifolium* 'Variegatum', creating a pleasing combination that changes with the seasons.

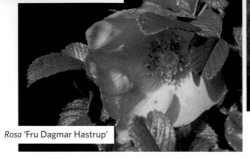

Rosa 'Cornelia'

Rosa Gertrude Jekyll

Rosa 'Fru Dagmar Hastrup'

Rosa 'Ballerina'

Rosa 'Ballerina'
1.2M × 1.2M (4 FT. × 4 FT.)

A dainty, modern shrub rose that produces sprays of delightful pink single flowers that are white toward the centre of each bloom. It flowers freely and profusely throughout summer and into fall. A delightful rose with blue geraniums, campanulas, and cottage-garden flowers.

Rosa 'Cornelia'
1.5M × 1.5M (5 FT. × 5 FT.)

This hybrid musk rose makes a loose shrub with dark green foliage and sprays of copper-pink double flowers, warmer in colour toward the heart of every flower. The fragrance is strong and delicious, and the flowers appear in flushes throughout summer and early fall. A superb planting partner for wine-red foliage shrubs or dark blue lavender.

Rosa 'Fru Dagmar Hastrup'
1.5M × 1.5M (5 FT. × 5 FT.)

An excellent rugosa rose with disease-free bright green foliage and large single pale pink blooms with golden stamens. The slightly fragrant flowers, produced in flushes through summer, are followed by large tomato red hips in fall. A good choice for light, sandy soils, and beautiful with silver-foliage shrubs such as *Brachyglottis* (Dunedin Group) 'Sunshine'.

Rosa Gertrude Jekyll
1.2M × 90CM (4 FT. × 3 FT.)

One of the best English roses, with strong, upright, quite thorny stems and healthy foliage. The large, rich pink blooms are deliciously fragrant and wonderful for cutting. Grow it with perovskia and purple sage.

Rosa glauca Pourr
1.2M × 90CM (4 FT. × 3 FT.)

This shrub, known as redleaf rose, has tall, arching, reddish arching stems that carry striking blue-grey, elegantly pointed leaves. Small cerise-pink flowers are followed by dark red hips. It is grown for the foliage rather than the flowers. Its light, airy habit means it fits into any planting scheme, and it is particularly stunning in a sunny border with red-orange *Crocosmia* 'Lucifer'.

Rosa Lady Emma Hamilton
1.2M × 90CM (4 FT. × 3 FT.)

An English rose with upright, arching stems and healthy dark, bronze-green foliage flushed red at the tips of the shoots. The buds are the colour of blood oranges, opening to glorious, globe-shaped flowers of warm apricot-orange. Their fragrance is deliciously fruity—strong, fresh, and appealing. A wonderful choice alongside the copper-bronze foliage of *Physocarpus opulifolius* 'Diable d'Or'.

Rosa 'Roseraie de l'Hay'

Rosa Lady Emma Hamilton

Rosa Rosy Cushion

Rosa ×*odorata* 'Mutabilis'

Rosa glauca Pourr

Rosa ×*odorata* 'Mutabilis'
1.8M × 1.5M (6 FT. × 5 FT.)

A fine, delicate tea rose that grows to form a light, open shrub with dark stems and dark green leaves with narrow leaflets. The delicate single flowers are carried in open clusters, and they open gold, flush pink, and change to soft red-purple. A spray of flowers resembles a flight of exotic butterflies or a bunch of sweet peas. Grow it at the back of a sunny border with *Deutzia* ×*hybrida* 'Strawberry Fields'.

Rosa 'Roseraie de l'Hay'
1.8M × 1.8M (6 FT. × 6 FT.)

A fabulously fragrant and free-flowering rugosa rose that tolerates poor, sandy soil. It is vigorous and bushy in habit, with bright green foliage and large red-purple double flowers that display golden stamens when fully open. It flowers freely and continuously through summer. Plant it alongside *Physocarpus opulifolius* 'Diablo'.

Rosa Rosy Cushion
1.2M × 90CM (4 FT. × 3 FT.)

A rounded shrub with healthy dark green foliage. The single dog rose–like blooms are carried in clusters; their petals are pink, paler toward the centre. The flowers are lightly fragrant, attractive to bees and pollinating insects, and produced continuously throughout summer. Grow it in a border with *Hebe albicans* 'Red Edge' and *Berberis thunbergii* f. *atropurpurea* 'Rose Glow'.

Rubus spectabilis 'Olympic Double'

Rosmarinus officinalis

Rubus cockburnianus 'Golden Vale'

Rosmarinus

This woody, aromatic herb has been grown in gardens since ancient times. Garden centres and nurseries often confine it to the herb section, and many gardeners overlook its value as an evergreen shrub. Rosemary likes a sunny position. It is very tolerant of drought and usually grows best on poor, dry soils. Prune in spring, if necessary, right after flowering. Old, woody plants do not always respond well if cut back; it is often better to replace them.

Rosmarinus officinalis
1.2M × 1.2M (4 FT. × 4 FT.)
Common rosemary has upward-sweeping stems and narrow, strongly aromatic grey-green leaves that are white on the undersides, giving the shrub a silvery appearance. Blue flowers appear among the leaves in spring. You can grow it as an informal hedge, and it is also an excellent plant for coastal gardens. Plant with cistus, helianthemums, and lavender in a warm, sunny border.

Rubus

Most ornamental brambles are unruly shrubs that are not suited for the tidy, orderly gardener. Many have thorns and vigorous arching stems, and many sucker and spread. However, in the right situation rubus can be very useful plants that cope with difficult situations and poor soil.

If you grow plants for their blooms, prune after flowering. Cut those grown for winter stems down to ground level every year or every other year.

Rubus cockburnianus 'Golden Vale'
1.2M × 1.8M (4 FT. × 6 FT.)
White-stemmed bramble has vigorous arching, thorny stems with bright golden yellow, fern-like leaves from spring through fall. In winter the leaves fall away and the reddish stems develop a more conspicuous white bloom, which gives them an almost ghostly appearance. Underplant with black *Ophiopogon planiscarpus* 'Nigrescens' for a striking combination in all seasons.

Rubus spectabilis 'Olympic Double'
1.2M × 1.2M (4 FT. × 4 FT.)
Upright tan-coloured stems, attractive in winter, carry fresh green foliage and double rosette-shaped blooms of cerise-purple from early spring to early summer. Salmonberry is a very versatile shrub that suckers a little in some gardens but generally behaves well. It is an excellent choice for rough ground and a good choice to plant under a purple-leaved plum.

Salvia officinalis 'Icterina'

Sambucus nigra f. porphyrophylla 'Eva'

Salvia officinalis 'Purpurascens'

Sambucus nigra f. laciniata

Salvia

Shrubby salvias include a variety of sun-loving, aromatic shrubs. Some are grown for their flowers, others for their foliage. They are not suited to cold gardens, wet soil, or exposed sites. Most are pruned in spring to remove any winter damage and stimulate new growth. I find the varieties of *Salvia officinalis*, common sage, most useful for their subtle foliage effects. They love good drainage, poor soils, gravel, and paved areas.

Salvia officinalis 'Icterina'
45CM × 75CM (18 IN. × 30 IN.)
A delightful common sage, with soft, aromatic, light grey-green leaves variegated with creamy yellow, forms a low-spreading mound. The blue flowers appear in spikes in early summer, but this is not the most free-flowering variety. A lovely partner for *Lavandula stoechas* subsp. *sampaioana* 'Purple Emperor' in a sheltered, sunny spot.

Salvia officinalis 'Purpurascens'
45CM × 75CM (18 IN. × 30 IN.)
Purple sage is one of the most versatile foliage shrubs for a sunny situation on dry soil. The soft mauve-grey foliage is perfect mixed with any other colour, but is at its best with pastels. It forms a low-spreading mound and will flow over the edge of a wall or onto paving or gravel. In early summer the spikes of bright blue flowers are magnets for bees. Plant it with *Convolvulus cneorum*, *Helichrysum italicum* 'Korma', and *Allium cristophii*.

Sambucus

Ornamental elders are excellent foliage shrubs that grow on any soil and tolerate both dry and wet conditions. They are particularly useful on chalk soils, and their naturalistic habit makes them ideal for country gardens. The purple-leaved varieties need sun for good foliage colour. Some yellow-leaved varieties scorch in full sun and are best grown in semi-shade.

Prune young plants hard in late winter to stimulate vigorous growth. Prune mature plants more lightly to stimulate side branching and summer flowers.

Sambucus nigra f. porphyrophylla 'Eva'
1.8M × 1.5M (6 FT. × 5 FT.)
This purple shrub, known as black elder and sometimes sold as *Sambucus* Black Lace, has vigorous upright stems that carry dark, almost black leaves, finely cut and softly shining. In early summer the pink flowers appear in flattened heads. Black berries follow, but they are usually inconspicuous. The light character of this shrub makes it an excellent mixer with roses, perennials, and other shrubs. A lovely planting partner for *Rosa glauca*.

Sambucus nigra f. laciniata
2.4M × 2.4M (8 FT. × 8 FT.)
Cut-leaved elder is a vigorous specimen with very finely cut, fern-like green foliage and large, lacy heads of tiny white flowers in early summer. The flowers resemble cow parsley, and bees and pollinating insects appreciate them greatly. Drooping clusters of dark red fruits follow in fall; wild birds enjoy these. This is a delightful shrub for a large country garden, and ideal to plant in rough grass or in the corner of a paddock.

Santolina chamaecyparissus

Santolina rosmarinifolia 'Primrose Gem'

Sambucus racemosa 'Sutherland Gold'

Sambucus racemosa 'Sutherland Gold'
1.8M × 1.5M (6 FT. × 5 FT.)

A golden-leaved elder, called European red elder or red-berried elder, with delicate leaves with lightly cut edges. These are bronze tinted as they emerge, and clear golden yellow when fully expanded. The flowers start to develop as the leaves unfurl. They appear early, but they are inconspicuous and easily missed. This variety does not scorch in full sun, but it is equally attractive in shade, where it will assume a more subtle shade of lime yellow. It is a good choice for any gold-and-green planting scheme and works well with *Choisya* ×*dewitteana* 'Aztec Gold' and *Lonicera nitida* 'Maigrun'.

Santolina

Santolinas are known as cotton lavenders, and they are sun-loving dwarf shrubs with very finely cut, soft, aromatic foliage. In habit they resemble lavenders, and in appearance the foliage is more like that of a conifer. They grow on most well-drained or dry soils and are ideal alongside paving or in gravel. You can also grow them in pots. Pruning is necessary to keep the plants tight and compact. You can prune in early spring, cutting back the whole shrub to where new shoots are emerging lower on the stems. Prune just before flowering if the blossoms are undesirable.

Santolina chamaecyparissus
45CM × 60CM (18 IN. × 2 FT.)

A small shrub with soft, woolly, grey foliage that forms a dense, soft mound. The foliage is soft silver-grey; the bright yellow button flowers open from grey buds in summer. Most gardeners remove these, although they are not unattractive in the right setting. One of the best and most tolerant silver-foliage shrubs; ideal for a narrow border or to soften the edge of paving. It is highly effective as part of a cloud bed with *Cistus obtusifolius* 'Thrive' and a small-leaved hebe.

Santolina rosmarinifolia 'Primrose Gem'
45CM × 60CM (18 IN. × 2 FT.)

A lovely santolina with soft green foliage that forms a loose, feathery mound. The pale primrose yellow flowers are produced on slender stems well above the foliage. It has a delightful habit and colour to plant with lavenders, and a contrast in texture when partnered with *Phormium cookianum* subsp. *hookeri* 'Cream Delight'.

Sarcococca

Sarcococcas, often referred to as sweet box or Christmas box, are excellent small evergreen shrubs that succeed on most soils in shade or semi-shade. They will often grow in sunnier positions, but their leaves tend to go rather yellow. They are not a good choice for containers. Most grow to form a suckering clump of vertical stems carrying shining, leathery leaves. Their

Sophora 'Sun King'

Sarcococca confusa

Skimmia ×confusa 'Kew Green'

main attraction is their tiny white-pink flowers, which appear in mid- to late winter and fill the whole garden with their sweet fragrance.

Sarcococca confusa
45CM × 60CM (18 IN. × 2 FT.)

Green upright, then arched, stems carry small, waved, deep green leaves. The white flowers appear in the leaf joints from midwinter, and their fragrance is sweet and heavy. The blooms are followed by black berries that sometimes persist and are still on the stems when the following year's flowers appear. This is an ideal shrub for cutting, both for its foliage and its fragrant flowers. Plant with *Viburnum davidii* and *Euonymus fortunei* 'Emerald Gaiety' for a simple, effective planting solution for shade under deciduous trees.

Skimmia

Skimmias are small evergreen shrubs, popular for their winter buds and berries. They grow on most well-drained, fertile soils and are excellent for pots and winter containers. They need shade for good, dark green foliage and tend to yellow in sun and on shallow chalk soils.

Normally they do not need pruning, but they are excellent for cutting for floral decoration.

The most widely sold and planted variety is *Skimmia japonica* 'Rubella', a male form with red buds and no berries. This is a good plant for winter containers, but not an ideal long-term garden shrub.

Skimmia ×confusa 'Kew Green'
75CM × 75CM (30 IN. × 30 IN.)

A small dome-shaped shrub with bright green leaves that do not go yellow and chlorotic in a sunnier position. Green flower buds in winter open to large clusters of deliciously fragrant creamy flowers in spring. This male form does not produce berries, but don't let this put you off planting it. Plant alongside *Osmanthus heterophyllus* 'Goshiki'.

Sophora

Sophoras are both evergreen and deciduous shrubs and trees of the pea family. They grow on all well-drained soils in sunny positions. They have pretty, fern-like foliage and showy flowers. The evergreens are more valuable in gardens. Prune after flowering to control shape and size.

Sophora 'Sun King'
2.1M × 2.4M (7 FT. × 8 FT.)

This shrub is known in the United States as kowhai. It is evergreen, with a loose, open habit and pretty dark green foliage. Golden yellow bell-shaped flowers hang from the branches in spring. It is rather sprawling, but you can train it against a wall or prune to control its size. It is remarkably free flowering, even as a young plant, and when in full bloom it is quite a spectacle in the spring garden. Striking underplanted with yellow daffodils or blue muscari. It makes a good planting partner for a yellow-variegated evergreen such as *Elaeagnus ×ebbingei* 'Viveleg', with *Euonymus fortunei* 'Emerald 'n' Gold' to add interest at ground level.

Spiraea

Sprireas are easy to grow deciduous shrubs tolerant of drought, poor soils, and exposure. They thrive in most gardens on all well-drained soils, especially chalk. They are at their best in full sun but tolerate some shade. Some are grown for their colourful foliage. All are free flowering and produce clusters of blossoms that are attractive to bees and pollinating insects. Prune early blooming varieties after flowering by cutting out some of the stems that have flowered. This is rarely necessary every year.

The varieties of *Spiraea japonica*, Japanese spiraea, are low, twiggy shrubs that flower over a long period of summer and early fall. Pruning consists of trimming over with shears in early spring before growth commences. This removes old flower heads and any straggly growth.

The golden-leaved forms are the most popular; these are cheerful shrubs that add a lot of colour for little effort. They mix surprisingly well with other shades, even though their hues can be strong. However, you'll never find a hard yellow; the flowers are usually red or pink.

Spiraea japonica 'Firelight' produces a fine display of deep pink flowers in early summer as the foliage turns gold from the glowing orange new shoots that appeared in early spring.

Spiraea 'Arguta'
1.2M × 1.2M (4 FT. × 4 FT.)
This graceful spiraea is often referred to as bridal wreath. Fine arched stems carry soft blue-green narrow leaves. Before the foliage develops, clusters of small white flowers garland the branches in mid- to late spring, creating a delightfully frothy display. The perfect shrub for an informal garden underplanted with forget-me-nots.

Spiraea japonica 'Anthony Waterer'
60CM × 60CM (2 FT. × 2 FT.)
A really useful shrub with upright stems and dark green willow-like leaves, occasionally variegated with white and pink. The flower heads of deep red buds open into bright red flowers. Lovely planted with *Brachyglottis* (Dunedin Group) 'Sunshine' and *Ceanothus thyrsiflorus* var. *repens*, or anything with purple foliage.

Spiraea japonica 'Firelight'

Spiraea 'Arguta'

Spiraea japonica 'Genpei' ('Shirobana')

Spiraea japonica 'Anthony Waterer'

Spiraea japonica 'Little Princess'

Spiraea japonica 'Firelight'
45CM × 60CM (18 IN. × 2 FT.)
One of the most popular golden foliage shrubs, 'Firelight' has superseded *Spiraea japonica* 'Goldflame', which tends to revert and produce plain green shoots. The foliage appears as bright orange new shoots in spring and then develops into soft, warm yellow that is greener in the heart of the plant. The tips of the shoots retain a red-orange hue and the foliage colours richly in fall in different shades of red. The fluffy, deep pink flowers are surprisingly attractive with the leaves. Good with *Berberis thunbergii* 'Admiration'.

Spiraea japonica 'Genpei' ('Shirobana')
60CM × 60CM (2 FT. × 2 FT.)
This shrub, similar in stature and habit to 'Anthony Waterer', has narrow green leaves and heads of deep pink-and-white flowers on the same plant. The effect is soft and pretty, and makes it a versatile plant that mixes well with other small shrubs. Creates a pretty combination with *Lavandula angustifolia* 'Hidcote' and *Potentilla fruticosa* 'Primrose Beauty'.

Spiraea japonica 'Little Princess'
30CM × 45CM (1 FT. × 18 IN.)
A dwarf compact shrub making a low mound of medium green foliage smothered with heads of deep pink flowers. Small enough for the tiniest garden, rock garden, or pot, or with carpeting alpines in gravel. Good to add summer colour when planted with winter-flowering heathers and compact conifers with blue foliage.

Symphoricarpos ×doorenbosii 'Mother of Pearl'

Syringa 'Red Pixie'

Syringa vulgaris var. alba

Symphoricarpos

Snowberries are not the showiest deciduous shrubs, but they thrive in shade, under trees, and in difficult conditions. Most form twiggy thickets of fine stems with small leaves and make excellent shrubby groundcover. The flowers are insignificant, but the berries are attractive from fall through early winter. Symphoricarpos are ideal in country gardens and naturalistic schemes. Pruning is unnecessary, but you can cut back the shrubs in early spring.

Symphoricarpos ×doorenbosii 'Mother of Pearl'
90CM × 90 CM (3 FT. × 3 FT.)
A compact form with fine arching stems and blue-green foliage that is light and feathery. The white berries are flushed with pink and can make an attractive display in winter. Use under trees with small-leaved variegated ivies and *Vinca minor*.

Syringa

Lilacs are enduringly popular for their fragrant late-spring flowers. They are hardy deciduous shrubs that thrive on most soils, including chalk. Many grow to form large shrubs of tree proportions and are too large for smaller gardens, but there are small-leaved, compact varieties that are easier to accommodate. Prune after flowering by cutting out some of the flowered branches to allow new growth to develop lower on the plants.

I have only included two varieties here, as lilacs generally have a short season of interest and rather plain foliage for the rest of the year.

Syringa 'Red Pixie'
1.2M × 90CM (4 FT. × 3 FT.)
Dwarf lilac is an upright and compact shrub with small, soft green leaves with purple leaf stalks. The tiny, fragrant flowers are red-purple in bud and open lilac-mauve in typical lilac flower heads. A shrub in full flower in late spring is a scented delight, even in a small garden. The foliage is pleasing after the flowers have faded, and little if any pruning is needed. A useful shrub to add structure to a bed of herbaceous perennials.

Syringa vulgaris var. alba
3M × 1.8M (10 FT. × 6 FT.)
There are many forms of *Syringa vulgaris* with single and double flowers. All flower in late spring and have medium green foliage. I would always choose this simple white lilac with its large heads of single, brilliant white, wonderfully fragrant flowers. It is a perfect background shrub for any large-garden green-and-white scheme with *Cornus alba* 'Elegantissima' and *Viburnum opulus* 'Roseum'.

Viburnum carlesii 'Diana'

Viburnum ×hillieri 'Winton'

Viburnum opulus

Viburnum davidii

Viburnum

Viburnums offer an array of deciduous and evergreen shrubs, including many of our most popular garden subjects. Most are easy to grow, hardy plants that thrive on most soils in sun or semi-shade. Some viburnums tolerate very shady conditions.

Pruning requirements vary according to variety. Some need to be pruned, while others are best left alone. Be sure to check before you cut.

Viburnum carlesii 'Diana'
1.2M × 1.2M (4 FT. × 4 FT.)
A rounded deciduous shrub of open habit, with soft green, slightly felted leaves. This shrub is usually grafted and is liable to produce suckers from the rootstock. You should remove these at the base before they take over and smother the plant. The rounded clusters of flowers appear at the end of the branches at the same time as the purple-tinged new leaves unfurl. Slender buds of coral pink open to tubular flowers that are pale pink on the inside and heavily fragrant. A good shrub to grow among perennials or roses. Alternatively, plant it with *Cornus alba* 'Sibirica Variegata'; the variegated leaves will prolong the season of interest.

Viburnum davidii
60CM × 60CM (2 FT. × 2 FT.)
A wonderful domed evergreen shrub with shining dark green ribbed leaves with red leaf stalks. Tiny clusters of grey-white insignificant flowers develop into blue-black berries on female plants. If you want a plant that fruits, buy it in berry. It makes an attractive low hedge and a good subject for a pot in shade. Excellent on any soil and very shade tolerant, and a good choice under trees planted with *Sarcococca confusa*.

Viburnum ×hillieri 'Winton'
1.8M × 1.8M (6 FT. × 6 FT.)
A fast-growing, semi-evergreen shrub of open habit with copper-coloured new leaves that become deep green, flushed red in winter. Clusters of creamy white flowers hang all along the branches in midsummer. These develop into red fruits that turn black on the branches before they fall. Underplant with *Cotoneaster dammeri* and *Pachysandra terminalis* 'Variegata'.

Viburnum opulus
2.1M × 1.5M (7 FT. × 5 FT.)
European cranberry bush is a large, deciduous shrub with upright stems and maple-like medium green leaves that colour brilliantly in fall. It grows in sun or semi-shade on any soil. In spring, lacecap heads of creamy white flowers appear; these are followed by clusters of redcurrant-like, glistening fruits in fall. This is a good wildlife shrub and ideal in a country garden setting or hedgerow.

Viburnum opulus 'Roseum'

Viburnum plicatum f. tomentosum 'Mariesii'

Viburnum plicatum f. tomentosum 'Summer Snowflake'

Viburnum opulus 'Roseum'
2.1M × 1.5M (7 FT. × 5 FT.)

'Roseum' is similar to *Viburnum opulus* but often more spreading in habit. The flower heads are balls of sterile florets that appear soft lime green, change to cream, then eventually turn white; they often blush pink before they fade. As they mature, they weigh down the branches for several weeks from midspring.

Prune after flowering, if necessary, by cutting back some of the older flowered branches. A glorious shrub planted alongside *Choisya ×dewitteana* 'Aztec Pearl'.

Viburnum plicatum f. tomentosum 'Mariesii'
1.2M × 1.8M (4 FT. × 6 FT.)

This wide-spreading deciduous shrub needs space to allow its wonderful layered, horizontal branches to develop. The lacecap flower heads are creamy white and poised all along the branches in late spring; often a few smaller flowers appear in fall. The pleated leaves turn rich shades of red, copper, and bronze in fall. Avoid pruning, which will spoil the natural shape. Plant as a free-standing specimen shrub or use as a focal point in a corner in sun or semi-shade.

Viburnum plicatum f. tomentosum 'Summer Snowflake'
1.2M × 90CM (4 FT. × 3 FT.)

'Summer Snowflake' is a better choice than 'Mariesii' for the smaller garden, as it is much narrower in habit. It does not have such obviously layered branches, but it produces small lacecap heads of white flowers from late spring through to fall. It requires no pruning. A perfectly matched planting partner for *Cornus alternifolia* 'Argentea'.

Weigela

These are hardy, deciduous, flowering shrubs that thrive in a sunny position on most soils, including chalk. They are tough, tolerant, and good in both town and country gardens. They are mostly grown for their late spring and early summer flowers, but some have the benefit of colourful foliage. These are the ones I use in planting schemes. Prune after flowering by cutting out some of the flowered stems to allow new shoots to develop.

Weigela 'Florida Variegata'

Weigela florida 'Foliis Purpureis'

Yucca flaccida 'Golden Sword'

Weigela florida 'Foliis Purpureis'
1.2M × 1.2M (4 FT. × 4 FT.)

A slow-growing shrub with arching, often horizontal branches and dark green leaves heavily flushed with dull purple. The mauve-pink trumpet flowers appear in late spring and make a pleasing combination with the leaves. This is not the showiest shrub, but a really useful mixer in planting schemes. Plant with *Spiraea japonica* 'Genpei' ('Shirobana') and *Brachyglottis* (Dunedin Group) 'Sunshine' for an easy, pleasing combination.

Weigela 'Florida Variegata'
1.2M × 1.2M (4 FT. × 4 FT.)

A compact shrub with loose branches carrying dark green and rich, creamy white variegated leaves. The trumpet-shaped flowers open deep pink and fade to a lighter shade. Usually both colours appear in the same cluster. Although the main flush of flowers is in late spring, some blooms appear in late summer and fall. Lovely planted with *Spiraea japonica* 'Anthony Waterer' and *Berberis thunbergii* f. *atropurpurea* 'Rose Glow'.

Yucca

Yuccas are members of the agave family. These architectural evergreens have rosettes of spiky leaves. They thrive in full sun and are much hardier than they look. In my garden they survive hard winters when phormiums and cordylines have failed. Some have very hard, sharply pointed leaves, while others have softer, friendlier foliage. I choose the latter. They require no pruning apart from removing dead leaves and flower stems.

Yucca flaccida 'Golden Sword'
60CM × 60CM (2 FT. × 2 FT.)

This excellent yucca forms a rosette of soft pointed leaves, often bent over at the tips with peeling filaments down the edges. Each bright green leaf has a broad golden band that makes this a bright and eye-catching shrub. In summer tall stems up to 1.2m (4 ft.) carry large, creamy white, bell-shaped flowers. Grow it in gravel or underplant with *Vinca minor* 'Illumination' for an eye-catching combination.

PLANTING AND CARING FOR SHRUBS

Shrubs are low-maintenance plants. Once they are planted and established, you do not need to do the regular lifting, dividing, and replanting that herbaceous perennials require. You do not have to replace them every year, and they tolerate a wide range of growing conditions. Most shrubs will fit in with your regime of garden maintenance, and most cope with neglect. However, you will compromise their potential with poor planting at the outset and subsequent lack of sensible cultivation, especially appropriate pruning. If you give shrubs a good start and a little aftercare once or twice a year, they will reward for many years to come, whether in the open ground or in pots on the terrace.

ABOVE Shrubs that are well positioned, well planted, and allowed to achieve their potential will reward season after season with little maintenance.

LEFT Spring bulbs and perennials fill the gaps and add colour in this newly planted bed of shrubs.

Shrubs in the ground

Many shrubs will be planted directly into the ground, if it exists in your garden. This is a straightforward practice, but you should consider a number of factors at the outset, such as planting distance, timing, and preparing the ground.

PLANTING DISTANCE

When you buy a small shrub, it is always difficult to envision its eventual proportions, even when you have the dimensions in front of you. And the ultimate size and spread is not an exact science; these measurements vary according to soil, climate, and growing conditions.

If you plant a bed with shrubs that are sufficiently spaced to allow each to reach its potential size, the space will initially look sparse—especially when planted with subjects that will grow into medium to large shrubs. You must decide whether to plant closer, and deal with overcrowding in the future, or fill the gaps with perennials, bulbs, and annuals.

It is virtually impossible to specify the optimum spacing for shrubs. You must use your best judgement. If two shrubs each have a spread of 90cm (3 ft.) within five years, plant them about 90cm (3 ft.) apart. The space will thus be covered within three to five years; in the meantime, you can fill the gap between the plants. If you plant shrubs too close together, you must be prepared to remove one in the future to allow the other to reach its potential. Although the ground will be covered, reducing the frequency of weeding and cultivation, the need for pruning will increase.

Commercial landscape schemes often use multiple plantings of a single variety. This practice fills the space quickly and achieves short-term impact. In a garden situation this is rarely appropriate when planting medium-size or larger-growing shrubs such as choisya, deutzia, or philadelphus. Your garden will look institutional. However, multiple plantings in groups of three or more are often appropriate with smaller subjects such as erica, calluna, lavandula, santolina, dwarf hebe, and sometimes roses. This increases the subject's impact and prevents a fragmented effect. Groundcover

ABOVE Multiple plantings of basic shrubs can make the garden look boring and institutional.

RIGHT Frost is not a problem for hardy shrubs after planting.

plants such as cotoneaster, hedera, vinca, and rubus are also planted in groups or drifts of one variety.

When you plan to group shrubs together to create pleasing planting combinations, consider their individual habits. Are they upright, spreading, loose, or compact? Give the individual shrubs enough space to showcase their growth habits, but do not plant them so far apart that they fail to relate to one another. Bear in mind that all plants are individuals. No matter how carefully you plan, they rarely all perform exactly as you expect. This is the magic of gardening.

TIMING

You can plant container-grown shrubs at any time of the year, but aftercare is always easier during the cooler months of fall, winter, and early spring. Bare root shrubs are planted only during the dormant season of late fall and winter. The threat of frost is often a concern to gardeners when planting. Frost after planting is not a problem for hardy shrubs, as the roots are better insulated in the ground than they are in a plastic pot. It is not a good idea to plant when the soil surface is frozen. This results in frost being buried during planting, which makes the soil colder for the roots and potentially causes damage.

PREPARING THE GROUND

No matter what you plant, you will achieve better results if you prepare the ground thoroughly and plant carefully. This may be easier said than done when replacing a shrub in an existing planting or adding to a planting scheme, but the success of your new shrub depends upon it.

First, fork over the planting area and ensure it is free from perennial weeds, especially those with creeping rhizomes or invasive roots. Fragments that remain in the ground will soon regrow and penetrate the rootball of your new shrub. The weeds are almost certain to prefer the container shrub's growing medium to your soil. If the site is badly infested, delay planting and kill off the weeds by applying a non-residual systemic weed killer.

On heavy clay soils, dig in some good garden compost or well-rotted manure to

Dig a hole much larger than the rootball of the shrub you are about to plant—at least twice its depth and three times its width. Fork over the base of the planting hole to encourage roots to grow down into the soil below.

If you have not already done so, thoroughly water the shrub in its pot. Dip it in a bucket of water and keep the pot submerged until it stops bubbling. If you plant a dry shrub, water will find it difficult to penetrate the rootball and your new subject will struggle to establish.

Mix a generous amount of shrub- and tree-planting compost into the bottom of the hole and with the heap of soil you have removed.

Add a couple of generous handfuls of slow-release general fertilizer to the bottom of the planting hole and the pile of soil and compost for backfilling.

Once you have prepared the planting hole, remove the plant from the pot and place it in the middle of the hole.

Place the shrub in the planting hole and check the depth of the shrub with the surrounding soil.

When you are satisfied with the position of the shrub in the planting hole, backfill around the rootball with the planting compost and soil mixture.

Use your toe or heel to firm the soil around the rootball, taking care not to damage the plant.

Water newly planted shrubs thoroughly, even if it is raining. This helps to settle the soil particles around the roots.

improve the soil structure. This is also beneficial on well-drained sites to improve the soil's water-holding capacity.

Many gardeners have traditionally used bone meal when planting. It provides phosphate for root development and some slow-release nitrogen. However, it is better to use a more balanced compound fertilizer that provides the main plant nutrients and trace elements. But remember to use an ericaceous fertilizer and lime-free planting compost when planting azaleas, rhododendrons, camellias, and other ericaceous plants.

Backfill the hole with the soil and planting compost; leave the planting hole just slightly deeper than the depth of the rootball of the shrub. Before you place the shrub in the planting hole, you can add dried mycorrhizal fungi. These granules are placed in the bottom of the planting hole, as they work only if they are in direct contact with the roots. Once in the ground, they grow and form a symbiotic relationship with the shrub's root system, helping the plant to absorb water and nutrients and thereby aiding establishment. Opinions vary on their effectiveness, but they are considered to be very beneficial on poor soils. They are also useful when planting roses, as they eliminate the possibility of rose replant disease and enable a rose to be planted where another was growing without changing the soil.

Planting in the ground

Some gardeners recommend teasing out the roots of a shrub before planting. But if the plant is a good-quality specimen and has not been in the pot for more than one growing season, there should be no need to do this. If you interfere with the rootball, you may damage the roots and hinder establishment. But if the shrub appears pot-bound and the roots are densely packed at the base of the pot, you can gently tease out a few roots at the bottom of the rootball before you plant.

Some shrubs, especially roses, do not form a compact rootball that holds together when removed from the pot. Keep as much of the rootball intact as you can. If it falls apart, plant the shrub firmly and pay particular attention to watering and aftercare.

WATERING AND FEEDING SHRUBS IN THE GROUND

Leave a saucer-shaped depression around the plant to make watering easier. Labels often instruct you to plant to the same depth as the shrub is in the pot, but it is important to cover the surface of the rootball with a thin layer of soil. If you do not, there is a danger that the roots will become exposed and that the rootball will dry out. Shrubs are increasingly grown in soil-less peat-substitute composts. These dry out easily from the surface of the compost if it is exposed, so if the rootball is not covered, it may become dry even if the surrounding ground is quite moist.

Water your newly planted shrubs regularly during the first season after planting to aid their establishment. When planting a new bed, border, or hedge, it is worth laying permeable or porous irrigation pipe over the soil surface and covering it with a layer of bark. This gradually delivers a supply of water and keeps the soil moist.

PLANTING BARE ROOT SHRUBS

In the dormant season you can plant some deciduous shrubs bare root, when they have lost their leaves and do not keep soil around their roots when lifted. It used to be common practice to plant bare root spiraea, potentilla, and forsythia, but this method is now mainly used for planting deciduous hedging whips, symphoricarpos, and roses.

When planting a bare root shrub, you can sprinkle mycorrhizal fungi directly onto the roots to aid root development and establishment.

However, roses are increasingly sold as containerized plants that are lifted from the field, potted, and sold.

The procedure for planting bare root shrubs is exactly the same as for container-grown ones. Before you plant, check the roots and cut out any broken or damaged ones. If the roots have become very dry, soak them in a bucket of water. Spread the roots out in the planting hole. Mycorrhizal fungi are particularly beneficial when planting bare root shrubs; make sure they are in direct contact with the shrub's roots. Backfill with soil and compost around the roots, then add slow-release fertilizer. Do not sprinkle the fertilizer directly on the roots, as it can harm the delicate new root hairs as they develop.

A bare root shrub may not be securely anchored into the ground, even if you have planted it firmly. If it rocks in the wind, the fragile developing roots may be broken. It is good practice to reduce the top growth of the shrub by one-third to one-half by cutting it back with secateurs. This reduces the shrub's wind resistance and makes for less foliage to support when the shrub comes into leaf. Although you may feel like you are taking a step backward by reducing the size of the plant, it will be well ahead by the end of the growing season.

Thorough watering after planting is essential, even in winter, to settle the soil around the roots. As with container-grown shrubs, attention to watering during the first growing season is essential for success.

Shrubs in containers

For most gardeners, seasonal bedding plants and bulbs are obvious choices for planting in pots and containers, but permanent planting with shrubs can be much more effective and rewarding. This practice saves both time and money, as shrubs can thrive in pots for many years, so you will not have to replant all your containers once or twice a year. The ideal situation is to plant some pots with permanent subjects and retain a few to replant with seasonal colour.

ABOVE Shrubs provide structure and year-round interest, whereas seasonal plants add colour and change the picture.

RIGHT *Acer palmatum* 'Sango-kaku' is beautiful in winter even without its foliage.

Phormium 'Yellow Wave' in a well-chosen pot makes a striking focal point.

Growing shrubs in pots allows you to position them where planting in the open ground is just not possible. Some gardens, courtyards, and balconies do not have any soil, so containers are the only option. Growing in pots also allows you to cultivate shrubs that would not thrive on your soil type.

But the idea of planting shrubs in containers raises a great deal of questions. Do all shrubs work in pots? If you read the labels, won't many shrubs grow too large for pots on the patio? How long will a shrub be happy in a pot? What soil do you use? Do you need to feed a shrub in a pot regularly? What happens when you need to repot it? The truth is, you can grow just about anything in a container if you choose a generous size and a good-quality, specially formulated growing medium.

A few shrubs do not do well in pots. Among the evergreens, daphnes and sarcococcas are poor choices. They seem to survive, but they also sulk and look unhappy. Although many deciduous shrubs grow happily in pots, you need to consider what they will look like in winter. Japanese maples (varieties) and deciduous azaleas (*Rhododendron* varieties) have attractive silhouettes and are good choices. Spiraea and potentilla will grow just fine, but they will be unattractive in winter.

CHOOSING THE RIGHT LOOK

Your shrub and your pot have to work together to make an attractive feature. A well-chosen container will look appropriate for the garden and suit the situation. A contemporary container might be out of place in a traditional setting, and vice versa. Beware of brightly coloured pots unless the design and planting of the garden demands it. A shiny blue-glazed pot may look stunning in the garden centre but could seem quite out of place when you get it home. Remember that your shrub should be the feature. The container is there to support and enhance.

CHOOSING THE RIGHT SHAPE AND SIZE

A traditional flowerpot shape—wider at the top than the base and deeper than wide—is the best choice for planting shrubs. This shape allows plenty of volume of growing medium and sufficient depth for good root development. Avoid containers that narrow at the rim. It is usually impossible to extract the plant without breaking the pot.

It is essential to choose a container that is large enough for the shrub to grow into.

ABOVE Plant a long-term container subject, such as a large Japanese maple, into a big pot as soon as possible.

LEFT It is always easier to extract an established shrub from a traditional flowerpot than from a container that is narrower toward the rim.

If you get it right, your shrub will be happy in its pot for at least five years and hopefully several more. If the container is not large enough, the growing medium will dry out quickly and will soon become exhausted of nutrients. As the shrub gets larger it will put up more resistance to wind, so if the container is too small it will be top heavy and likely to blow over. Gardeners working on exposed sites should choose heavy containers that are broad at the base.

As a rough guide, the pot you choose for your shrub should be two to three times the size of its first container home. For a more mature shrub already in a container larger than 40cm (15 in.) in diameter, choose a pot that is at least 7.5cm (3 in.) more in diameter and depth than the existing container. Do not repot into a container that is only slightly bigger than the existing one. You are wasting time and effort on questionable benefits.

CHOOSING THE RIGHT PLANTING MEDIUM

Many gardeners are bewildered by the array of available potting soils. The term *compost* in and of itself is confusing. In the United Kingdom it means growing media and material used to improve soil in the open ground, while in North America the term refers only to the latter. Tree- and shrub-planting compost is used for soil improvement, not for growing in pots.

Never use garden soil in pots and containers, no matter what you are growing or how good your soil is. Micro-organisms, spores, invertebrates, and weed seeds that are harmless in the open ground can cause problems in the confined environment of a pot. Always use a specially formulated growing medium. For permanent subjects like shrubs, loam-based potting soil is your best bet. This is made from sterilized soil, often with the addition of peat or peat substitute, so it has fine particles that hold on to water and nutrients. It will also drain freely and have the right amount of air space between the particles.

Loam-based, lime-free planting medium is not dependent on the wetting agent

For ericaceous subjects such as camellias, rhododendrons, and azaleas, use lime-free, soil-based planting medium.

PLANTING IN CONTAINERS

Place a few broken crocks or flat stones in the bottom of the pot to keep the drainage hole open. This is essential to avoid waterlogging.

Water your container-grown shrub as if you were planting in the open ground.

Add a layer of growing medium in the bottom of the pot and position the rootball of the shrub in the centre of the container, leaving an even gap between the rootball and the pot. The surface of the growing medium should be about 4cm (1.5 in.) below the rim of the pot. If it is below this, lift the shrub out and add more compost; if above it needs to go deeper, adjust accordingly.

Fill around the rootball, firming the compost with your fingertips as you go. When the growing medium is halfway up the rootball, add a small handful of controlled-release fertilizer, more if the pot and plant are large. Then fill to the top, covering the rootball with a thin layer of growing medium. The finished surface should be below the rim of the pot to allow for easy watering. This may seem obvious, but many gardeners make the mistake of leaving the shrub too high in the pot.

You may find it easier to plant the pot, rather than the shrub. Slip the well-watered shrub out of its pot and then position the growing pot inside the container, leaving the shrub on one side. It is easy to see if the pot is at the right level in the final container without leaves and stems in the way.

Carefully take out the plastic growing pot and drop in the rootball of the shrub; it will be a perfect fit. Spread a thin layer of growing medium over the rootball of the shrub and water thoroughly. Once you have used this technique to pot a plant, you will never do it any other way.

contained in the peat-based material, so it gives better long-term results. After a few years the effectiveness of the wetting agent may deteriorate, and you will have trouble delivering moisture to the roots of the shrub.

WATERING AND FEEDING SHRUBS IN CONTAINERS

Shrubs growing in pots need regular watering throughout the year, even in winter when the pots are not frozen. Do not be fooled by rainfall. A shrub in a pot may cover the soil surface with such a canopy of foliage that rainwater rarely penetrates the growing medium. Pots under the eaves of a house or in the rain shadow of a wall rarely get much natural watering. Evergreens can be particularly vulnerable after freezing weather, which can be very drying. It is important to check pots regularly throughout the year, and to keep a close eye on them in warm and windy weather when shrubs are in full leaf.

You can reduce the need for watering by using a quality loam-based growing medium and large, good-quality containers. Do not be tempted to use water-storage granules. Permanent subjects in pots will not benefit from the additional water-storage properties, and freezing conditions may cause a waterlogged pot to split, which will certainly cause root damage.

You can also reduce the need for watering and make watering easier by grouping containers together. This practice shades the sides of the containers, which keeps them cooler and reduces water loss. It also looks better and gives you the opportunity to create attractive planting combinations and change them easily.

When it comes to feeding shrubs in pots, it is always better to use a slow- or controlled-release powdered or granular fertilizer rather than liquid feeding. All you

ABOVE Group pots together to make watering easier and to reduce the need for watering. It looks more interesting, too.

TOP LEFT Check pots regularly for watering, especially when the foliage covers the growing medium and prevents rainfall from penetrating.

BOTTOM LEFT In spring, top dress your shrubs in pots with a controlled-release fertilizer and a little fresh growing medium.

LEFT *Salvia officinalis* 'Icterina' and *Rosmarinus officinalis.*

RIGHT *Leucothoe* Lovita

need to remember each spring is to scrape off the top 2–3cm (1 in.) of the growing medium, add a handful of controlled-release fertilizer, and top up with fresh growing medium. A controlled-release fertilizer is always a granular formulation and releases nutrients only when there is adequate moisture and the temperature is high enough. It is practically impossible to overfeed with a controlled-release fertilizer, so this is ideal in the confined conditions of a pot. Ericaceous plants are known as light feeders because they require smaller amounts of nutrients. Use a fertilizer that is specifically formulated for ericaceous plants.

A few good shrubs for pots in shade

Acer palmatum 'Beni-maiko'
Buxus sempervirens 'Elegantissima'
Camellia japonica 'Jury's Yellow'
Euonymus japonicus 'Green Rocket'
Fatsia japonica

Leucothoe Lovita
Pieris japonica 'Little Heath'
Skimmia ×confusa 'Kew Green'
Viburnum davidii

A few good shrubs for pots in sun

Acer palmatum 'Shaina'
Berberis thunbergii 'Admiration'
Convolvulus cneorum
Coprosma 'Lemon and Lime'
Cordyline australis 'Torbay Dazzler'
Hebe 'Frozen Flame'

Laurus nobilis
Photinia ×fraseri 'Little Red Robin'
Pittosporum tenuifolium 'Tom Thumb'
Rosmarinus officinalis
Salvia officinalis 'Icterina'

ABOVE A deutzia will still grow
and bloom happily if you do
not prune it for a year or two.

LEFT Pruning is not a daunting
task if you approach it logically.

Pruning shrubs

The task of pruning baffles many gardeners, both beginner or experienced, who see it as a complicated task that requires specialized knowledge. They tend to approach pruning randomly, without thought and consideration of the consequences. The bad reputation that shrubs have with many gardeners is a result of such thoughtless, and often unnecessary, pruning.

Remember that you do not have to prune. Pruning is an activity born in the formal gardens of yesteryear, when the whole structure of the garden was based on trimming and training woody plants to make shapes and patterns. In nature, the elements, pests and diseases, and grazing animals take care of pruning. While many shrubs do not have to be pruned at all, pruning improves the performance of others, so it is important to understand the requirements of the shrubs in your garden. If you fail to prune a shrub that benefits from the practice—such as a deutzia or philadelphus—for a year or two, it will still grow happily and bloom as expected. You can then resume the pruning regime at a later date, but it is important to do it at the right time of year.

There is an optimum time for pruning most shrubs, and a great deal depends on the season and the local climate. Choosing the right time to prune is a logical process. If a shrub flowers, prune after flowering. The new growth that develops after pruning will ripen and flower the following season. If a shrub is grown mainly for its foliage, prune just before a flush of new growth is produced: cutting back existing growth results in healthy new shoots. If you only remember one piece of advice in this section, remember to prune after flowering. It is the key to unlock the mystique of pruning.

REASONS FOR PRUNING

There are a number of reasons for pruning, and it is important to understand them before you reach for the secateurs. Pruning for the sake of pruning can have disastrous results.

Pruning to control shape and size

It is often necessary to prune a shrub that has simply grown too big for a situation. Perhaps you chose the wrong shrub in the first place, or maybe you want to keep it

ABOVE This deutzia, a flowering shrub, is pruned after flowering. Cutting out some of the flowered stems encourages new shoots to develop.

CENTER Cutting some of the older branches out of this rosemary controls its size and spread and preserves its natural growth habit.

RIGHT *Cornus sanguinea* 'Midwinter Fire' is improved if cut right back in late winter or early spring.

You can cut back an old photinia hard in late winter to rejuvenate it. The shrub may take a year or more to recover.

under control. Regularly clip hedges and topiary subjects such as boxwood and yew to achieve the desired shape and keep them to the intended size. Other shrubs may need occasional selective pruning to help them stay within the bounds of the garden and to avoid too much competition with neighbouring plants.

The way you approach pruning to control shape and size has a profound effect on the plant's growth. The objective should be to preserve the natural habit, rather than to create a rounded dome or trimmed ball. Reserve this type of pruning for topiary and formally trained subjects. Too often a gardener uses the shears or the hedge trimmer regularly on any shrub to keep it in check. This results in dense, twiggy growth on the outside of the branch framework and a characterless shape. It is particularly inappropriate on deciduous flowering shrubs, which are left with ugly twigs, awkwardly held leaves, and a few flowers in the heart of the plant.

Pruning to stimulate vigorous growth and superior-quality foliage

In most cases hard pruning results in vigorous growth. For example, if *Cornus sanguinea* 'Midwinter Fire' is cut down to just a few centimetres above ground in early spring, it will respond with strong upright shoots that look fantastic the following winter. If pruned less severely it produces thinner, weaker stems with side branches of inferior colour. If *Sambucus porphophylla* 'Eva' is pruned to 30cm (1 ft.) above the ground in late winter, it will respond with vigorous upright stems and fabulous, finely cut foliage.

Pruning to rejuvenate a shrub

Because hard pruning normally stimulates vigorous growth, you can do it on some old, woody shrubs to rejuvenate them. For example, you can rejuvenate an old lilac, *Syringa vulgaris*, by cutting back some or all of the old woody stems to within 30cm (1 ft.) of the ground, either in winter or right after flowering. If you feed and water, it will respond with strong young shoots that will mature and flower the following year.

If you cut back old evergreen shrubs such as mahonia, euonymus, elaeagnus, and photinia in late winter or early spring, they usually respond with vigorous growth and good-quality foliage. Just be prepared for the devastated, unattractive appearance of the shrub while it recovers.

Pruning to encourage flowering

Pruning flowering shrubs influences and stimulates flowering. Prune after flowering to encourage the shrub to produce new growth, which will develop and flower the following season.

Do not prune after flowering anything grown for its fruit, such as *Viburnum opulus*, pyracantha, cotoneaster, and deciduous euonymus. Prune these after birds have taken the fruit. Where a pyracantha or cotoneaster is trained as a wall shrub, you can cut back the new shoots that are produced during the summer to where the fruit is carried on the branches to display the berries to greatest advantage. This also helps to restrict the growth and keep the shrub in check.

ABOVE Prune a cotoneaster after the fruit has disappeared. Note that this practice may be at the expense of some of the following year's flowers and fruit.

LEFT An old, leggy mahonia can be cut back to just above any whorl of foliage. It will respond with new, vigorous shoots and fresh foliage.

Pruning to control pests and diseases

Pruning to control insect pests and diseases is an annual winter activity for gardeners growing productive fruit trees and bushes. You also have to do winter pruning on some ornamentals, especially roses. Cutting out any damaged or diseased wood in winter removes the spores of fungal diseases and overwintering eggs of insect pests. When you are dealing with insect infestations and severe cases of leaf-spot fungal diseases, it is sometimes better to cut the shrub back to bare wood and start again rather than employ a chemical cure. This works well on evergreens such as photinia.

LEFT Pruning in early spring is a good way to control leaf-spot disease on photinia.

BELOW Shoots that appear from the base of grafted shrubs are probably suckers from the rootstock. Remove these as soon as they appear.

Pruning to remove suckers

Suckers are shoots that grow from the rootstock of a shrub, so they occur only on plants that have been grafted or budded. Roses are the best-known shrubs that produce suckers, but they also occur on some viburnums, especially *Viburnum carlesii* and *Viburnum ×burkwoodii*, and on witch hazels, *Hamamelis ×intermedia* varieties. Remove suckers as close to the point of origin as soon as possible. If you allow them to grow, they will weaken the plant and are liable to take over because the rootstock is usually more vigorous than the subject grafted onto it.

Pruning to remove reversion

Variegated shrubs are liable to produce reverted, plain green shoots; some shrubs are particularly prone to this, such as *Elaeagnus pungens* and *Euonymus japonicus* varieties. If left to grow, these plain green shoots grow more vigorously than the variegated plant. They may eventually take over, leaving the desired shrub to fade away. Cut them out completely into wood carrying variegated leaves.

PRUNING TOOLS

Before you can prune, you need the right equipment. The most important tool is sharp bypass secateurs. Invest in a good-quality pair. Bypass secateurs cut like scissors, whereas anvil secateurs have one sharp blade that cuts onto a fixed flat blade. Although anvil secateurs can be easier for cutting through tough stems, they also tend to crush the stems, especially if they not very sharp.

A light pair of quality loppers is also useful for reaching down into shrubs and up to higher branches. Geared loppers make it possible to cut thicker branches and are easier to use. You also need good-quality gardening gloves. Gauntlet gloves, which have wide cuffs that protect your wrists, are excellent when pruning shrub roses and larger shrubs that you need to reach into.

For some shrubs you can use hedging shears, and these are obviously the best tools for trimming hedges or topiary. They are also a better choice for trimming fine, twiggy deciduous shrubs, such as *Spiraea japonica* and *Potentilla fruticosa* in late winter. In these cases you are just clipping off last year's faded flower heads and the thin wispy stems. Cut back by about 15cm (6 in.).

Once you have your bypass secateurs in hand, it's time to get to work. Aim to develop a well-branched shrub with an open habit and few competing branches. Try to cut back to outward-facing buds or shoots, or those that will develop to fill a gap.

RIGHT A pair of good-quality bypass secateurs is the most essential pruning tool.

BELOW Cut out this plain green shoot on *Euonymus japonicus* 'Bravo' before it takes over.

Remove weak, feeble shots and any diseased or damaged branches as you go. If you keep in mind how the shrub will respond with every cut, you will not go wrong.

ABOVE Prune forsythia in mid- to late spring by cutting back flowered shoots to where new vigorous shoots are emerging.

LEFT You can clip potentillas with shears in late winter.

PRUNING FLOWERING SHRUBS

Gardeners usually prune flowering shrubs to stimulate flowering and to control size and shape. These operations are usually one and the same, and are generally carried out soon after flowering. If a shrub flowers in early spring, prune in mid- to late spring. If it flowers in early summer, prune in midsummer.

It is easy to tackle early season deciduous flowering shrubs if you remember that they flower on wood produced the previous year. After flowering, examine the shrub. You will find vigorous new shoots developing low on the branches. These shoots will grow and flower the following year. Cut back between one-half and two-thirds of the stems that have just flowered to where these new shoots are emerging low down on the branches. After that, leave the shrub unpruned until the same time the following year. If you prune in fall, you will be cutting off the coming year's flowers. If you cut back the ends of the shoots in fall, you will steal the natural habit of the shrub.

If a shrub flowers in late summer or fall, leave pruning until late winter. Examples include caryopteris, buddleja, perovskia, and ceratostigma. Earlier pruning may stimulate new growth, which frost could damage. Also, the old growth that pruning will remove often helps to protect the lower part of the plant through winter. These shrubs will not have vigorous new shoots emerging, but if you examine the lower part of the shrub you will usually see growth buds. If you cut back the stems to this point,

LEFT Prune late-flowering *Hydrangea paniculata* in late winter.

BELOW Buddlejas are best cut back hard to 60–90cm (2–3 ft.) above the ground in late winter.

these buds will develop through spring and summer and be ready to flower at the end of the season. Most late-flowering shrubs, such as *Buddleja davidii* and *Hydrangea paniculata*, are hard pruned to stimulate vigorous growth and upright stems. You may cut these back by two-thirds or more, usually to the same point each year.

You can selectively prune older flowering shrubs to control size and shape in winter at the expense of some of the following season's flowers. Without the foliage, you can see the framework of the shrub more easily. You can cut back some of the older stems to within 20cm (8 in.) of the ground, encouraging new shoots to develop from the base of the shrub. These older stems are usually duller in colour than the younger wood and thus easily identified. This pruning is the same as winter pruning of deciduous foliage shrubs.

Laterally branched growth is desirable on some shrubs, as more side shoots may mean more flowers. For example, a lightly pruned shrub rose will result in a bushy plant with lots of roses. If the same plant is pruned more severely, it will respond with long shoots with the flowers carried way up in the air. Incorrect pruning is the main reason some gardeners are disappointed with some shrub roses or English roses. Hard pruning turns them into monsters.

Midsummer pruning is performed on roses when dead-heading. This is now usually referred to as *summer pruning* to underline its importance, and to prevent gardeners from merely snipping off the dead flowers when they should be thinking about the next crop of blooms.

PRUNING DECIDUOUS FOLIAGE SHRUBS

Prune in winter to control the size and shape of deciduous foliage shrubs such as *Physocarpus opulifolius*. Again, cut back the longer, taller stems to where younger, light-coloured shoots are emerging lower on the branches. Alternatively, remove whole stems to ground level to encourage new growth to develop from the base. This is the best way to prune varieties of *Cornus alba* and *Cornus sericea* grown for their variegated and colourful leaves. This hard pruning can also promote the production of better-quality foliage.

PRUNING EVERGREEN SHRUBS

Evergreen shrubs are normally pruned to control their size and shape, and to promote fresh growth and good-quality foliage. When pruning an evergreen subject, such as *Choisya ternata*, the best approach is to cut the longer branches back by about one-third. This means cutting back into the middle of the shrub, which encourages any new growth to be produced lower down on the existing stems. You will preserve

RIGHT Pruning a choisya in spring involves cutting back some of the longer shoots by about 30cm (1 ft.) into the shrub to encourage new growth from lower in the plant.

BELOW Deciduous foliage shrubs such as physocarpus are more easily pruned in winter, when it is easier to identify the older stems.

ABOVE Prune santolina in
summer, when it is about to
flower. This removes the hard
yellow flowers and stimulates
the growth of silver foliage.

LEFT Clip over winter-flowering
ericas in spring to remove
the faded flowers and to
promote bushy growth.

the natural irregularity of the shrub's outline and avoid the regular clipped effect that would result from snipping back the shoots over the whole shrub. If you work logically and carefully over the shrub in this way, using a sharp pair of secateurs, you will gradually achieve the desired shape and size. Do this type of pruning after flowering to allow new growth to develop and bloom. You may have to do it in winter if there is frost damage or die back to remove.

In the case of evergreens grown purely for their foliage, prune just before growth commences in spring or when a new flush of growth is desirable for the appearance of the plant. This is the case with *Photinia ×fraseri*, grown for its bright red young leaves. If you prune in mid- to late summer, the shrub still has time to produce colourful new foliage that will hold its colour through winter.

PRUNING HEATHERS

Prune ericas and callunas, whether grown for their flowers or their foliage, after flowering. Hedging shears are the best tool to crop off the flowers and tip back the top growth to promote bushy, compact plants. If you leave the shrubs unpruned for several years, they become leggy and bare in the middle.

SILVER-FOLIAGE SHRUBS

As with other flowering shrubs, prune lavender right after flowering by cutting back to just below the base of the flower stems. This should stimulate fresh silver-green foliage that remains in good condition through winter and prevents heavy, wet flower stems from damaging the shrubs.

In the case of shrubs grown purely for their silver foliage, such as varieties of helichrysum and santolina, it may be better to prune just before flowering to remove undesirable brightly coloured flowers. Cut back as you would lavender. You can also cut back older plants in spring by cutting back to where new shoots are emerging on the stems.

ERICACEOUS SHRUBS

Ericaceous shrubs such as pieris, camellia, and rhododendron rarely require pruning. However, older shrubs can become misshapen and leggy, and you can successfully rejuvenate them by pruning right after flowering. Most produce new vigorous shoots from the bare wood, even from low down on the stems.

You can keep camellias more compact by pruning lightly right after flowering. This can be an advantage in small gardens, in containers, or where you require a formal

LEFT Most Mediterranean subjects, such as cistus, lavender, helichrysum, and santolina, refuse to shoot from old wood, so never cut back to bare stems if there are no signs of new shoots emerging.

RIGHT Hard prune deciduous azaleas after flowering to rejuvenate old, leggy plants. Mulching and watering after pruning is particularly important to stimulate new growth.

Allow *Cornus controversa* 'Variegata' to grow naturally. Prune only to remove dead or damaged growth.

shape. However, it is successful only with camellias that are naturally upright and compact in habit.

WHEN NOT TO PRUNE

One final word about pruning: When in doubt, leave pruning out. Some shrubs resent pruning, especially as older plants. Some evergreen ceanothus, cytisus, and cistus fall into this category. These are not long-lived plants, so replacement is often a better option than trying to rejuvenate by pruning.

Never prune a shrub unnecessarily that is grown for its unique growth habit, such as *Cornus controversa* 'Variegata' or *Viburnum plicatum* f. *tomentosum* 'Mariesii'. Pruning may rob the plant of its beautiful natural growth habit.

Shrubs are physically forgiving, but they will appreciate fertilizer, water, and perhaps mulch after pruning. As with anything growing in your garden, a little attention to cultivation reaps big rewards.

Feeding shrubs

Shrubs are usually at the end of the queue at feeding time. Most of us usually remember to feed our roses, and maybe scatter the remains of a packet of fertilizer on the border. But we rarely think to regularly feed the established shrubs in the garden.

Most shrubs are tough, tolerant plants that grow adequately even without occasional feeding, especially because most soils contain sufficient nutrients to support plant growth. However, shrubs are long-term garden plants, and you want them to look their best year after year, so regular feeding is beneficial for healthy foliage and flower production. Feeding becomes even more important when shrubs are put under stress by extremes of rainfall, or through regular watering through periods of drought. This stimulates vigorous growth, which exhausts nutrients and causes soluble ones to washed away. This can result in weaker growth, which is more susceptible to disease.

Feeding is always more important on poor soils that are low in natural nutrients. Shallow soils, sand, and gravel-rich soils that drain freely contain less nutrients because watering and rainfall regularly wash them away. You can improve nutrient retention on these soils by adding organic matter in the form of garden compost and well-rotted manure. Peaty acid soils are also usually low in nutrients, but you can make them more fertile by adding loam, mineral-rich soil with fine particles.

ABOVE This informal *Spiraea*
'Arguta' hedge will benefit
from regular feeding to
improve its flower power.

LEFT Flowering shrubs deliver
an amazing display year after
year. Do you need to feed
them to guarantee results?
Rhododendron 'Horizon Monarch'
with *Berberis* ×*stenophylla* 'Etna'.

However, ericaceous plants, which grow on acid, peaty soils, are light feeders and require low nutrient levels.

Where shrubs are in competition, as in a hedge, slower growth because of lack of soil fertility can be an advantage. If you make them grow more, you may have to prune more often. However, if you do not feed occasionally, the hedge may eventually become weak and deteriorate.

MAIN PLANT NUTRIENTS

All packeted fertilizers tell you what is in the box in terms of nutrition. But it is worth knowing what the main plant nutrients do, as this information will help you decide whether a fertilizer is going to give a shrub what it needs. The three main plant nutrients are nitrogen (N), phosphorus, usually referred to as phosphate (P), and potassium, usually referred to as potash (K). A plant uses nitrogen for the growth and development of leaves and stems, phosphate for roots, and potash for flowers and fruit.

Traditional fertilizers were used to deliver specific nutrients according to requirements. For example, bone meal, a rich source of phosphate, is traditionally used when planting to encourage root development. Potash fertilizer is used around shrubs reluctant to bloom to encourage flower production.

MINOR PLANT NUTRIENTS AND TRACE ELEMENTS

In addition to the three main nutrients, plants also require other nutrients in smaller quantities. These are the vitamins and minerals of the plant world. The best known is iron, because this becomes unavailable to ericaceous plants on alkaline soils through a complex relationship between the nutrient and soil pH. This lack of iron results in yellowing foliage, lack of growth, and often the death of the shrub.

ORGANIC VERSUS INORGANIC FERTILIZERS

In simple terms, organic fertilizers, derived from something that was once living, gradually break down in the soil and slowly release their nutrients. However, their nutrient content is usually low and difficult to ascertain accurately. Overfeeding is

ABOVE A light application of potash fertilizer is often used around shrubs that are shy to flower. It also hardens new growth and makes it less susceptible to frost damage, as with *Magnolia ×loebneri* 'Leonard Messel'.

RIGHT Rhododendron leaves showing yellowing because of lack of iron. This may be the result of alkaline conditions or just a lack of nutrients in the soil.

Feed and water cornus grown for their winter stems after you cut back in early spring.

unlikely, especially as the fertilizer rarely breaks down when there is insufficient moisture in the soil.

An inorganic fertilizer is manufactured and of chemical origin; nutrient content is usually high and can be accurately stated. It breaks down quickly in the soil and makes nutrients immediately available to the shrub. However, rainfall or watering easily washes away these nutrients. If you apply too much fertilizer, the concentration of nutrients in the soil water can be too great, resulting in damage to the roots of the shrub.

CHOOSING THE RIGHT FERTILIZER

There is little point in testing your soil to determine which nutrients are in short supply, then trying to correct this by applying fertilizers that provide the missing ones. It is far better to apply a quality general slow-release fertilizer that contains all the major and minor nutrients, as well as trace elements. An organic-based fertilizer is the ideal option. That means an organic fertilizer that has been enriched to provide a greater source of nutrients, including all the minor nutrients and trace elements.

Specific rose fertilizers are also a good choice for most flowering and foliage shrubs. Roses are greedy feeders, so these contain high proportions of nitrogen and potash, as well as all the minor nutrients and trace elements a shrub requires.

It is important to use specific fertilizers for ericaceous plants. These are free of lime and release nutrients in small amounts to avoid overfeeding.

DETERMINING THE BEST TIME TO FEED

The ideal time to feed is usually just before growth gets under way in spring, and perhaps again in summer to give shrubs a boost for the latter part of the season. This second application is particularly important for roses after the first flush of flowers to equip the plants for the next performance and to keep foliage healthy for the rest of the season.

It is good practice to feed right after pruning flowering shrubs that are trimmed on a regular basis. This ensures a healthy supply of nutrients ready for the shrubs to make new growth. Scatter the fertilizer over the soil surface around the shrub, mostly toward the drip line. This is where the branches extend to and where the roots will be most active. Work the fertilizer into the soil surface using a hoe or small fork and leave the rain to do the work; alternatively, water it in thoroughly.

ABOVE Roses are hungry shrubs. A rose fertilizer is also a good choice for any other flowering and foliage shrubs.

LEFT You can use grass clippings as mulch around large, mature shrubs and under hedges. Do not pile them up too close to the main stems.

Mulching shrubs

Mulching is the practice of spreading a layer of organic material over the soil surface above the roots. This keeps the soil cool in summer, reducing water loss and suppressing weeds. It also insulates the ground and may reduce the penetration of frost. Most mulches gradually break down into the soil, increasing the organic matter content and thereby improving the soil structure. Mulches usually consist of well-rotted organic matter, such as composted garden waste, partly composted bark, bracken, or straw.

Shrubs are tough, woody plants, so you can use non-composted material such as shredded garden waste and grass cuttings around large, strong-growing shrubs and under hedges. This non-composted waste gives off heat in the composting process and takes nitrogen from the soil. This can slow the growth rate of plants and cause damage to sensitive subjects. Avoid clippings from lawns that have recently been treated with herbicide.

Mulches are highly beneficial if applied when the soil is moist and after the application of slow-release fertilizer. Mulching is not a substitute for feeding. When applying mulch, avoid heaping it up around the base of the stems, as this may interfere with growth.

Gravel or stone chippings are often used as inorganic mulch around Mediterranean subjects and other shrubs that dislike wet soil beneath their leaves and stems. This also conserves moisture and keeps the ground insulated, but does not increase the organic matter content.

Watering shrubs

All plants need regular watering after planting until they become established. This may be for a few weeks, months, or up to a year depending upon the weather, season, and climatic conditions. Frequency of watering also depends on these factors, so you will have to use your best judgement. A container-grown shrub planted in fall, when rainfall is frequent through winter, will need watering thoroughly after planting. You can likely leave it alone until the following spring, when it may need watering as it

ABOVE An irrigation system is useful on newly planted beds, but can encourage roots to stay near the surface if you use it permanently.

RIGHT Feel beneath the surface of the soil and judge how dry the ground really is, especially around newly planted shrubs.

starts to grow, particularly if the weather is dry. The best practice is always to keep an eye on a shrub and see how it behaves.

On the other hand, a container-grown shrub planted in spring will need regular watering every few days, perhaps every day if the weather is warm, dry, and breezy. You can gradually reduce the frequency of watering after two or three months, once you are satisfied that the plant is becoming established. The secret of success is vigilance. A dry shrub tells you it needs water when foliage loses its lustre and new growth starts to wilt. Left without water, the leaves of many deciduous shrubs go brown and crisp at the tips and the leaves of evergreens often drop.

Once shrubs are established, regular watering should be unnecessary if you choose the right shrubs for your growing conditions. For example, if the soil is normally dry or you expect regular periods of drought, choose shrubs that are adapted to a dry climate—particularly those with small and narrow leaves, silver foliage, or thick, waxy, or oily leaves; these are designed to resist desiccation. Shrubs with lush growth and thin, soft deciduous leaves need regular watering in these conditions, so they are best avoided.

The objective is to encourage your shrubs to form a healthy and extensive root system where the roots reach down into the soil in search of water. If you supply too much water on the soil surface, the roots are likely to stay there.

This is often the problem with permanent irrigation systems. From the outset shrubs establish their roots near the soil surface because that is where the moisture is. They will grow, sometimes too well, but they become dependent on that regular supply of surface water and they suffer if it is not available. Porous or permeable irrigation pipe on the soil surface can be helpful around newly planted shrubs, especially along hedges. However, in the long term an irrigation system is undesirable in a garden based on shrubs.

Lovely *Acer palmatum*
'Ozakazuki' sets the garden
ablaze in fall with its fine foliage.

Further Reading

Anderton, Stephen. *Rejuvenating a Garden.* London: Kyle Cathie, 1998.

Brickell, Christopher, and David Joyce. *The Royal Horticultural Society Pruning and Training: The Definitive Practical Guide to Pruning Trees, Shrubs, and Climbers.* New York: Dorling Kindersley, 2011.

Buffin, Michael W. *Winter-flowering Shrubs.* Portland, Oregon: Timber Press, 2005.

Cooke, Ian. *Shrubs: A Gardener's Handbook.* Ramsbury, Wiltshire: Crowood Press, 2012.

Cushnie, John. *Shrubs for the Garden.* London: Kyle Cathie, 2004.

Dirr, Michael A. *Dirr's Encyclopedia of Trees & Shrubs.* Portland, Oregon: Timber Press, 2011.

Dirr, Michael A. *Hydrangeas for American Gardens.* Portland, Oregon: Timber Press, 2004.

Dirr, Michael A. *Viburnums: Flowering Shrubs for Every Season.* Portland, Oregon: Timber Press, 2007.

Gardiner, Jim. *The Timber Press Encyclopedia of Flowering Shrubs: More Than 1700 Outstanding Garden Plants.* Portland, Oregon: Timber Press, 2011.

Gossler, Roger, Eric Gossler, and Marjory Gossler. *The Gossler Guide to the Best Hardy Shrubs: More than 350 Expert Choices for Your Garden.* Portland, Oregon: Timber Press, 2009.

Hillier Nurseries. *The Hillier Manual of Trees and Shrubs.* London: Royal Horticultural Society, 2014.

Hogan, Sean. *Trees for All Seasons: Broadleaved Evergreens for Temperate Climates.* Portland, Oregon: Timber Press, 2008.

Houtman, Ronald. *Variegated Trees and Shrubs: The Illustrated Encyclopedia.* Portland, Oregon: Timber Press, 2004.

McIndoe, Andrew. *Shrubs: The Hillier Gardener's Guides.* Devon: David and Charles, 2005.

Miller, Diana M. *400 Trees and Shrubs for Small Spaces: How to Choose and Grow the Best Compact Plants for Gardens.* Portland, Oregon: Timber Press, 2008.

Photography Credits

The Bransford Webbs Plant Company, pages 84 top left, 87 centre left, 88 bottom right, 166 top right

Jonathan Buckley, pages 109 bottom right, 159 centre

David Edge, Forest Edge, pages 138 centre, 157 centre

fotolia.com, pages 163 centre left, 183 top left, 206 left

Will Giles, The Exotic Garden, page 110

Lynn Keddie, pages 210 top centre, 214

Osberton Nurseries, pages 99 centre, 101 centre left, 126 centre right, 193 right, 194 left, 194 centre, 195 top right, 196 right

All other photographs by Andrew McIndoe assisted by Alexander McIndoe and Rosamond McIndoe

Index

JULIAN WINSLOW

About the author

Andy McIndoe is managing director of Hillier Nurseries and Garden Centres in Hampshire, England. As designer of the Hillier exhibit at the Chelsea Flower Show for more than two decades, he has upheld the company's unprecedented record of consecutive gold medals at the show.

He has more than 30 years' experience in retail and production horticulture and specialises in planning and advising on private garden design. He is especially interested in sustainable schemes that achieve colour and interest throughout the year with minimal input using shrubs, roses and perennials.

Andy contributes regularly to blogs, magazines, newspapers, and BBC radio and television. He lectures widely to gardening groups and societies at home and abroad and leads numerous gardening tours. His previous books also reflect his enduring interest in hardy shrubs, trees, herbaceous perennials, flower bulbs and garden design.

His gardening knowledge has been acquired through hands-on experience following his graduation from Bath University with a degree in horticulture. He and his wife, Ros, are both keen gardeners. Their two-acre garden at Sherfield English near Romsey, which is naturalistic in style with an extensive wildflower meadow and informal planting, welcomes visitors by appointment. Andy blogs at my-garden-school.com/blog/.